The Fantastic in Holocaust
Literature and Film

The Fantastic in Holocaust Literature and Film

Critical Perspectives

Edited by JUDITH B. KERMAN *and*
JOHN EDGAR BROWNING

Foreword by JANE YOLEN

CRITICAL EXPLORATIONS IN
SCIENCE FICTION AND FANTASY, 49

Series Editors Donald E. Palumbo *and* C.W. Sullivan III

McFarland & Company, Inc., Publishers
Jefferson, North Carolina

Jane Yolen, "Foreword: The Rumpelstiltskin Factor," reprinted by permission of Jane Yolen. Original publication in *The Journal of the Fantastic in the Arts* 5, no. 2 (1993): 11–14. Copyright © 1993. Gary K. Wolfe, "Introduction: Fantasy as Testimony," reprinted by permission of *The Journal of the Fantastic in the Arts* 5, no. 2 (1993): 3–10. Copyright © 1993. Judith B. Kerman, "Uses of the Fantastic in Literature of the Holocaust," reprinted by permission of *The Journal of the Fantastic in the Arts* 5, no. 2 (1993): 14–31. Copyright © 1993. Michael Yogev (here as Michael P. McCleary), "The Fantastic in Holocaust Literature: Writing and Unwriting the Unbearable," reprinted by permission of *The Journal of the Fantastic in the Arts* 5, no. 2 (1993): 32–49. Copyright © 1993. Joan Gordon, "Surviving the Survivor: Art Spiegelman's *Maus*," reprinted by permission of *The Journal of the Fantastic in the Arts* 5, no. 2 (1993): 81–89. Copyright © 1993. Jules Zanger, "*The Last of the Just*: Lifting Moloch to Heaven," reprinted by permission of *The Journal of the Fantastic in the Arts* 5, no. 2 (1993): 49–59. Copyright © 1993. Ellen R. Weil, "The Door to Lilith's Cave: Memory and Imagination in Jane Yolen's Holocaust Novels," reprinted by permission of *The Journal of the Fantastic in the Arts* 5, no. 2 (1993): 90–104. Copyright © 1993. Leon Stein, "A Holocaust Education in Reverse: Stephen King's 'The Summer of Corruption: Apt Pupil,'" reprinted by permission of *The Journal of the Fantastic in the Arts* 5, no. 2 (1993): 60–79. Copyright © 1993.

LIBRARY OF CONGRESS CATALOGUING-IN-PUBLICATION DATA

The fantastic in Holocaust literature and film : critical perspectives / edited by Judith B. Kerman and John Edgar Browning ; foreword by Jane Yolen.

    p.   cm. — (Critical Explorations in Science Fiction and Fantasy ; 49)
    [Donald E. Palumbo and C.W. Sullivan III, series editors]
    Includes bibliographical references and index.

ISBN 978-0-7864-5874-5 (softcover : acid free paper) ∞
ISBN 978-1-4766-1873-9 (ebook)

    1. Fantasy literature—History and criticism.   2. Fantasy films—History and critcism.   3. Holocaust, Jewish (1939–1945), in literature.   4. Holocaust, Jewish (1939–1945), in motion pictures.   I. Kerman, Judith, 1945– editor.   II. Browning, John Edgar, editor.
PN56.F34F3555 2015
809.3'8766—dc23   2014037040

BRITISH LIBRARY CATALOGUING DATA ARE AVAILABLE

On the cover: *The Shoes on the Danube Bank*, a war memorial in Budapest by sculptor Gyula Pauer (George Robertson/Dreamstime)

Printed in the United States of America

McFarland & Company, Inc., Publishers
 Box 611, Jefferson, North Carolina 28640
  www.mcfarlandpub.com

Acknowledgments

The editors wish to thank the authors who contributed to this collection for their professionalism, patience, support, and brilliant insights, and we are indebted to Brian Attebery, editor of *Journal of the Fantastic in the Arts (JFA)*, who granted us permission to reprint here the original "seed" articles from *JFA* 5, no. 2 (1993). Our thanks also goes to Leslie Gerber for his help with proofreading.

The images reproduced in this book are used solely for educational purposes. The copyright for these images is most likely owned by either the individual party whose permission we obtained to reproduce the image or the publisher or distributor of the image.

Table of Contents

Foreword
The Rumpelstiltskin Factor
Jane Yolen

A number of years ago, while working with fairy tale material, I was puzzling over the story of Rumpelstiltskin, the Grimm version. It is a tale related to the English "Tom Tit Tot" and many European variants (tale type 500). The amorality of the story bothered me, for here we had a miller who lies, his daughter who is complicitious in that lie, a king who swallows the lie whole (being either stupid, disingenuous, or greedy—or a combination of all three). And the only character who seems genuinely moral, that is who does not lie, who says exactly what he plans to do is the little man, Rumpelstiltskin.

Only what happens to him? He tears himself up at the end and disappears into oblivion.

Why? That was the question that kept troubling me. Why?

He says he will spin the straw into gold for the miller's daughter, who is in peril of her life. (Fairies traditionally could spin such magical stuff.) He asks for a token in return. When she has, finally, nothing to give him, he asks for what would surely be an impossible promise. Her first child. She gives the promise freely, then tries to renege on it later.

Why? The story, after first showing the little man to be a savior, casts him in the villain's role: he wants to steal her child for some unknown and unnamed rite. Blood guilt. I began to see a pattern.

The little man is often pictured with a large nose. He has an unpronounceable name. He trades in gold, exchanging it.

Could it be that what we have encapsulated in the body of this German tale is an anti–Semitic story? (In the British version, interestingly,

1

the little man is described as "a black thing"; and in an Ipswich variant the little black man is replaced by a Gypsy woman.)

This story is not, of course, the only folktale that carries inside it a warning against trafficking with "the other." Folk stories have often used magic to underscore the warnings of culture mixing, of *mongrelization* (to use the Nazis' own word).

There is but one small step between genuine folklore and what folklorists like to call "fakelore," it is magical tales—literary fairy tales or the literature of the fantastic.

I was reminded of my musings about Rumpelstiltskin as I read the following papers about the uses of fantasy literature in writing about the Holocaust. Sometimes it is necessary to take a step back from the abyss, substituting seven-league boots for the hobnails, transforming what *was* into *what could not possibly be.*

There are critics of this kind of telling; there are problems of "ownership" of events. But it seems to me that just as *Rumpelstiltskin* fed its quiet racism into generations of eager young ears, so these subversive recountings of the Holocaust can make *even more* real what—at the remove of fifty years—seems not real. Magic is like that.

I have written two books and a short story entwining the Nazi Holocaust with the fantastic. In *The Devil's Arithmetic* it is time travel that allows a modern child (and thus the modern child reader) to both be in— and be outside of—the events in a concentration camp. In my adult novel *Briar Rose* I use a fairy tale framework to implode Holocaust material on a very real life. And in the story "Names," working with the guilt of a survivor's child, I use the incantatory power of the roll call of death in the camps as a method of mnemonic reckoning. Each of these pieces of writing has had advocates and detractors. The advocates have felt the fantasy added to the power of the piece; the detractors that the Holocaust itself is a powerful enough Event that is made less by the use of the fantastic.

Those two opposite poles of criticism are addressed in the essays in this book, a first—but one hopes not a last serious look—at how the nature of evil can be defined, redefined, refined, and made manifest by writers of the fantastic who, nevertheless, never deny that a real and terrible evil was visited upon millions of innocents in a once upon a time that was only fifty years ago in our actual past.

Editors' Preface

JUDITH B. KERMAN *and*
JOHN EDGAR BROWNING

Gary K. Wolfe asks, in the introduction to this anthology, "Can the Holocaust be represented with sensitivity and historical verisimilitude in an imaginative mode so often associated in the popular mind with escapism and 'irreality'?" He continues, "If the reality of the Holocaust challenges the imagination—or transcends it, as Elie Wiesel and others have argued, what can the fantastic imagination possibly bring to the table?" This present volume is interdisciplinary in scope, including print literature and film, animation, graphic novels, and various other media. Within these media, we concern ourselves with the fantastic, a form which, "by its very nature," Wolfe aptly comments, "violates the norms of realism that have dominated not only Holocaust texts but virtually the whole body of what has been received and taught as 'serious' literature for the past two centuries. Fantastic literature suggests fairy tales, myths, science fiction—the impossible or at least the improbable." We have sought here to collect essays that, while not necessarily in agreement with one another or reducible to a single medium or theoretical approach, engage in dialogue with each other and together produce a comprehensive whole.

But why write about the Nazi Holocaust? And why read about it? Survivors, as Judith B. Kerman acknowledges later, "have needed to bear witness, and for many the idea of bearing witness gave meaning to their sufferings even as they occurred, helping them to survive." However, she suggests "writings by non-survivors are a more complicated matter, and reading about these events is similarly complex." Inquiry into the nature and purpose of Holocaust texts inclusive of fantastic elements is "not really separate from these broader issues, which concern the ontological as well as the moral nature of the Holocaust itself." We might ask the same of any catastrophe, natural or man-made, that

> reminds us of how thin the thread is that keeps us from either misery or savagery. Cambodia. Hiroshima. Kuwait City and Baghdad. Even the lives of our own homeless. Yet, to the extent that our everyday lives continue in relatively unruffled comfort, these experiences are in fact fantastic to contemplate, which is why almost every account reports refusal by most European Jews to believe the warnings they received, even as they were herded onto the trains.

Those who were soon to be victims believed that these reports had to be "fairy tales," madness, as Jane Yolen terms it in *The Devil's Arithmetic* (1988). Kerman asks, "When the real is so fantastic, what literary effects will succeed in making it credible, and in helping the reader to comprehend its human meaning?"

To respond meaningfully to such a challenge, one approach is made available by the techniques of the fantastic, the "condensation of images which allows it to affect its readers at many levels and in many different ways" (Kathryn Hume, *Fantasy and Mimesis* [1984], 196). "Any tacit agreement," Wolfe points out, "that the Holocaust is 'off-limits' to the imagination may well have the paradoxical effect of mythologizing it further, as the historical event recedes, and the surviving texts take on the status of icons." If the Holocaust is "to remain a continuing confrontation with almost unimaginable evil," Wolfe continues, "it must, as Caryn James implies, be re-imagined for succeeding generations on their own terms." This anthology aims to interrogate literary and filmic texts in which the Holocaust and the fantastic are articulated together in various ways, some more successful than others, in order to wrestle with dilemmas of representation and memory.

Many of the essays in the book make available to today's readers a body of work originally published in a special Holocaust issue of the *Journal of the Fantastic in the Arts* in 1993. The essays were based on papers given at the International Conference on the Fantastic in the Arts. They were sparked by Michael P. McCleary's paper, "The Fantastic in Holocaust Literature: Writing and Unwriting the Unbearable," originally given in 1988 (published then under Michael Yogev) and included in this volume. That issue of the *Journal* is now out of print.

The first sections begin by exploring potential uses of and conceptual approaches to the fantastic in Holocaust narratives. In "Uses of the Fantastic in Literature of the Holocaust," Judith B. Kerman contends that in order to respond meaningfully and ethically to the Holocaust, "writers need to incorporate moral and emotional complexity" and one way to do this "is made available by the techniques of the fantastic." Michael P. McCleary's original paper interrogated "whether fictionalized or fantastic accounts of Holocaust provide escape from its horrors," or whether audiences "should ever 'appreciate' or take pleasure in the aesthetic quality" of fictional works that take as their subject one as sad and abominable as the Holocaust. Ultimately, McCleary argues that the "fantastic is often integral to the power of the works of [Holocaust] writers," and its use is not only "appropriate for depicting the Holocaust" but "it may indeed be, paradoxically, the most 'natural' mode in which to re-present this age of extremity."

The remaining essays in this section take a case study approach to the fantastic mode in Holocaust literature. In "Surviving the Survivor: Art Spiegelman's *Maus*," for example, Joan Gordon uses Art Spiegelman's *Maus, A Survivor's Tale* (1986; the second volume, *Maus: And Here My Troubles Began*, was published in 1991) "to discuss the laws of Holocaust writing and why *Maus* violates them in order to answer the question ... of survival in a post-heroic world."

The essays in the rest of the collection extend these concerns to film television, and drama as well as fiction written since 1993. Eric J. Sterling's "The Fantastic Search for Hitler: The Führer's Defense in His Own Words," explores fantastical and sentimental drama about the Shoah and takes as his particular example *The Portage to San Cristobal of A.H.* In the next essay, "'Hidden in Plain Sight': On Holocaust Fantasy in the Metaphysical Detective Story," Patricia Merivale takes "fantasy," as it is applied to Holocaust fiction, to encompass non-"realistic" fictional strategies like magic realism, myth, and parable that are situated in such genres as fantasy (Narnian), folk- and fairy tale, horror stories, science fiction, and alternate history. She also extends this to the "metaphysical" or "postmodern" detective story. In "The Summons of Freedom: Fantastic History in Jonathan Safran Foer's *Everything Is Illuminated*," Paul Eisenstein argues that the novels and letters Alex and Jonathan exchange in *Everything Is Illuminated* "converge powerfully on the issue of the writer's, and our own, radical freedom to believe (or not) in the impossible and indecent truths of the past." While Jules Zanger's "*The Last of the Just*: Lifting Moloch to Heaven" treats the spiritual aspects of Holocaust fantasy narratives, several essays examine Jane Yolen's important Holocaust-related stories for young audiences, like Ellen R. Weil's "The Door to Lilith's Cave: Memory and Imagination in Jane Yolen's Holocaust Novels," Vandana Saxena's "Mother Goose Tales: Intergenerational Storytelling and the Holocaust in Jane

Yolen's *Briar Rose* and Peter Rushforth's *Kindergarten*," and Carol A. Senf's "*The Devil's Arithmetic* and Time Travel: Truth and Memory."

Finally, a number of essays deal with film and television representations that refer to the Holocaust either directly or by allusion. In "A Holocaust Education in Reverse: Stephen King's 'The Summer of Corruption: Apt Pupil,'" Leon Stein examines how King's novella raises important issues and offers "some valuable insights on the unique, extreme intentionality of the Nazis, on the assembly-line methods of killing during the Holocaust, and on the charismatic appeal of Hitler and the Nazis to the German people." John Edgar Browning's "Holocaust-as-Horror, Science Fiction, and the 'Look' of the 'Real/Reel' in *V* (1983)" looks at how the television series *V* represents the horrors of the Holocaust using a fantastic mode of narration like science fiction while incorporating simultaneously the cinematic techniques of horror and documentary film. What we find, according to Browning, is that the grammars of science fiction and horror enable *V* to challenge dominant or classic representations of the monstrous in Holocaust narratives. In "A Dishonest Reckoning: Play-'Acting Through' Personal Trauma and the Shoah in Martin Scorsese's *Shutter Island* (2010)," Kristopher Mecholsky is concerned primarily with the fantastic *as* a mode and its reconciliation with "legitimacy" in Holocaust narratives. Exploring *Shutter Island*'s use of Holocaust imagery, Mecholsky probes several important questions along the way, like: What are the limits of fiction in representations of the Shoah? Can genre fiction ever appropriately or legitimately represent it? And, what is appropriate and legitimate when it comes to Holocaust representation? Finally, Caroline Joan (Kay) S. Picart's "Going Beyond Horror: Fantasy, Humor and the Holocaust" looks at how one goes about analyzing cinematic genres that reference the Holocaust, but substitute the (privileged) documentary mode for more fantastic modes of narrativizing. For Picart, *Pan's Labyrinth* and *Life Is Beautiful* tell us much about how we can use less realistic formats to collectively work through the trauma of the Holocaust.

As recent history amply demonstrates, the lessons of the Nazi Holocaust remain to be learned throughout the world. The authors in this collection examine the usefulness of fantastic modalities in the arts for exploring relevant ontological and moral issues.

Introduction
Fantasy as Testimony
Gary K. Wolfe

The impetus for the special issue of *The Journal of the Fantastic in the Arts* began with a paper which Michael P. McCleary presented (as Michael Yogev) at the Eleventh Annual International Conference on the Fantastic in Fort Lauderdale, Florida, in 1990. That paper (reprinted here in a revised form) sparked considerable discussion about fantastic treatments of the Holocaust among other conference attendees, including that year's guest of honor, Jane Yolen. Yolen's own 1988 young adult novel *The Devil's Arithmetic* had been the focus of some controversy over the very issue that McCleary's paper raised—namely, can the Holocaust be represented with sensitivity and historical verisimilitude in an imaginative mode so often associated in the popular mind with escapism and "irreality"? If the reality of the Holocaust challenges the imagination—or transcends it, as Elie Wiesel and others have argued—what can the fantastic imagination possibly bring to the table? "The Holocaust, a half century later, is still not to be played with," writes John Updike; "it still gives off a poisonous heat, and perhaps none but those who actually endured the camps, like Primo Levi and Tadeusz Borowski, should be licensed to make art of them. But, of course, the artistic conscience rebels against any such prohibition."[1]

Our discussions led to forming two entire panels on the topic for the following year's conference, and the essays included here by Judith B. Kerman, Joan Gordon, Jules Zanger, and Ellen R. Weil were all presented in earlier form at those panels. Jane Yolen also participated in the discussions in 1991, and her intriguing notion of the possible anti–Semitic implications of "Rumpelstiltskin"—mentioned in her special foreword—was first presented as an idea for exploration at those panels. Upon learning of these discussions, historian Leon Stein mentioned his interest in the Stephen King story "Apt Pupil," and was asked to prepare a new essay on that story—which, while not strictly fantastic, is the work of an author so closely associated with fantasy and horror that it seemed more than worthy of explanation.

Since work on the special issue of *The Journal of the Fantastic in the Arts* began, the central questions it addressed have gained increased prominence. The second volume of Art Spiegelmant's *Maus* received a special Pulitzer Prize in 1991, and a number of popular novels have appeared which have raised the issue anew. In England, Martin Amis's *Time's Arrow* (1991) combined the fantastic notion of reversing the flow of time with the story of a physician who worked in the death camps in Nazi Germany; and Robert Harris's *Fatherland*, about a victorious Nazi Germany seeking to suppress knowledge of the Holocaust, became a major bestseller in both England and the United States. An alternate-history Holocaust scenario is at the center of Janet Guthman and George Guthridge's *Child of the Light* (1992), and a Holocaust survivor is able to draw on the power of his vanished compatriots in Dan Simmons's horror novel *Carrion Comfort* (1989). The 1992 volume of Gardner Dozois's *Year's Best Science Fiction* anthology contains two stories which touch upon Holocaust themes, and Jane Yolen's 1992 novel *Briar Rose* represents her second fictional treatment of this theme.

Nor is this trend confined to literature. In a March 1, 1992, article in the *New York Times*, critic Caryn James writes that "in recent years some of the most moving and evocative renderings of the Holocaust have been both deeply respectful and filled with fancy. Artists too young to remember World War II are breaking the mold of documentary realism, infusing their work with fantasy and pop culture, and incorporating a sophisticated sense of how the mass media control images of the past."[2] James cited not only Amis and Spiegelman, but also a fantasy sequence in Agnieszka Holland's film *Europa, Europa*, Günter Grass's 1959 novel *The Tin Drum* (and the 1979 film made from it), the work of the young German painter Anselm Kiefer, Michael Verhoeven's 1989 film *The Nasty Girl*, and Donald Margulies 1992 play *Sight Unseen*. While not all these works might qualify as fantastic in the sense implied by most of the essays that follow, James has nevertheless identified a growing willingness on the part of artists and writers to move away from the tradition of documentary realism that has so long dominated artistic responses to the Holocaust. "The farther the war recedes into the past, the more imagination is needed to wrench it into the present," James wrote.[3] A similar point is made by Ethan Mordden in his *New Yorker* review of Spiegelman's *Maus*: "The Holocaust is so ter-rifyingly picturesque—so beyond what we think of as real life, what we think of as possible—that its commentators keep dressing it, styling it. It cannot be described to normal men and believed, so it must be conjured up artistically, almost invented."[4]

Yet it would be misleading to argue that the use of fantastic tropes to explore the meaning of the Holocaust is entirely a recent phenomenon. There is something undeniably apocalyptic about the event itself—as there is about the whole self-imposed myth of Nazism—and it should not be surprising that the Holocaust and the fantastic share a history that in some cases almost predates the event itself. A popular science fiction pulp writer named Nat Schachner parodied Hitler and his notions of racial purity in the pages of *Astounding Stories* as early as 1933, and Katherine Burdekin's remarkable 1937 feminist novel *Swastika Night* was among the first works to speculate on the implications of a world dominated by Nazis. In the early years of the war itself, films such as Charles Chaplin's *The Great Dic-tator* created fantasy scenarios to lampoon Hitler and his anti–Semitism. And even in the years after the war, alternate-history stories of Nazi vic-tories appeared with some regularity from authors such as "Sarban" (John W. Wall; *The Sound of His Horn*, 1952), Philip K. Dick (*The Man in the High Castle*, 1962), and William L. Shirer ("If Hitler Had Won World War II," *Look*, 1961).

It wasn't really until the 1960s, following the TV and film productions of *Judgment at Nuremberg*, the Broadway and film productions of *The Diary of Anne Frank*, and—perhaps most important—the widely publi-cized capture and trial of Adolf Eichmann in 1960, that the Holocaust began to take on a historical identity distinct from that of World War II. By then, the combat aspects of the war—strategy, tactics, espionage—had given rise to whole genres of popular fiction, film, and television, and it became apparent that few of these popular treatments had included any significant references to the experiences of Hitler's victims. Still later, when the memoirs of actual survivors such as Elie Wiesel, Primo Levi, and Tadeusz Borowski gained wide prominence and when increasing numbers of other survivors began to speak more openly about their experiences, the conviction grew among writers and historians that the literary mode best suited for confronting the Holocaust—perhaps, indeed, the only appropriate mode, was that of testimony. While the graphic violence and phantasmagorical imagery of a novel such as Jerzy Kosinski's *The Painted Bird* (1965) could earn praise as the work of a survivor (and in part because of its ambiguous status between autobiography and invention), non-survivors such as Romain Gary, Leslie Epstein, and William Styron seemed to invite charges of trivialization (sometimes justified) when dealing with similar, or even less charged, material. In her essay, Ellen R. Weil quotes Theodor Adorno's famous statement that to write poetry after Auschwitz is barbaric and Elie Weisel's claim that "Holocaust literature" itself is an oxymoron, while Joan Gordon explores the restrictions she still feels today in trying to write about a body of literature whose previous criticism "tends more the legislative than the descriptive." And indeed, the most commonly applied critical test of any text that presumes to represent the Holocaust is to measure it against the words of the survivors, or to ask what survivors might think of it. It may be that no other modern historical event has laid such a privileged claim to language and imagination.

And yet the testimony of survivors is by its very nature limited in time and space. It is limited in time for the obvious reason that there are a finite number of aging survivors, and it is limited in space because the sheer volume of testimony being collected by historians threatens to overwhelm all but the most dedicated students and scholars of the event. While a few works of survivors, such Elie Wiesel's *Night*, bid fair to become classics of world literature, most of the first-hand accounts are destined to remain the province of the scholar and the historian. Thus, any tacit agreement that the Holocaust is "off-limits" to the imagination may well have the paradoxical effect of mythologizing it further, as the historical event recedes, and the surviving texts take on the status of icons. For the Holocaust to remain a continuing confrontation with almost unimaginable evil it must, as Caryn James implies, be re-imagined for succeeding generations on their own terms.

But what if those terms include the fantastic? Fantastic literature, by its very nature, violates the norms of realism that have dominated not only Holocaust texts but virtually the whole body of what has been received and taught as "serious" literature for the past two centuries. Fantastic literature suggests fairy tales, myths, science fiction—the impossible or at least the improbable. When I mentioned to a friend that I was working on a special issue of *JFA*, his first response was to ask if the whole concept of the Holocaust and the fantastic didn't seem to imply that the Holocaust itself was a kind of fantasy, an exaggerated or even imagined event not unlike that described in the nut-fringe literature of historical "revisionists." The question reveals a common confusion among the various meanings of "fantasy"—the innocent daydream, the psychotic construct, the propagandistic manipulation, the literary invention. As a literary mode, "fantasy" comes with more semantic baggage than it really needs or deserves, and the intersection of this mode with the fantastical reality of the Holocaust creates complex problems of rhetoric and narrative strategy. As Lawrence L. Langer observes,

> Fantasies have become literally true—a principle, as we shall have occasion to see, that was to have a profound shaping effect on the writer's conception of his world. Fantasy, of course, had been employed for centuries by artists, for its own sake and to offer commentary on the human scene—Bosch populated his canvases with creatures of fantasy; and the records of myth and literature, from the Minotaur to the Houyhnhnms and beyond, are crowded with comparable distortions of reality—sometimes comic, sometimes tragically earnest—and though the reader or observer is often absorbed by these universes of the imagination, he never mistakes them for literal reality.... But when fantasies become literally true, the artist, the writer, must record a reality that has become an *expression* of the impossible, at the same time convincing his audience that whatever distortions he employs do not negate, but clarify reality and subject it to an illuminating metamorphosis.[5]

The question Langer raises is addressed, in one form or another, by each of the essays which follow. The works discussed range from young adult literature (Jane Yolen's *The Devil's Arithmetic*) to the "graphic novel" presented in comic-book form (Art Spiegelman's *Maus*), from France (André Schwarz-Bart's *The Last of the Just*) to Argentina (Jorge Luis Borges's "Deutsches Requiem") to Hasidic tales, from stories by best-selling writers (Stephen King, Romain Gary) to works originally published as genre literature (Lisa Goldstein's *The Red Magician*). But these essays represent only the beginning of the discussion. As far back as 1980, Sidra DeKoven Ezrahi concluded her study of Holocaust literature by noting an increasing number of writers who chose to confront the Holocaust by means of "a leap into fantasy charged with historical possibilities."[6] Ezrahi's observation has proved more prescient than she might have suspected; more than a third of the texts listed in the admittedly incomplete bibliography, which follows the essays, date from 1980 or later. While a few of these listed works are demonstrably exploitative, many represent sincere attempts to find, among the resources of fantastic literature, some means of sustaining our confrontation with the most shocking event of the twentieth century, and to keep it from receding into the pale shadows of history.

NOTES

1. John Updike, "Books: Nobody Gets Away with Everything," *The New Yorker*, May 25, 1992, 86.

2. Caryn James, "Putting the Unimaginable to Imaginative Use," *The New York Times*, March 1, 1992, sec. 2:1, 14.

3. Ibid., 14.

4. Ethan Mordden, "Books: Kat and Maus," *The New Yorker,* April 6, 1992, 91.

5. Lawrence L. Langer, *The Holocaust and the Literary Imagination* (New Haven, CT: Yale University Press, 1975), 23–25.

6. Sidra DeKoven Ezrahi, *By Words Alone: The Holocaust in Literature* (Chicago: University of Chicago Press, 1980), 216.

Uses of the Fantastic
in Literature of
the Holocaust

JUDITH B. KERMAN

Why write about the Nazi Holocaust? And why read about it? Many survivors have needed to bear witness, and for many the idea of bearing witness gave meaning to their sufferings even as they occurred, helping them to survive.

But writings by non-survivors are a more complicated matter, and reading about these events is similarly complex. Questions about the nature and purpose of Holocaust texts which incorporate fantastic elements are not really separate from these broader issues, which concern the ontological as well as the moral nature of the Holocaust itself.

First, although we know that these events took place, it is difficult to understand the relationship between events like the Holocaust and the realities of everyday life. A personal example: when I visited Germany, and especially Dachau, I was baffled by the way in which they were just places in the real world; my understanding of their cataclysmic historic meaning, especially for me personally as a Jew, did not mesh with their ordinariness. Even Dachau is only a place: a railroad station, a pleasant suburb, barbed wire fences and concrete. Which is real, the concentration camp or comfortable middle-class life? Is it only a question of 45 years, or different universes?

One might ask the same question about any catastrophe, natural or man-made, which reminds us how thin the thread is which keeps us from either misery or savagery. Cambodia. Hiroshima. Kuwait City and Baghdad. Even the lives of our own homeless.

Yet, to the extent that our everyday lives continue in relatively unruffled comfort, these experiences are in fact fantastic to contemplate, which is why almost every account reports refusal by most European Jews to believe the warnings they received, even as they were herded onto the trains. As Jane Yolen's novel, *The Devil's Arithmetic*, frames it,[1] these reports were clearly "fairy tales," madness. Even today, the efforts of some revisionist "historians" to question whether the Holocaust really happened are psychologically aided by the contradiction between most people's everyday experience and such unmitigated horror.

A major difficulty in dealing with the Holocaust in literature is precisely that these events seemed to be, should have been, fantastic, like the torture stories Tzvetan Todorov describes as "scenes of cruelty"[2] in his study of the fantastic as a genre. He clearly considers them only literary phenomena, and yet any torture victim can attest to their potential for reality. When the real is so fantastic, what literary effects will succeed in making it credible, and in helping the reader to comprehend its human meaning?

A second question concerns the Nazis and their collaborators, how any human being can do what the Nazis and others did, thousands and thousands of apparently normal people who committed repeated atrocities. Would any or all of us do the same, under similar conditions? What was the difference between those who participated and those who resisted? Was effective resistance possible? What is the nature of the minds that could plan or carry out the death camps? We cannot argue that they were not human. Again, Nazism is not the only example, just the paradigm: torture is as old as human history, from ancient times down to today's Iraq, Syria, South Africa, El Salvador. And planning nuclear war after Hiroshima and Nagasaki is not so very different from planning the industrial-style system of the death camps.

How can literature accommodate the character of a torturer or a comfortable, everyday military man with the capacity for mass murder?

A third question concerns the victims themselves. Why did they cooperate in their destruction? Were the survivors merely lucky, were they somehow stronger than those who died, or did they collaborate, implicating themselves in the evil processes that destroyed their fellows, like the *Judenrat* members and the Kapos? Primo Levi declares[3] that one had to find a way to become relatively privileged within the system to survive, while Viktor E. Frankl declares[4] the necessity for each prisoner to find a meaning for his or her life, a reason to keep struggling. Here literature has fewer problems, because identification with the reporter is a familiar mode. But as Levi points out, few of those who had the most extreme, perhaps the purest, experience of the concentration camps lived to tell about it. And many of the survivors (such as Elie Wiesel at several points in *Night*) accuse themselves of cowardice, complicity or selfishness.

I am not sure it is possible to find settled answers to these kinds of questions, but in asking them we struggle with the human meaning of the Holocaust. The moral questions are much more complicated than Good versus Evil. Although without any question the concentration camps and ghettos were unmitigated evil, as soon as we look at individual human beings rather than a social system, motivation becomes complicated— even Mengele, even Hitler, was once an innocent child. And since Freud we have not been able to rest comfortably with that adjective. Fairy tales, as Bruno Bettelheim has taught us in his major study, *The Uses of Enchantment: The Meaning and Importance of Fairy Tales*, arise from, and speak to, those parts of the mind which were never innocent. It is no surprise, seen from this perspective, that they should foreshadow terrible realities, the psychopathologies of entire societies. (For a provocative Freudian reading of Nazism as psychopathology, see Richard Rubenstein's *After Auschwitz: Radical Theology and Contemporary Judaism*.)

Thus the moral discourse needed to consider the Holocaust is much more complicated than it might at first appear. Mimesis is inadequate to deal with these questions. Repeated exposure to survivor stories is numbing; the repetitions of horrific scenes and actions weaken their impact, so that, as Kathryn Hume suggests,[5] we begin to need novelty to experience the shock of horror afresh. In addition, the uniqueness of each ordinary individual pales against the background of such horrific extremes. Even Elie Wiesel, under the guise of realism, adopts a literary and sometimes melodramatic tone in his attempt to find a workable aesthetic distance from his experiences, to keep them from being alternately overwhelming or numbing and to insist on their moral significance.

To respond meaningfully to such a challenge, writers need to incorporate moral and emotional complexity; one approach is made available by the techniques of the fantastic, the "condensation of images which allows it to affect its readers at many levels and in many different ways."[6] I would like to consider several examples which use the fantastic in a number of different ways, some more successful than others, to wrestle with these questions.

A striking example to consider is *The Last of the Just*, published by Andre Schwarz-Bart in 1959. The novel is built around the Jewish legend that there are 36 Just Men, the Lamed-Vov, upon whose shoulders the world reposes and into whose hearts all the sufferings of the world are taken. It traces the history of the Levi family, into which a Just Man is born in each generation, often to be martyred. About one third of the book considers the early history; the remainder is the story of three generations: Mordecai, Benjamin, and finally Ernie, who dies in a death camp.

The novel hovers very delicately at the edge of the fantastic. In addition to the legend itself, which is either fantasy or religion depending on your point of view, the histories of the Levi Just Men are told with a light touch, a sense of the ridiculous and yet great affection for people who are often wise but equally often foolish. The voice is the voice of folktale and legend rather than reportage, even in the accounts of pogrom and martyrdom. Although the style becomes more realistic as it approaches contemporary time, new elements of the fantastic enter, first Ernie Levy's childhood perspectives and imaginings, and later his behavior when he escapes Nazi-occupied France and begins to live as a dog. And of course this increasing realism of style plays against the increasingly fantastic events we know to be historical. Finally, in a startling reversal, Ernie's wedding takes place on a level and in a setting which can only be "fantasy" (unless it is heaven) at the very moment that he is entering into the horror tale, the hell-made-real, of the death camps.

These uses of the fantastic serve several functions. First, the light and legendary tone of the history of the Levis, especially the martyrdoms, immediately sets up a tension with what the reader knows will be the future—the reality of the ghettos and death camps undercuts and underlines this tone and makes it impossible to take these early martyrdoms as merely legend. Beyond this, Ernie's experiences, in particular, are often presented with hallucinatory vividness, using the resources of poetry and fantasy to make events and emotions more real in their impact on the reader than mimesis can do.

Several events in Ernie's childhood show anti–Semites actualizing their own fantasies: when his schoolmates reenact the Crucifixion, they accuse him of killing Christ and beat him up; later, when he has learned of the legend of the Just Men and decided, with a child's idealism, that he must be one, his attempts to absorb the suffering of a Gentile neighbor child lead to a pogrom, as the child's abusive mother accuses him of a "dirty Jewish" assault on her daughter.

Ernie's character, always slightly dreamlike, balances aspects of the archetype and the ordinary man, making his final sacrifice consistent with the moral resonance of the legend of the Just Men.

An interesting contrast is provided by the *Hasidic Tales of the Holo-*

caust compiled by Yaffa Eilach. These are brutally realistic tales in most ways, much more unsparing in their tone than, for instance, Elie Wiesel's *Night* or Bernard Gotfryd's *Anton the Dove Fancier.* Yet they are marked by many elements which "depart from consensus reality."[7] The stories are full of blessings by rabbis which heal or save the protagonist, prophecies, dreams which are either prophetic or which save the protagonist's life, miraculous survivals. Eilach describes the function of the Hasidic tale as

> to restore order and to mend the broken lines of communication between man and his fellow man, and between heaven and earth, at a time and place when faith and prayer failed.... Despite the scope of human destruction, the Hasidic tale believes that there is a way out of the inferno, not just a way into it. The normal and physical struggle against evil provides man with a normative and historical link with a pre–Holocaust past and a post–Holocaust future.[8]

These stories, like the legend of the 36 Just Men, raise questions about the definition of fantasy as departing from consensus reality. The stories were collected from survivors; the tales are true. The question of who constitutes the consensus upon which to base judgments about reality suddenly becomes urgent, raising questions that Todorov, for example, totally ignores. For the superstitious or mystically religious, many "fantastic" events are part of the reality of their consensus group, just as for torture victims the "tale of cruelty" describes lived experience.

Lisa Goldstein's effort to incorporate the Holocaust into a sorcery tale, *The Red Magician,* speaks directly to the ontological question of the Holocaust, what is real and what is fantasy, in several places. She provides a useful, if not terribly fresh, image of the ambiguity of the real in the shadow of the death camps when she says, "This was the real world that lurked beneath the other one like a skull beneath skin, the world of death."[9] More optimistically, her hero says, "After all, if nightmares are real, then miracles should be too."[10]

In theory, high fantasy should be able to capitalize on its own sense that there is another world beneath the facade of everyday reality and its tradition of battles between good and evil, and so provide a new perspective on our century's most awful nonfictional example. But in spite of evidently higher ambitions, *The Red Magician* fails to rise above genre fiction. The novel finally seems trivial as it frames a concentration camp narrative within the context of a battle of magic between two wizards.

The evil of the wizard rabbi, refusing to listen to the magician Vörös's warnings about the coming disaster, seems a matter of possessiveness, egoism and denial, hardly complex or profound enough to lend mythic resonance to the battle of magics. The battle itself and the "miracles" are standard genre magic.

The historically actual evil looming in the story's context demands a villain whose motivation, while perhaps mysterious, cannot be questioned by the reader, explained away or reconciled, and a battle which amazes and appalls in the way that death-camp narratives do. The story's sense of miracle must somehow speak to the deeper issues of the real history Goldstein invokes.

The reader consensus on which the high fantasy genre depends, in fact, is precisely that its devices are *not* real; but the reader of *The Red Magician* viscerally understands the urgency of the historic context and the actual mystery of the historic evil. This historic reality flattens out any inherent moral resonance the genre devices might have still carried, demanding that the author penetrate the genre to its deeper meanings, not only in occasional statements but in every detail and movement of the story. Unfortunately, by this standard *The Red Magician* fails. Although its characters ask some of the central ontological and moral questions,[11] the structure and texture of the story itself do not.

Jane Yolen's *The Devil's Arithmetic* also depends on genre fantasy— the time-travel story—and Yolen also raises the ontological question— how do we encompass these events within our sense of the "real?" However, her device and her purpose are well-suited to each other, and she successfully engages the reader's identification with her child heroine in order to teach a lesson precisely about the continuing importance of *stories* about the Holocaust. Although Yolen's work is clearly a "juvenile" as well as a "fantasy," it is supported by strong characterization and narrative detail; more significantly, the time-travel idea is the mechanism by which the story grapples with precisely the problems of belief and reality which are at issue, deepening and justifying her use of genre and finally allowing her to transcend it.

Similarly, even if we do not accept the literal efficacy of miracles, of a rabbi's blessing or a dream, the Hasidic stories use their fantastic elements, as Eilach comments, for a purpose integrally related to the deepest issues of the Holocaust: to express a faith that, at least for these survivors, human and divine care was not shattered by the death camps. This is in powerful contrast to the theme of the uncaring sky, the birds singing as the death machine grinds up its victims, the emptiness where God should be, in Wiesel, Schwarz-Bart and others, and to the revelation of human evil in both fictional and nonfictional accounts.

Eilach implies[12] that the Hasidic stories also mark survival itself as a moral victory in the universe of the Holocaust. Yet the complexity of this position too is suggested by Leslie Epstein's powerful and grotesque novel, *The King of the Jews*. This fictional history of an apocryphal Polish ghetto and its *Judenrat* uses fantasy and farce, comic and fantastic set-pieces including a sleepwalking scene and a burning apartment building worthy of the circus, to explore the problems of survival and collaboration. The novel's voice is the voice of Jewish folk humor. As in Schwarz-Bart, as the circumstances of its characters become more historically dire, Epstein uses fewer overtly fantastic effects in direct narrative, but he never entirely abandons farce. A hallucinatory piece of anti–Semitic street theatre occurs early in the book; an extraordinary performance of *Macbeth* by the Jewish orphans in the midst of the deportations occurs almost at the end.

Although I.C. Trumpelman, the President of the *Judenrat*, is the most striking character, the most extraordinary scenes in the novel are those in which the members of the *Judenrat* are chosen and later attempt to make terrible decisions, sacrificing some in the vain hope that more would thus be saved, enslaving and punishing their own people in the effort to save them. We know that the Nazis historically placed Jews in such awful moral dilemmas; these scenes consistently mix farce with terror, and the farce somehow sharpens the horror as the comically-drawn characters, exaggerated Everymen from a Yiddish theatre skit, struggle with their impossible choices. Little in *The King of the Jews* is fantastic in the sense of being literally impossible, but the tone insistently distances the reader from realism, and in doing so highlights both moral and ontological issues.

Art Spiegelman's remarkable two-volume graphic novel, *Maus: A Survivor's Tale* and *Maus II: A Survivor's Tale—And Here My Troubles Began*, also deals centrally with the moral ambiguity of survival. Spiegelman casts his complex narrative as a comic book and simultaneously as a fairy tale with animal characters. In this tale within a tale within a genre within a genre, the son of two survivors struggles with his relationship to his parents, especially his father, as the father tells the story of the parents' survival. Although both the survival story and the story of the son's relationship to the parents would stand on their own as survivor narratives, the use of the comic book format and the animal characterizations adds amazing richness and tension, as the use of legend and fantastic effects did in the case of *The Last of the Just*.

We are used to dealing with comic books as fantasy of a flat and trivial kind; the fact that this is a personal history of unusually rich and honest emotion and moral complexity plays against the simplicity of the drawings and the expectation of "comic book" flatness. We are used to dealing with fairy tales about talking animals as allegory or, in Bettelheim's terms, an opportunity for imaginative working through of complex personal problems; here the childlike allegory of Jews as mice, Nazis as cats and Poles as pigs adds to the sinisterness of the events.

Further, in *Maus II*, scenes showing characters as humans in mouse masks[13] add another layer to the ambiguity of historical and perhaps of moral role; if Artie and his survivor psychiatrist are now humans pretending to be mice, what is their moral status? What does it mean to see yourself (or present yourself) as a victim if this is not the whole truth? This device, uniquely available through the combined cartoon/fairy tale format, opens yet another dimension of the story, suggesting ways in which the problems of the Holocaust extend into the next generation.

The moral and also in some sense ontological problem of the nature of Nazism, of how ordinary people can become torturers, is raised by stories which go into the mind of the Nazi. Romain Gary's novel *The Dance of Genghis Cohn* begins with the promising and overtly fantastic premise of a *dybbuk*, the ghost of a murdered Jew, possessing the Nazi who murdered him. "Genghis" Cohn, the murdered Yiddish stand-up comic, possesses the outwardly-respectable police chief, interrupting his superficially-moral life with uncontrollable Yiddish-flavored outrageousness and threatening the policeman's reputation. Unfortunately, rather than exploring the character of the Nazi and the conflict between him and his *dybbuk*, the novel soon wanders into an elaborate and unsatisfying allegory about the causes of war and mass murder. The novel provides good evidence for Kathryn Hume's contention that "character-based fantasy is difficult to create and sustain."[14]

A much more successful short tale, noted by Hume, is Jorge Luis Borges's, "Deutsches Requiem." While it is stunningly convincing as a look inside the mind of a fanatic, the relationship of this story to the fantastic requires further examination. Hume makes the point that "the mind of a Nazi who tortured Jews ... is as alien to some readers as is a rabbit's,"[15] and it is possible to rest her contention that it is a "character fantasy" on that fact alone. However, for the most part the story seems a "realistic" interior monologue, and rather less "fantastic" than many stream-of-consciousness works. Hume comments that "Borges manages to maintain the full impact of his creation because he does not stretch it so far that the character comes to seem ordinary,"[16] but at first glance the extraordinariness of Otto Dietrich zur Linde seems more closely related to the ontological question of the Holocaust's place in human moral history than to the use of techniques of the fantastic.

However, the story also opens up a complex puzzle-box tied to the nature of Borges's entire oeuvre; familiarity with more of his work suggests that the situation is not so simple. As Emir Rodriguez Monegal and Alastair Reid note in their introduction to *Borges: A Reader*, "Few writers' works are more intimately one ... almost any text of his ... can be used to reconstruct the whole body of his work."[17] In fact, we cannot understand "Deutsches Requiem" without exploring its relationship to his other works.

Borges clearly felt outrage and disgust toward Nazism. His essay "Portrait of the Germanophile," for instance, evidences little ambiguity when it characterizes the admirer of Hitler as someone "cheered by wickedness and atrocity ... a secret and sometimes public admirer of vicious cleverness and cruelty."[18] He called Nazism "...uninhabitable; men can only die for it, lie for it, kill and wound for it. No one, in the intimate depths of his being, can wish it to triumph."[19]

Borges accused putative "Germanophiles" of "complete ignorance"[20] of the great accomplishments of German culture, including the German thinkers and writers, such as Schopenhauer, whose names are touchstones in Borges's works. By contrast, he declared his own love for that culture in the fervent late poem, "To the German Language."[21] But Otto Dietrich zur Linde, the Nazi murderer of "Deutsches Requiem," is, like Borges himself, well-educated in German culture and a particular lover of Nietzsche, Spengler and Schopenhauer, as well as Brahms, composer of the monumental *Ein Deutsches Requiem*. And Borges's attitude toward mental systems such as Nazism is always ambiguous, in spite of the clarity of his moral stance in the "real world." In the major fantasy, "Tlön, Uqbar, Orbis Tertius," he writes,

> [In the early 1930s], any symmetrical system whatsoever which gave the appearance of order—dialectical materialism, anti–Semitism, Nazism—was enough to fascinate men. Why not fall under the spell of Tlön and submit to the minute and vast evidence of an ordered planet?[22]

Borges seems to view this fascination with contempt; yet, throughout his works, he is himself clearly fascinated with just such created worlds, inventing them almost obsessively as free-standing fantasies and endlessly linking them to the world of consensus reality through the very seamlessness of his oeuvre.

Even Borges's attitude toward zur Linde himself is made ambiguous by the mirroring of zur Linde in "Three Versions of Judas." This work of overt fantasy purports to be a critical essay about a scholar, Runeberg, whose lifework speculates that Judas himself might have been the man of sorrows, a man whose "unlimited asceticism" extends even to vilifying and mortifying his spirit.[23] The man of sorrows's sacrifice, if it were indeed to be perfect, had to include sin itself:

> Judas sought Hell, because the happiness of the Lord was enough for him.... God made Himself totally a man but a man to the point of infamy ... reprobation and the abyss.... He chose the vilest destiny of all: He was Judas.[24]

In eerily similar terms, zur Linde describes his dedication to companions and cruelties he finds personally revolting, for the sake of his "lofty purpose."[25] He sees his life as "preordained"[26] in a manner analogous to Judas's,[27] and equates his appointment as subdirector of a concentration camp to the lives of "Paul, servant of Jesus," and Raskolnikov, whose destiny of banal evil and guilt he sees as "more arduous than the undertaking of Napoleon."[28]

Finally, he celebrates even the destruction of Germany,

> in order to construct the New Order.... If victory and injustice and happiness are not for Germany, let them be for other nations. Let Heaven exist, even though our dwelling place is Hell.[29]

The puzzle-box extends even to the nature of Nazism's crimes. In his complex and baffling essay, "A New Refutation of Time," Borges raises a question which must appall anyone who thinks about the moral meaning of the Holocaust, and yet whose logic, as always in Borges, is hard to disallow entirely. After an extended argument concerning the repetitive nature of time, he writes,

> the Sanhedrin of the Mishnah declares that, for the Justice of God, he who kills a single man destroys the world; if there is no plurality, he who annihilated all men would be no more guilty than the primitive and solitary Cain, which is orthodox, nor more universal in his destruction, which can be magic. I believe that is true. The tumultuous general catastrophes—fires, wars, epidemics—are but a single sorrow, illusorily multiplied in many mirrors ... what one person can suffer is the maximum that can be suffered on earth.... There is no point in being overwhelmed by the appalling total of human suffering; such a total does not exist. Neither poverty nor pain is accumulable.[30]

This chilling conundrum recalls Dostoevsky: if a single child suffers, how can God be just? Yet, intuitively, one must repudiate a position which denies the special enormity of genocide.

Finally, the story's title—"Deutsches Requiem"—must be considered. At one level, the story can be read as a requiem for Germany, the erudite and twisted character of zur Linde a demonstration that the glories of German culture which Borges loved did not protect Germans from infamy.

Indeed, Borges implies in "Tlön..." and elsewhere that the very love of abstraction, a particular characteristic of German thinking, might have been part of the problem.

But Brahms's *Ein Deutsches Requiem* itself, a work which is often somber but finally radiantly affirmative, insists that "they that mourn ... shall be comforted,"[31] that "the souls of the righteous are in the hand of God, and there shall no torment touch them."[32] Reading "Deutsches Requiem," hearing the self-justifying voice of the fanatic tormentor and murderer in the context of that gloriously humane music, one must ask a final question: How shall they, the survivors; how shall we, who come after, be comforted? Somehow this question encompasses all the unanswerable questions raised by the Nazi Holocaust and confronted by writers and readers alike. As George Steiner writes,

> The notion of "coming to terms" with the Holocaust is a vulgar and profound indecency. Man cannot, he must not ever "come to terms," historicize pragmatically or incorporate into the comforts of reason his derogation from the human within himself. He must not blur the possibility that the death-camps and the world's indifference to them marked the failure of a crucial experiment: man's effort to become fully human.[33]

In the face of issues of such difficulty and human urgency, consensus reality is an inadequate category and realistic strategies falter. Fantastic modalities risk trivializing their subject or, conversely, appearing trivial in such a context. Yet we must, by whatever means are available to us, attempt answers to the unspeakable questions posed by the Nazi Holocaust. Sometimes, as some of the works I have discussed demonstrate, the fantastic can provide serviceable approaches, however partial, to this crucial undertaking.

NOTES

1. Jane Yolen, *The Devil's Arithmetic* (New York: Viking Kestrel, 1988), 67.
2. Tzvetan Todorov, *The Fantastic: A Structural Approach to a Literary Genre* (Cleveland: Press of Case Western Reserve University, 1973), 133.
3. Primo Levi, *The Drowned and the Saved* (New York: Vintage, 1988), 17.
4. Viktor E. Frankl, *Man's Search for Meaning: An Introduction to Logotherapy* (New York: Washington Square, 1963), 117.
5. Kathryn Hume, *Fantasy and Mimesis: Responses to Reality in Western Literature* (New York: Methuen, 1984), 40.
6. Ibid., 196.
7. Ibid., 21.
8. Yaffa Eilach, *Hasidic Tales of the Holocaust* (New York: Vintage, 1982), xix–xxi.
9. Lisa Goldstein, *The Red Magician* (New York: Pocket Books, 1982), 126.

10. Ibid., 101.

11. Ibid., 143.

12. Eilach, *Hasidic Tales of the Holocaust*, xxi.

13. Art Spiegelman, *Maus II: A Survivor's Tale—And Here My Troubles Begin* (New York: Pantheon, 1991), 41–47.

14. Hume, *Fantasy and Mimesis*, 161.

15. Ibid., 162.

16. Ibid.

17. Emir Rodriguez Monegal and Alastair Reid, Introduction to *Borges: A Reader*, ed. Emir Rodriguez Monegal and Alastair Reid (New York: Dutton, 1981), x.

18. Jorge Luis Borges, *Borges: A Reader*, ed. Emir Rodriguez Monegal and Alastair Reid (New York: Dutton, 1981), 129.

19. Ibid., 154.

20. Ibid., 128.

21. Ibid., 320.

22. Ibid., 122.

23. Jorge Luis Borges, *Labyrinths: Selected Stories and Other Writings*, ed. Donald A. Yates and James E. Irby (New York: New Directions, 1964), 97.

24. Ibid., 98–99.

25. Ibid., 143.

26. Ibid.

27. Ibid., 96.

28. Ibid., 144.

29. Ibid., 147.

30. Borges, *Borges: A Reader*, 184.

31. Matthew 5:4.

32. Wisdom of Sol. 3:1.

33. George Steiner, "Through That Glass Darkly," *Salmagundi* 93 (Winter 1992): 48.

The Fantastic in Holocaust Literature
Writing and Unwriting the Unbearable[1]

MICHAEL P. MCCLEARY

> *... the conscious impotence of rage*
> *At human folly, and the laceration*
> *Of laughter at what cease to amuse.*
> —T.S. Eliot ("Little Gidding," *ll.* 135–37)

Holocaust literature raises a number of complex theoretical problems. Artistic decorum, in a profoundly moral sense, becomes an issue when artist employ fantastic characters, events, or narrative devices to portray an all too real historical abomination. While many readers may share Stephen Dedalus's sentiment that "History is a nightmare from which I'm trying to awake," brute fact has made the Holocaust a proper noun, an indelible mark on Western Civilization—despite the National Front in England and other neo–Nazi groups that deny it ever occurred. Indeed, the existence of such groups lends a particular urgency to the question of whether an author can effectively render the horrifying actuality of the Holocaust with purely imaginative characters or events, and whether such fictive presentations strengthen or undermine its historicity.

An equally complex issue arises in the question of whether fiction-alized or fantastic accounts of Holocaust provide escape from its horrors. Another dimension to this problem of artistic effect is the problem of whether an audience should ever "appreciate" or take pleasure in the aesthetic quality of a work of fiction whose subject is the abominations of the Holocaust?[2] Is the reader's experience of the text here at odds with the author's presumed intent to evoke a moral horror at the Nazis' systematic attempt to exterminate the Jews, Gypsies, and other "degenerate" groups? And what role, if any, does an author's own careful artifice play in the dynamics of preserving the memory of or drawing ethical conclusions from the Holocaust?

Psychological recoil in the face of the graphic horror of the Holocaust is one key component of the aesthetic problematics of "the literature of atrocity." Witness accounts of the Holocaust, like Elie Wiesel's autobiographical novel, *Night*, profoundly shock most readers' sensibilities. Yet as Lawrence Langer points out, they may ultimately have the opposite effect:

> Most of the autobiographies concerned with *"l'univers concentrationnaire"* numb the consciousness without enlarging it and providing it with a fresh or unique perception of the nature of reality, chiefly because the enormity of the atrocities they recount finally forces the reader to lose his orientation altogether and to feel as though he were wandering in a wilderness of evil totally divorced from any time or place he has ever known—a reality not latent in, but external to, his own experience.[3]

Encountering such a reality can initiate a desire in the reader to escape this assault on his fundamental sense of normalcy. One reaction is a state of moral shock that has an odd, distancing effect, much as extreme physical trauma activates the body's self-numbing capacities. It is partly this self-defensive numbness that has cause some Holocaust survivors (including Wiesel) to remain silent for many years before writing of their experiences—if they ever write at all. In his essay, "No News from Auschwitz," A.M. Rosenthal writes of the disturbing sense of mundanity he experienced on visiting this death camp, obliquely suggesting how time, distance, and even nature add to our tendency to disengage psychologically from the events of the Holocaust. While we may acknowledge the eloquence of George Steiner's argument that silence is the only appropriate response to the Holocaust, such a position can underwrite disengagement rather than forcing us to face the enormity of all the Holocaust represents.

The task of writing the Holocaust remains, therefore, despite our reticence, or psychological and political forces that would unwrite it: "Without the Holocaust, such literature would not have been possible; with it, by a curious inversion, literature has taken as its task *making* such a reality 'possible' for the imagination."[4] Together with authors like Toni Morrison and Louise Erdrich, who recreate the historical atrocities committed against other minority groups, Holocaust writers play an essential role in piquing a cultural consciousness—and conscience—only too ready to go to sleep and forget the facts of history. The use of the fantastic is often integral to the power of the works of these writers, and in this essay I will argue that not only is the fantastic appropriate for depicting the Holocaust, it may indeed be, paradoxically, the most "natural" mode in which to represent this age of extremity. The universe of the death camps is so imbued with hitherto unthinkable brutality and horror that it becomes literally fantastic; indeed, the most detailed and dispassionate witness accounts are often filled with apocalyptic images, ghostly figures, and fiery visions.

The two writers I will discuss do not focus on the death camps or on accurately representing the Holocaust experience itself. Instead, Leslie Epstein and Romain Gary create fantastic characters and comic narratives that deliberately establish an ironic distance from the unbearable experiences witness literature so graphically depicts. But Epstein and Gary then powerfully subvert the reader's comfort zone. Rather than allowing reader the luxury of staying at an ironic remove from their texts, Epstein and Gary collapse the ironic distance at certain points in their books and thereby produce an intense emotional engagement with the human reality of the Holocaust. Langer usefully outlines the dynamics of their narratives in his discussion of Jakov Lind and Picasso's *Guernica*:

> By a process of carefully controlled disorientation, these artists first "lose" the attention of their readers—sometimes gradually, as the unreal and the fantastic encroach almost instantaneously, as in the works of Jakov Lind, where an atmosphere of illogic and lunacy prevails from the beginning— then "regain" that attention, its premises having been thoroughly altered.[5]

As we will see, Epstein's book follows the first tack above, demonstrating in its use of metaphor and description the slowly encroaching unreality of life in Ghetto Lodz. Gary's book, on the other hand, is from the outset a thoroughly fantastic and grotesque vision. In both cases, readers are shocked into acknowledging, however reluctantly, their membership in the interpretive community whose recent past includes the Holocaust— along with the other versions of genocide practiced on the Armenians, Cambodians, and Kurds. Black humor and savage satire combine with the fantastic in Epstein's and Gary's books to produce a searching critique of humanity that is the root of comedy; as Langer notes in his discussion of the works of Jakov Lind, there is no place for tragedy in the Holocaust:

> Lind thus manages to eliminate from the story the same dimension of tragedy which history had eliminated from life, at least during the period

of the Holocaust, *when an atmosphere of fantasy had corrupted the moral clarity that breeds tragedy* (my emphasis).[6]

My contention is that it may take the combination of humor and fantasy to suggest in any way the true horror of the Holocaust for many nonvictim readers. The narrative dynamics of Epstein's and Gary's novels leave us particularly vulnerable to those moments where these writers forthrightly and unambiguously state the hard moral truths the Holocaust has to teach us about human nature.

Critical response to Leslie Epstein's 1976 novel, *King of the Jews*, underscores the aesthetic dilemmas I have outlined thus far. Writing in the *Yale Review*, Edith Milton is put off by Epstein's technique of patching together bits of historical truth and his own fictionalized and "flip" variations on them. She admits she "cannot recognize … the alien sensibility" which produced the book, and believes that Epstein has produced an "angry fairy tale, an adolescent fantasy in which the outside world exists dimly."[7] Milton concludes that "such distortion" makes Epstein's book itself "an atrocity" because it "tackles a ghastly subject and, God help us, makes it fun."[8] Robert Alter, on the other hand, praises Epstein's skill in creating a narrative of ironically understated horror by using such devices as renaming the Nazis as "Deaths-Headers" or "Others" to enhance the "peculiar generalizing effect of the novel as a whole,"[9] a universalization of the moral implications of the Holocaust. How can two critics reach such radically opposed assessments of the moral vision behind Epstein's work?

King of the Jews draws upon historical documents and testimony from a few escapees about the liquidation of the Lodz ghetto, the last concentration of Polish Jews to be sent off to the death camps. The book's namesake is one Isaiah Chaim Trumpelman, based on the actual figure of Mordechai Chaim Rumkowski, who headed the *Judenrat* that oversaw the factory work the ghetto's slowly starving residents were forced to do in order to remain alive. Ironically dubbed "the king of life," King Chaim was also the man designated by the Nazis to select those who would be transported during each "action" as the extermination of the Jews proceeded apace. Epstein lends his Trumpelman an exaggerated measure of the actual Rumkowski's arrogance, a megalomaniac's desire for power he justified as the only way to keep the ghetto's productive capacity high and thereby save—for a time—the lives of the Jews.[10]

Trumpelman forms the center of the narrative, but Epstein also skillfully evokes the increasingly unreal reality of ghetto life in his use of grotesque and fantastic imagery. The sun, for example, serves as a visual leitmotif. On the opening page of the novel we encounter the odd metaphor of "the yellowish lozenge of the Polish sun,"[11] and Epstein proceeds to undo our instinctive associations of the sun with life-sustaining warmth, stability, and continuity; it becomes "a bare bulb on a cord,"[12] "like the blade of a sawmill, shining, gleaming, spinning around,"[13] and "like an egg yolk slipping down the glossy side of the sky."[14] These grotesque images violate our sense of naturalism and heighten the horror of one fantastic scene in which Bettsack, the abject and half-mad schoolteacher, attempts to reassert the order of the universe. As a lesson on the orbital patterns of the planets, he arranges young people holding vegetables as stars, and then sets each of them spinning around a center, which he occupies as he revolves with a large squash. The comic aspect of the crazed schoolmaster and his dizzy students (including one who streaks about as a comet) gives way to a rising sense of terror when Bettsack collapses and the children anxiously question him about the possible extinction of the sun. Bettsack tries to dispel their fears, but ends up as Epstein's dark, ironic spokesman, stating enigmatically that "There is nothing science cannot achieve."[15]

The children's panic is calmed only by the arrival of the charismatic Trumpelman, who gathers them to him as together they watch a lovely sunset—through Epstein's characteristic filter:

> There, on the horizon, the real sun was leaking something. Red stuff, like jam, came out of it.... "Like a raspberry drop," said Usher Flicker ... the sun, cut by the earth's edge, still pumped that sweet-looking stuff from its center.[16]

Epstein's descriptions of the various residents of the ghetto likewise reflect the process of creeping dehumanization that made the mechanical elimination of the Jews a problem of engineering for the Nazis. For example, we meet Putermilch, who looks "like a root that had been dug up from the ground. A tuber. A yam."[17]

Such metaphoric transmutations of the sun or of characters are not, in themselves, enough to justify *King of the Jews* as more than an angry fairy tale. The most effective moment in the novel, to my mind, is the chapter in which the historical fact that there were theatrical performances inside the Lodz ghetto provides Epstein with the idea of staging a play few of his ghetto residents had ever encountered, *Makbet*. The ironies of choosing this of all plays are apparent enough; the ghetto residents quickly identify Shakespeare's tragic couple who makes a pact with evil as Trumpelman and his wife, who are seated in the places of honor but increasingly uncomfortable in the first row. Epstein's naïve audience has little of Coleridge's capacity for a willing suspension of disbelief; their ghetto world itself teeters on the brink of the inconceivable. For his part, Trumpelman begins to view the play as a direct challenge to his authority; he interrupts action onstage with verbal self-justifications and blustering threats that further attenuate the already blurred line between the fiction of the play and the incipient violence looming over the ghetto.

Epstein then collapses Shakespeare's fantastic drama into the historical present in a brilliant narrative stroke; at his second meeting with the witches, Macbeth sees the vision of the child-kings who will succeed him, but the eerie laughter of the hags is provided by the half-crazed and paranoid Trumpelman. In the silence that falls on the audience, Trumpelman than demands to k now who was responsible for this subversive performance, but before he can extort or cajole an answer, he is cut off:

> At that moment the owl hooted again. Everyone searched for the bird, for its lit-up eyes. It wasn't there. Not on its perch. Not anywhere. But the hoot-hooting continued, louder than before. It seemed to be coming from far off, perhaps from outside the theater completely. And drawing nearer, too. The audience stirred. People who had pocket watches took them out. From either side of the stage the curtains were coming together. Still no sign of the bright green eyes! What could it mean? Then someone, a person inside the House of Culture, declared, "The train!"[18]

Epstein inverts the dynamics of Aristotelian catharsis here; rather than having their fear and pity purged by witnessing violence and terror on stage, Epstein's literally captive audience (of which, we, the readers, are a part) finds itself suddenly in the grip of a reality even more chilling than Macbeth's. The ghetto residents will not be able to fulfill the psychological dialect of returning to and functioning within normal society after leaving the play; Epstein's black, ironic touch has them remain for the end of the play, choosing to endure the fictive hell of Macbeth rather than face the unbearable reality of their imminent shipment on to the death camps. Seeking a temporary escape from the unbearable, Epstein's characters find themselves ever more enmeshed in it. They are caught in a historical text that art cannot unwrite, and their terror becomes ours, for beyond the margins of art lies an unspeakable fate.

In the "Makbet" chapter, Epstein implicitly recognizes and at the same time defuses the moral objections to his use of fantastic or fictive events in writing about the Holocaust; we share a palpable shock of horror with the ghetto audience when the owl's hooting is recognized as the transport train. Moreover, our simultaneous appreciation of the irony and art whereby Epstein collapses this play within a fiction into the literal facts of the Holocaust enhances that shock, at the same time as it effectively adumbrates the issue of creating art out of the Holocaust that troubles Epstein's critics.

Epstein's novel manipulates a hodgepodge of historical facts and anecdotes into a grotesque and sometimes fantastic depiction of Holocaust reality, but Romain Gary's astonishing 1968 novel, *The Dance of Genghis Cohn*, operates from its outset on a thoroughly fantastic level. The first-person narrator is a former Yiddish comedian, stage-named Genghis Cohn for his viciously satiric humor. Gary makes only one concession to narrative realism: Cohn is among forty thousand victims mass-executed and buried by the Nazis at Babi Yar. But in a moment of comically perverse heroism as he stands naked on the edge of the mass grave, Cohn "moons" the firing squad and shouts "Kush mir in tokhes" ("Kiss my Ass") before he is gunned down. From this grotesque act emerges Gary's narrative premise: the officer in charge of this slaughter, named Schaltz, is so struck by this Jew's defiance that he looks up Cohn's name on the list of victims. This plants Cohn into his subconscious mind as a mythical Jewish demon, a *dybbuk*, and it is from this fantastic perspective that the novel is narrated.

Eli Pfefferkorn has noted that in Genghis Cohn "Gary has found the appropriate metaphor to fuse fact with fantasy ... a character whose dual nature allows him to straddle reality and fantasy."[19] The namesake of *The Dance of Genghis Cohn* is not only obsessed, but himself an obsession, and his running monologues alternate between "burlesque frivolity and historical-philosophical commentary."[20] While Cohn's bitter standup routine moves fluidly from the present back to the scene of his execution and then forward into scenarios of the future, the narrative present Gary creates is also at once real and fantastic. Schatz has become Commissioner of Police in a German town ironically named Licht ("light"), and his unenviable task is to solve a series of motiveless murders occurring in the nearby Forest of Geist ("spirit"). From the opening pages of the text, we thus encounter a fantastic narrator and a novel whose chief action is a hagiography, a sort of Ur-drama; the perpetrators of the murders are one Lily, who represents humanity's insatiable desire for fulfillment, and Florian, the gardener who plants—in humanity's collective grave—the various adventurers who struggle but inevitably fail to satisfy Lily's craving.

Gary's formulation of this universal urge in humanity to achieve the impossible fulfillment of its spirit is couched in crude terms: "Millions of heroes fucked themselves dead trying to fuck humanity happy."[21] Freudian overtones aside, Gary touches here also on the messianic urge George Steiner discusses in his disturbing study of the psychology of religion, *In*

Bluebird's Castle,[22] where he argues that Jews are responsible for giving to the world three impossible ideals. Pfefferkorn summarizes Steiner's argument as follows:

> According to Steiner this [Jewish] tradition manifested in the Books of the Prophets, in the sermons and parables of Jesus, and postulated in its secularized version by Marx and Trotsky has put intolerable demands on Western man. Judaism became the bearer of a messianic message and the Jew, in his very presence, the lacerating reminder of unattained ideals.[23]

We may debate the validity of Steiner's explanation for endemic anti–Semitism here, but Gary parodies his sense of the presence of the Jew in Western consciousness in Cohn's description of his bond to Schatz:

> The most important thing right now is to recover my sense of identity. There are moments when I begin to feel that both of us are merely *humans, tfou, tfou, tfou,* and thus the Nazi is capable of turning up in the Jew and the Jew in the Nazi: we are both part of the same semen of the species.[24]

Gary's book may be the most sustained use of grotesquely black humor and irony since Swift's *Gulliver's Travels,* and its strength lies in the narrator's ability to lance a reader's sensibilities even as s/he laughs. As Cohn ironically observes with a verbal leitmotif from Montaigne, "laughter is a deeply human characteristic,"[25] and Gary makes certain the reader is aware of the ambiguity behind the instinct to laugh, what Bergson saw as the dehumanizing element of comedy. This ambiguity is the chief effect of the grotesque, in which "the guffaw becomes a grimace,"[26] but for Gary it also highlights the problematics of any artistic re-creation of the Holocaust. Where Epstein is indirect, allowing his narrative art to make the point, Cohn is brutally speculative and topical:

> The thought occurs to me that thousands of artists have made works of great beauty out of the suffering of Christ. They have feasted on it. I also remember that out of the mutilated corpses of Guernica Picasso created "Guernica," and Tolstoy milked war and peace for his *War and Peace.* I've always believed that if we still talk about Auschwitz and Treblinka, it's because the thing has not yet been redeemed by a beautiful work of literature.[27]

Gary's genius in this book is to insert such deadly serious statements in the midst of his Yiddish comedian's dark stream of consciousness that the humor does not deflate or deflect but rather intensifies the philosophical points he intends to make. Typical of this narrative dynamic is the point at which Cohn reflects on the definition of culture:

I have had all my leisure to reflect peacefully on exactly what "culture" meant, and I finally found a rather good definition, when reading the newspapers a year or so ago. At that time, the German press was full of accounts of atrocities committed by the savage Simbas, in the Congo. The civilized world was indignant. So let me put it this way: the Germans had Schiller, Goethe, Holderline, and the Simbas of the Congo had nothing. The difference between the Germans, heir to an immense culture, and the savage Simbas is that the Simbas ate their victims, whereas the Germans turned them into soap. *This need for cleanliness, that is culture.*[28]

Even more pungently, Cohn admires a bit of comic wisdom he hears from his neighbor at their collective graveside: "Culture is when mothers who are holding their babies in their arms are excused from digging their own graves before being shot."[29]

The net effect of such an oscillation between philosophical speculation and blackest irony is a breakdown in the reader's ability to sit comfortably and read this book; appalled at the same instant we laugh, we undergo the uneasy psychological dynamic of the grotesque in "the co-presence of the laughable and something incompatible with the laughable."[30] The moral force of Gary's narrative hinges on the timing of Cohn's painful punchlines, for otherwise we fall into a state of comic overdose, or more disturbingly, see that overexposure can turn into culture amnesia. As Harpham puts it, "One can't be shocked forever.... Domesticating our grotesqueries, we applaud, or admire them, and finally pay them the ultimate tribute of ignoring their deformity"[31]; the current U.S. fad of trading cards that describe in detail the exploits of famous criminals and murderers is just one example of this latter tendency, for here young people are literally *paying for* their deformity.

Gary's book will not allow such a domestication, for the only relief we have from savagely comic Cohn is an escape to the Ur-drama of Florian and Lily. This proves not an escape at all, however, but a magnification of the fate suffered by the Jews onto a universal scale. In Part Three of the novel, called "The Temptation of Genghis Cohn," Gary presents Cohn with Schatz's offer to forgive and forget, a gesture of the German people offering the Jews full partnership in humanity. Cohn reads this as an attempt to implicate him in his own extermination, and in a typically raucous paragraph expands on his refusal:

I have finished disentangling myself from their brotherhood, which had landed on my head with a thousand tons of pity, a hundred grams of pardon, ten cents of forgiveness, a pound of compassion, one love song, a milligram of honor, a bit of napalm, six pair of French electrodes for Algerian testicles, one Ouradour-sur-Glane, three wise men stealing gifts from a stable in Bethlehem, a Messiah running away as fast as his legs will carry him, a Mona Lisa still soliciting with her dirty smile, one French grandeur and the roundup of Jews in Paris by the French grandeur of 1943, a new German awakening, and a can of gasoline for self-sacrifice but a great deal more than gasoline will be needed to cleanse their brotherhood.[32]

Gary's point here is that it is not enough for us to simply opt for brotherhood—or applaud German reunification—and forget the past. Cohn's bitter catalog reflects Gary's conviction that Hiroshima, Cambodia, Vietnam, and China all represent the same impulse that led to the madness of the Holocaust—and to its unwriting (or more cynically, its underwriting) as art.

This novel's sustained assault on our moral sensibility leaves us gasping for some sort of positive alternative, and it offers us a version of one in a moving passage where Cohn the *dybbuk* seems to recede and Gary the author steps forth:

All there remains of me is my old Jewish hope that one day humanity will be created. That she will emerge at least from the old primeval ocean where she is still dreaming her confused dream of a spiritual birth. One day the world will be created and only then the word *brotherhood* will mean something other than an offer of partnership in guilt and shame.[33]

But Gary will not let us off the hook, for he follows this chapter with the offer of brotherhood that Cohn rejects above, and reinforces this rejection in the next chapter, where Cohn, hiding in the Forest of Geist, meets a returned Christ who is angered and bitter at the inhumanity sanctified as art in his image. In a fury, the Messiah persuades Cohn to join him, and they begin to stone the great masters who appear in the Forest to beseech Christ's cooperation:

Michelangelo, Leonardo, Cimabue, Raphael, and *tutti-frutti*, all of them with paints and brushes ready and their faces slit from ear to ear with greedy smiles…. We let them have another handful, they hide in the bushes, but go on whining, all they ask for is an hour of posing, they don't give a damn for the rest, one hour of posing on the cross for Culture's sake, He has no right to refuse.[34]

Cohn and Christ's identities converge by the novel's end, signifying in a fantastic mode the broadest artistic spectrum of violence celebrated as art. But Gary's novel itself represents a response to the aesthetic as escape or cultural amnesia by its obsession with justice and memory; Cohn's painful moral barbs support Hitler's own judgment that "Conscience is a Jewish invention…. It is a blemish like circumcision."[35] If conscience makes cowards of us all, writers like Epstein or Gary will not allow us to turn away from our past, or rest easier in an artistic version of the horrors that our century has wrought. Todorov defines the fantastic as *"that hesitation experienced by a person who knows only the laws of nature, confronting an apparently supernatural event."*[36] Through the use of the fantastic, Epstein and Gary force readers to confront their hesitation (or inability) to acknowledge membership in the interpretive community of the Holocaust, modern humanity. To paraphrase Groucho Marx, we would rather not be part of this community precisely *because* it has us all, victims and criminals, as its members; we cannot avoid being part of this twentieth century club. Writers of Holocaust literature make us pay our dues.

NOTES

1. A version of this essay was first delivered at the Eleventh Annual Conference on the Fantastic in the Arts, Fort Lauderdale, Florida, March 21–25, 1990.

2. I am not addressing specifically here the disturbing issue of the complex voyeuristic thrill, what Eli Wiesel has called the "pornography of violence," sometimes present in an audience viewing even the most barbarous cruelty. As I will show, Gary's novel addresses this in some of Genghis Cohn's most bitterly caustic moments.

3. Lawrence Langer, *The Holocaust and Literary Imagination* (New Haven, CT: Yale University Press, 1975), 75.

4. Ibid., 8.

5. Ibid., 3.

6. Ibid., 214–15.

7. Edith Milton, Review of *King of the Jews*, by Leslie Epstein, *Yale Review* 69 (1979): 94.

8. Ibid., 95–96.

9. Robert Alter, Review of *King of the Jews*, by Leslie Epstein, *New York Times Review of Books* 84 (1979): 1.

10. See the description of Rumkowski in Leonard Tushnet, *The Pavement of Hell* (New York: St. Martin's Press, 1972), 34 ff. Tushnet cites eyewitness accounts of Rumkowski's flowing capes, florid speeches, and horse-drawn coach as evocative of his extravagant character. Epstein has Trumpelman riding a white stallion around the ghetto. Recent events in Rumania have fueled controversy surrounding the chief rabbi of the Rumanian Jewish community, Moses Rosen, who effectively sheltered the Jews from Ceausescu's endemically anti–Semitic regime in return for large payments of cash. Rosen, like Rumkowski, has both admirers and detractors, but is akin to Epstein's Trumpelman in his taste for luxurious accommodations and his capacity for couching the brutal policies of the state in palatable terms. See the *Washington Post* story by Glenn Frankel, "The Rabbi and the Dictator," reprinted in *The Seattle Times*, February 10, 1990, A10–11.

11. Leslie Epstein, *King of the Jews* (New York: Coward, McCann & Geoghegan, 1979), 11.

12. Ibid., 45.

13. Ibid., 163.

14. Ibid., 192.

15. Ibid., 120.

16. Ibid., 120–21.

17. Ibid., 55.

18. Ibid., 262.

19. Eli Pfefferkorn, "The Art of Survival: Romain Gary's *The Dance of Genghis Cohn*," *Modern Language Studies* 10 (1980): 78.

20. Ibid., 79.

21. Romain Gary, *The Dance of Genghis Cohn* (New York: World Publishing, 1968), 63–64.

22. George Steiner, *Bluebird's Castle: Some Notes Toward a Redefinition of Culture* (New Haven, CT: Yale University Press, 1971).

23. Pfefferkorn, "The Art of Survival," 82.

24. Gary, *The Dance of Genghis Cohn*, 65. The famous Milgram electrical shock experiments at Yale in the 1950s are a disturbing confirmation of Cohn's anxiety here.

25. Ibid., 28.

26. Geoffrey Harpham, "The Grotesque: First Principles," *Journal of Aesthetics and Art Criticism* (Summer 1976): 67.

27. Gary, *The Dance of Genghis Cohn*, 125.

28. Ibid., 59.

29. Ibid.

30. Philip Thomson, *The Grotesque: The Critical Idiom*, ed. John D. Jump (London: Methuem, 1972), 3.

31. Harpham, "The Grotesque," 463.

32. Gary, *The Dance of Genghis Cohn*, 210.

33. Ibid., 205.

34. Ibid., 217–18.

35. Hermann Rauschning, *Hitler Speaks* (London: Putnam, 1939), 232, 220 respectively (quoted in Pfefferkorn, 82). Pfefferkorn points out that "Rauschning, former Nazi chief of Danzig, deserted Hitler and escaped to the U.S." and that prior to this "he was a close intimate of Hitler's inner circle and privy to his master's reflections" (82).

36. Tzvetan Todorov, *The Fantastic: A Structural Approach to a Literary Genre* (Cleveland: The Press of Case Western Reserve University, 1973), 25.

Surviving the Survivor
Art Spiegelman's Maus[1]
JOAN GORDON

Maus, a comic book about the Holocaust, is an oxymoron, guaranteed to shock by its mere existence and thus violating the laws of Holocaust literature.[2] But *Maus I: A Survivor's Tale* (1986) and *Maus II: And Here My Troubles Began* (1991) are not the tale of a survivor of the Holocaust but the tale of the survivor of survivors, a frame tale in which the frame overwhelms the central story (see Figure 1). *Maus* is Art Spiegelman's autobiographical expression of the journey not of the hero but of the hero's son. Joseph Campbell traces the hero's archetypal journey into the under-world (*katabasis*) and his return to tell the tale and to teach what he has learned. Vladek Spiegelman, the author's father, and every other Holocaust survivor, has experienced a literal *katabasis*, and we recognize the impor-tance of the journey and the obligation to witness. But what of the hero's life after *katabasis*, and what of the hero's child? How did Telemachus survive having Odysseus for a father? I want to discuss the laws of Holo-caust writing and why *Maus* violates them in order to answer the question about Telemachus, of survival in a post-heroic world.

The editors of *An Anthology of Holocaust Literature* (1975), in their introduction, illustrate how criticism of Holocaust literature tends more to the prescriptive than the descriptive. The editors, Jacob Glatstein, Israel Knox, and Samuel Margoshes, set up a law code that is representative of Holocaust literary criticism. According to the rules, first-hand witness takes precedence over second-hand description and the resulting work must be realistic; any fiction dealing with the Holocaust must spring from the absolutely confirmable set of objective facts. These facts form a sacred testimony which is the only acceptable stance for Holocaust literature;

that is, as a holy commemoration of the martyrs. This commemoration should be uttered in an authentic Jewish voice, something which also exists in some objective manner. The editors describe the goal of Holocaust literature: "a modern sacred book ... commemorating forever the six million, as an enduring temple for their spirit." This "book of Books, out of the depths of the Sacred Martyrdom, will not find its first and original home in English or French or Russian, but in Hebrew and Yiddish."[3] The ideological necessity for scientific, objective, Aristotelian realism leads to a Platonic ideal—a "Book of Books." And this Platonic sacred text would be untranslatable, a mystery finally, in its witnessing of an experience impossible to communicate, an experience that is ultimately subjective. Such a code violates our current assumptions about the nature of objectivity and authenticity in its insistence on the tangible existence of a Jewish voice and of a concrete set of facts somehow beyond interpretation and communication, while at the same time it admits that the voice cannot be translated nor the set of facts communicated, even though both translation and communication are considered a holy duty. It is no wonder that George Steiner, in *Language and Silence* (1967), and many others have suggested that silence is the only valid response to the Holocaust.

Figure 1. Cover design for *Maus II: And Here My Troubles Began* (1991).

As I realized these conflicting, paradoxical strictures, I felt angry and frustrated in a number of ways. First, I felt myself boxed in by a set of rules which would be judged unacceptable in any other literary criticism. Next, I felt callous and guilty for not feeling those constraints myself, for suggesting merely by listing them that they should not be there, for even suggesting that I might consider Holocaust literature in any other but the legislated way. Finally, I felt resentful because these laws suggested that I would never be able to understand the literature, that my role as critic of such literature is simply to be another passive receptor of the act of witnessing. In short, I felt a lot like Art Spiegelman as he writes the story of writing his father's story.

James E. Young deals wisely with the conundrum of Holocaust literary criticism by exploring "the crucial role interpretation played in the events themselves" (3) and I plan to do something similar here, to examine how the interpretations of events by the Spiegelmans shaped *Maus*, and how that shaping resulted in a work which violates the letter while remaining true to the spirit of the prescriptive laws I have sketched.

Law Number One

First-hand witness takes precedence over second-hand description. *Maus* violates it. The graphic novel begins with a first-hand memory— Art's—of his own childhood, when he fell down and his friends skated away without him. How does his father, Vladek, the Holocaust survivor, comfort him? "FRIENDS? Your friends? ... If you lock them together in a room with no food for a week.... Then you could see what it is, friends! [ellipses in original]."[4] After that, every chapter begins and ends with Spiegelman *fils* dealing with the recording of his father's story in the "present." That "present," by the way extends from 1980 to Vladek's death in 1982, although the publishing of the comic books extends from 1980 to 1991. Chapter Five of the first volume provides an exception to this frame, containing Spiegelman's 1973 comic, *Prisoner on the Hell Planet*, in which he deals with his mother's suicide. These frames lead us to understand that the book is really about Art's life and how his father's interpretation of the devastating events shaped his son. We are not, then, coming to *Maus* to learn about the Holocaust—that is not its subject—but about how the generation after is shaped by it and how they see the event. Soon, of course, as the survivors themselves die, that next generation will provide the most direct link to the Holocaust.

Law Number Two

The work must be realistic—violated. Cartoon mice, or more accurately, cartoon people with cartoon mouse heads, are not realistic. In fact, the non-realistic representation of ethnic groups by particular animals is the most troublesome aspect of *Maus*. Spiegelman represents all Jews of any nationality, including the French convert Francoise, as mice, thus identifying them with the weak, the meek, the victim. Germans are cats— natural enemies of mice; all Poles are pigs—unclean; Americans are dogs— friendly and obtuse; the French, are, predictably, frogs. These portrayals offend because they support ethnic stereotypes, simplify and misrepresent political situations, and allude to the very unserious, unsacred world of Loonytoons. Why would Art Spiegelman not only violate the laws of realism (one can think of several valid answers for that), but do so in such a calculated and offensive manner?

First, as he explained to a Polish press attaché when he applied for a visa, "these aren't my metaphors. These are Hitler's."[5] But this is only part of the truth, as Spiegelman admits to the attaché when he adds, "considering the relationship between Poles and Jews for the last few hundred years, it seemed appropriate to use a non-kosher animal."[6] But it is also a potentially insulting metaphor as well, and ignores the much more complex relationship between Jews and other Poles before World War II.

And that reveals a second reason: these choices reveal his anger, and not only at the Jews. Spiegelman, or at least, Art, the character in the comic, is angry with the Jews for being victims, for making *him* a victim. Precisely speaking, he is angry at three Jews, his parents and himself. Although he listens to his father tell him about his ingenuity, his toughness, his powerful will to survive, and hears through his father about his mother's similar courage, what Art, the character in the graphic novel, *feels* is that his parents were victims. The people Art knew were weak, twisted by the events into less-than-perfect parents, not men (or women), but mice. His mother gave in—she committed suicide. His father gave in—he let the experience of the Holocaust shape everything he did, drive everyone away from him. The Art Spiegelman of both the "past" and "present" of the book is a mouse through and through and *his* weakness shapes the vision; that mouse sees his parents as mice.

The author Spiegelman (the human cartoonist with the mouse mask in the books) knows this is a childish interpretation of a mother who had been depressive before the war, and of a father with every reason to carry the awesome baggage of horror. As Spiegelman says later, outside the covers of the books, in the commentary on the graphic novels called *Metamaus* (2011):

> The story of *Maus* isn't just the story of a son having problems with his father, and it's not just the story of what a father lived through. It's about a

cartoonist trying to envision what his father went through. It's about choices being made, of finding what one can tell, and what one can reveal, and what one can reveal beyond what one knows one is revealing.[7]

This makes clear the difference between Art, the character, and Spiegelman, the author, and why the choice to use animal stereotypes is an artistic one rather than simply an emotional response.

Adam Gropnik suggests a third reason for violating the law of realism by turning human beings into stereotypic animals; beneath the historical references, beneath the anger, Gropnik sees a similarity in Spiegelman's mask-like mouse heads with human bodies to the theriocephalic illustrations in the *Bird's Head Haggadah*, a thirteenth-century Ashkenazic illuminated manuscript.[8] In that manuscript the awe and sacredness of remembering the Jewish Diaspora are expressed through the mysterious images of human beings with mask-like birds' heads. As Gropnik explains it:

> The medieval artist had a subject too holy to be depicted; the modern artist has a subject too horrible to be depicted. For the traditional illuminator, it is the ultimate sacred mystery that must somehow be shown without being shown; for the contemporary artist, it is the ultimate profanity that must somehow be shown without being shown.[9]

By sacrificing the realistic for the impossible, Spiegelman uses cartoons to allude to the inexpressible, transcending the same anger his cartoon images represent. *Maus*, by this reasoning, acknowledges the need for "a modern sacred book," though not one meant, in this case, primarily to "commemorate the six million." Looking back on the review by Gropnik, Spiegelman says that although he had not been aware of the *Bird's Head Haggadah*, "the reference seemed dead on." Spiegelman connected it to the Jewish "commandment against making graven images of God" of which he was aware "despite my shoddy religious training."[10]

Law Number Three

Any fiction about the Holocaust must arise from a confirmable set of facts—Spiegelman obeys, but in a way that questions the possibility of absolute confirmation. Spiegelman gets his facts from his father, a witness and survivor, but surrealism can arise as surely from facts as can realism. The work's frame shows Art interviewing Vladek, insisting that his father tell the story of his trip to the underworld in an orderly, chronological way. Art travels to Auschwitz and Buchenwald in order to depict those scenes more clearly, and he provides maps, charts, a microscopic view of a louse to convince us, and perhaps himself, that the facts are straight.

Spiegelman the author, however, recognizes that eye-witness accounts may be limited by the witness's memory or circumstances. Vladek, for example, does not remember an orchestra at Auschwitz, but there is plenty of evidence from other eye-witnesses and from photographs that there was one. In *Metamaus*, Spiegelman describes how he would deal with such discrepancies. Sometimes he would "triangulate the event and allow his [Vladek's] memory to be subsumed in the grander memory." In the case of the orchestra, because

> there was ... [a] personal reason for him to remember differently—because it was something he specifically says he saw, or because of the importance and weight it seemed to have in the conversation—then I went with his version and tried to make a visible correction if necessary.[11]

Spiegelman decided, in the case of the orchestra, to have Vladek say that he remembered no orchestra but, in the drawing he shows "little bits of the cello and the silhouettes of the musicians behind the marching figures to insist that they were there."[12] Neither Art, the character in the books, nor Spiegelman, the author, disputes the reality of the Holocaust and the author goes to great pains to research and confirm those facts. But the author recognizes that memory is not an objective device.

Spiegelman's purpose in collecting all these facts and in recording them is not to be a witness to the witness or to transmit the experience of the Holocaust. Instead, he aims to understand his father, who has been shaped by the Holocaust: "My focus really had to do with trying to understand how damaged Vladek was, and whether he had been damaged before the war or not, and what the implications of those psychological issues might be."[13] So, although *Maus* uses facts from his father's experience, those facts are not the work's *raison d'être*. The report on the Holocaust is encased by that dominating frame, the son's attempt to understand the father surrounding the father's experience, like layers of nacre covering the irritating center of a pearl. The difficulty of such an attempt is indicated by the eleven years between the publication of the first chapter (1980) and the final one (1991).

Spiegelman, throughout the novels, has a very careful and sophisticated relationship to this matter of confirmable facts. Both Vladek and the character Art are portrayed as "damaged," and therefore their witnessing of events is flawed as well. Nevertheless, the author, Spiegelman, goes to great lengths to confirm and portray events with meticulous accuracy, all the while showing his characters as fantastic theriocephalous beings. The tension between that attention to facts and the surreal nature of the characters reminds us of the subjectivity of individual perceptions in any work that attempts objectivity. Winston Churchill said that "History is written by the victors." *Maus* illustrates how every person who witnesses events sees them through his or her own subjectivity. While Spiegelman indeed adheres to the confirmable facts of the Holocaust in *Maus* he also acknowledges that complete and totalizing objectivity is impossible, even dangerous.

Law Number Four

Use an authentic Jewish voice and language—violated. When he shows himself writing the comic strip, Spiegelman portrays himself as a man with a mouse mask, as if he does not really feel like an authentic Jew while he writes *Maus*. Beyond this expression of inauthenticity of Jewish voice is Spiegelman's medium of expression. What could be further from authenticity than a comic book? At first this seems an exploitive, shocking choice—the single most disturbing aspect of *Maus*, more disturbing than the stereotypic animal representations, because it uses a form linked with the frivolous, the ephemeral, the merely popular. Strangely, these attributes form Spiegelman's closest agreement to the stern arbiters of Holocaust literature. As Elie Wiesel says, "Auschwitz negates all literature.... Holocaust literature? The very term is a contradiction."[14] Explaining his seemingly perverse choice of narrative form, Spiegelman explains:

> That invests it with a certain lack of hubris. It's not an *opera* about the Holocaust; it's something modest, it's a comic strip—a medium that has a history of being without pretensions or aspirations to art. And perhaps if there can be no art about the Holocaust, then there may at least be comic strips.[15]

So, though he asks, "Have I exploited the dead?" his choice of voice is meant to do the opposite.[16]

Had Spiegelman adhered to this law, writing in Hebrew or Yiddish, the potential audience for his book would have shrunk drastically, of course, and that particular law, claimed as it was in an anthology of literature about the Holocaust written in English, has always seemed to me particularly self-defeating, or perhaps symbolic. Yes, *Maus* is written in English, but that is Art's authentic language. Vladek's testimony is written in the idiosyncratic grammar that represents his accented English, and that is his authentic language to his son. On the final page of the second volume, Vladek says to his son, "More I don't need to tell you. We were both very happy, and lived happy, happy ever after."[17] His words are both authentic and untrue. The novels show us that "happy ever after" was not an option in a work that would be true instead to the psychological impact of the Holocaust.

Conclusion

Three out of four rules broken. Spiegelman does not break those rules to commit sacrilege and break hearts. Instead, he does so to break away from the content of his story, to its frame, the son's experience, and in doing so, to break through to some understanding of his relationship with his parents and with history.

All this breakage leads me back to my set of mythic questions, questions which may have led a person to expect more Jung and Joseph Campbell than he or she is likely to get. But there is some. Campbell traces the hero's journey from the call to adventure through a series of tests, into the underworld, and up to his return to the world we know, where he will tell the tale. While we can see how Vladek Spiegelman did indeed go through a series of tests, experience hell, return, and tell of his trials, the real thing dwarfs the map. Being a Jew in Europe during the 1930s was not exactly a voluntary call to adventure, there was no reward for surviving the nadir, and the jury is out on whether the act of witnessing will restore any world order. More significantly, the nadir of this particular journey was shared by more than six million Jews, most of whom did not return, and not one of them wanted to take the trip, while the hell was man-made, quite divorced from the divine. Nevertheless, the staggering feat of survival must surely be viewed as heroic, even on a mythic plane. The real gap between Campbell's heroic map and the human realm, however, is that it is a closed loop. A mythic tale like the *Odyssey* drops its heroic aspect as soon as Odysseus returns, and we never learn of Odysseus's later life. What is the price of *katabasis*?

The closed loop also shuts out Telemachus. The hero's journey is so overwhelming that it dominates his post-*katabasis* half-life and shrinks the significance of the next generation. Art is our Telemachus. Though the son may struggle to make sense out of it, asking to hear the tale in chronological order, he can never understand that overwhelming experience, and will never be understood by his father except in terms of it. How then is the son to survive? By making his own story, one which surrounds his father's, and frames it, one which acknowledges that the father's story must be confronted though it cannot be understood, one which makes his father's *katabasis* the mysterious core of his own story, and one which makes its aim a connection to the father. To tell his own story, the son must break the laws of the father's story, except for the law about the facts, so none will mistake his *Bildungsroman* for an epic, or his comic book for the Book of Books. Spiegelman says, "The subject of *Maus* is the retrieval of memory and ultimately, the creation of memory."[18] Art's story shows how to survive the survivor by showing what happens to memory when it leaves the mind of the one who remembers.

NOTES

1. This is a slightly expanded, revised, and updated version of the article that originally appeared in Gary K. Wolfe's special issue of the *Journal of the Fantastic in the Arts* (1993).

2. Since its publication in two volumes and one collected volume, followed by its extremely favorable reception over time with the rise in respectability of the form, *Maus* has been dignified by the name "graphic novel."

3. Jacob Glatstein, Israel Knox, and Samuel Margoshes, eds., *An Anthology of Holocaust Literature* (New York: Atheneum, 1975), xiv.

4. Art Spiegelman, *Maus: A Survivor's Tale* (New York: Pantheon, 1986), 5.

5. Claudia Dreifus, "The Progressive Interview: Art Spiegelman," *The Progressive* (Nov. 1989), 37.

6. Ibid.

7. Art Spiegelman, *Metamaus* (New York: Pantheon, 2011), 73.

8. Theriocephaly refers to the portrayal of beings with human bodies and animal heads, usually associated with religious associations, as, for example: Anubis, the jackal-headed Egyptian god; Ganesha, the Hindu god; and the Christian portrayal of St. Christopher with a dog's head. Georgio Agamben has something to say about theriocephaly in *The Open: Man and Animal* (2004). He speculates that the portrayal of theriocephalous beings, at least in a thirteenth-century Hebrew Bible in the Ambrosian Library in Milan, "suggest[s] that on the last day, the relations between animals and men will take on a new form, and that man himself will be reconciled with his animal nature." See Georgio Agamben, *Open: Man and Animal* (Stanford, CA: Stanford University Press, 2004), 3. I have found, however, that in graphic novels, theriocephalous beings are usually metaphors for human beings (think of Goofy, the Disney character); that is certainly true in *Maus*.

9. Adam Gopnik, "Comics and Catastrophe: Art Spiegelman's *Maus* and the History of the Cartoon," *The New Republic* 22 (June 1987): 33.

10. Spiegelman, *Metamaus*, 117.

11. Ibid., 30.

12. Ibid., 30; the frame described is in Art Spiegelman, *Maus: A Survivor's Tale II: And Here My Troubles Began* (New York: Pantheon, 1991), 54.

13. Spiegelman, *Metamaus*, 73.

14. Qtd. in Eileen R. Weil, *The Holocaust in Literature* (Chicago: Roosevelt University External Studies Program, 1990), 4.

15. Dreifus, "The Progressive Interview," 35.

16. Ibid.

17. Spiegelman, *Maus: A Survivor's Tale II*, 136.

18. Spiegelman, *Metamaus*, 73.

The Fantastic
Search for Hitler
The Führer's Defense
in His Own Words

ERIC J. STERLING

There are taboos that must be broken or they will continue to choke us. —George Tabori, Holocaust playwright[1]

Introduction

Traditional Holocaust plays of the 1950s and 1960s such as Frances Goodrich and Albert Hackett's *Diary of Anne Frank* (1955) were sentimental and melodramatic. They were inoffensive, well-meaning literary pieces that tugged at the audience's heart strings. Nazis were clearly identified as the undisputed villains, with Jews being portrayed as helpless, innocent victims. The plays portrayed, among other themes, Jewish passivity and the struggle for survival. Because it was considered taboo by many for playwrights to deviate from historical truth or realism (for fear of trivializing the suffering of the victims and giving fodder to Holocaust deniers), sentimental and predictable dramas dominated the first decades of Holocaust drama. But then followed a movement away from what George Tabori called "sentimental pity, sanctimonious judgment, and that hypocritical philo–Semitism which, to many, is the reverse side of anti–Semitism."[2] One reason is that sympathy for the victims seemed ineffectual and passive, leaving audiences to ponder why Jews failed to resist the evil forces that attacked them. Subsequent dramatists found that sentimental theatre was too predictable and simplistic, inhibiting audiences from examining the complex moral, social, and historical situations that occurred during the Shoah—real scenarios that necessitated significant and life-changing moral decisions and sometimes even what Lawrence Langer labeled "choiceless choices."[3]

Starting in the 1980s, therefore, playwrights started penning more imaginative, complex, and non-traditional works that did justice to the unique, sophisticated, and three-dimensional issues that victims actually encountered during the Holocaust. Playwrights eventually found that one of the most useful ways to explore complex issues was through non-traditional theatre, such as Holocaust comedies and serious dramas that involved the fantastic. These issues involved Jewish collaboration, moral dilemmas such as survival at the expense of one's values and ethics or of the lives of others, decent and law-abiding Germans who mindlessly—but not always maliciously—followed orders without thinking of the consequences, and presentation of historically inaccurate situations to encourage more profound understanding of the human condition under unprecedented adverse and horrific conditions. The taboo against non-traditional theatre was shattered by bold dramatists such as George Steiner, Christopher Hampton, Peter Barnes, and George Tabori. As Ray Bradbury has remarked, "Each fantasy assaults and breaks a particular law." This essay will explore Christopher Hampton's stage adaptation of George Steiner's novella *The Portage to San Cristóbal of A.H.* (1981) and the valuable contributions this fantastic play makes to Holocaust studies.

When arguing against using sentimental and realistic drama about the Shoah to entertain and stir the emotions of audiences, Holocaust author George Tabori wrote, "It would be an insult to the dead, to beg for sympathy, or to lament their crushed nakedness. The event is beyond tears."[4] Tabori felt that sentimentality and the evocation of pathos are impotent responses to the Shoah and cannot do justice to the suffering of Holocaust victims, so theatre has to extend beyond sympathetic situations and toward fantastical scenarios, such as in his play *Cannibals* in which two Auschwitz survivors and the sons of camp victims in the same cell block attend a dinner party after the war and reenact the moral dilemma of whether to eat an obese, recently-deceased Jewish inmate—clearly a fantastical theme. In the production notes to their Holocaust drama *Throne of Straw*, Harold and Edith Lieberman say, "Any work on the Holocaust is bound to produce emotion, but care must be taken to avoid any sentimentality. This is especially true during those moments of moral choice."[5] Like German playwright Bertolt Brecht, the Liebermans felt that sentiment and emotional involvement in a play distracted audiences from thinking critically and delving deep into moral issues.

The Portage to San Cristóbal of A.H. also purposely avoids sentimentality and emotion; even when the characters die, the audience, having failed to identify with them, sheds no tears. One manner in which to create some distance between a theatrical work and the emotions of the audience is through the employment of the fantastic, as exemplified in *The Portage to San Cristóbal of A.H.*

A fantastical play functions differently than a traditional drama because audience members' intellectual and emotional realization that the action never happened, and could never happen, allows them to think about the drama's issues with reason and objectivity. S.C. Fredericks observes that fantastic literary works are unique in their "deliberate violation of norms and facts we regard as essential to our conventional conception of 'reality,' in order to create an imaginary counter-structure or counter-norm ... [, with] this 'counter-reality' principle [being] essential."[6] W.R. Irwin asserts that such literature is "based on and controlled by an overt violation of what is generally accepted as possibility."[7] In *The Portage to San Cristóbal of A.H.*, for instance, audience members understand that the premise of Adolf Hitler surviving World War II and being alive in 1979 violates reason and historical fact, but the play is still entertaining and thought-provoking. Tzvetan Todorov claims that the fantastic exists in cases where, "in a world which is indeed our world, the one we know, a world without devils, sylphides, or vampires, there occurs an event which cannot be explained by the laws of this same familiar world."[8] The world is familiar, but logically the events cannot have happened, which causes audiences, rather than being immersed in a heavily emotional way, to be conscious that they are watching a play. They do not establish distracting emotional attachments with the characters because they know that either the situations or the characters (or both) are not historically accurate. Freddie Rokem believes that "fantastic elements are probed as a means to address and confront the issue of the incomprehensibility and the incommunicability of the Shoah."[9] Rokem correctly asserts that the fantastic can be employed effectively to demonstrate seemingly incomprehensible situations while also showing how the Holocaust cannot be adequately explained. Such scenarios could include not only how Adolf Hitler might have survived his Berlin bunker in 1945 and escaped to South America, but also how such a ruthless dictator could have inspired a civilized and highly educated nation to commit horrific and arguably unprecedented genocidal violence. However, although the fantastic and the non-historical may be used well to stimulate analytical and provoking thoughts about the Holocaust, it should be mentioned that some important scholars (such as Theodore Adorno and even George Steiner himself) and victims of the Shoah have often cautioned that it is morally and artistically unacceptable to create fictions (and consequently fantastical situations) about the Holocaust.

Adorno and Steiner

It is widely known that renowned philosopher and social critic Theodor Adorno stated that it would be barbaric to write poetry after Auschwitz. Although Adorno's meaning is disputed by critics, it is doubtful that he meant that no one should ever create works of art after the Holocaust or even about the Holocaust. It is likely, rather, that he meant that artistic creations (including fiction, poetry, and drama) can never adequately portray or replicate the horrors that victims and survivors encountered, nor can readers and viewers of these works ever comprehend what the victims and survivors endured. Therefore, artistic creations have the potential to trivialize these atrocities. Another concern about creative works written about the Holocaust is that they can create material for Holocaust deniers, who can employ these works to advance their insidious political agendas. For instance, deniers who watched the realistic film *Schindler's List* claimed that the movie constituted proof that talented artists such as Steven Spielberg possess the ability to create lifelike, realistic films, photographs, and other works of art about the Holocaust that look genuine and historical when the works are, in fact, reproduced skillfully through modern technology, great camerawork, and fine editing in film studios. Thus deniers disingenuously posit that many actual films and photographs from the Holocaust were created artistically after the Holocaust and crafted to appear as genuine.

Adorno is not the only critic who expressed concerns about creative art and even language about the Shoah. In *Language and Silence* (1967), George Steiner himself wrote, "The world of Auschwitz lies outside speech as it lies outside reason. To speak of the *unspeakable* is to risk the survivance of language as creator and bearer of humane, rational truth. Words that are saturated with lies or atrocity do not easily resume life."[10] How can one express through language, Steiner asked, the inexpressible, the illogical, and the unfathomable? According to Lawrence Langer, Steiner believed at one time "that the reality of the Holocaust addresses the contemporary mind most effectively with the authority of silence."[11] In other words, because creativity, art, and language cannot effectively express the suffering and horrific acts during the Holocaust, it is better to say nothing and be respectfully silent rather than to speak or express oneself through an art form.

The Intertwining of the Real and the Fantastic in the Play

Steiner obviously changed his mind because he penned his fantastic novella *The Portage to San Cristóbal of A.H.* (1981), which British playwright Christopher Hampton adapted faithfully into a play of the same name in 1982.[12] In the play, a concentration camp survivor and Nazi hunter named Emmanuel Lieber, obsessed with capturing Nazi dictator Adolf Hitler, who he—but few others in the world—is convinced has survived the war, sends out an Israeli team to locate the war criminal in the Amazon jungle, capture him, and bring him back clandestinely to Israel for a trial. The team suffers through intense heat, rain, swampy conditions, and mosquitoes that pervade the Amazon, and they successfully capture Hitler. However, they lack the resources and good health to bring Hitler out of the Amazon, so, knowing that they cannot deliver him to Lieber, they decide to stage their own ad hoc trial in the Amazon. Meanwhile, the team loses the ability to communicate with Lieber, who is waiting and giving orders from Israel, because of a faulty radio. Government agents of Russia, England, France, Germany, and the United States intercept the radio transmissions and contemplate whether they should steal Hitler from his kidnappers and even murder the Israeli team to ensure that they themselves gain possession of the former Führer. It becomes apparent that the capture of Adolf Hitler is about more than justice and retribution: it is also about politics and power.

It is widely known and well documented that Nazi dictator Adolf Hitler shot himself to death in his Berlin bunker on 30 April 1945 and that his body was then burned beyond recognition before the Russian army arrived. However, in his novella *The Portage to San Cristóbal of A.H.,* which was nominated for the PEN/Faulkner Award for Fiction, Steiner posits the fantastical question: What if Hitler had survived the war and escaped to South America? What if Nazi hunters finally captured him in May 1979, at the age of ninety, in the Amazon jungle in Brazil? Holocaust drama specialist Robert Skloot admires the controversial novella and

Hampton's faithful play adaptation, and he writes that although the "story is a fantastic lie [...] [it] is intended as a moral fable, one that uses the 'archvillain' of the twentieth century as protagonist in order to advance certain understandings about history, art, and the relationship between them."[13] As "a moral fable," the play allows audiences to ponder a dilemma that history did not allow: What should have been done with Hitler had he survived the war? Because it is a historical fact that Hitler died in his bunker, only a fantastic work can create this moral dilemma.

In a sense, *The Portage to San Cristóbal of A.H.* demonstrates the intertwining of the real and the fantastic because Hitler was a real person and the work delves deeply into the historical events surrounding the Führer's last hours, yet it is almost universally understood that Adolf Hitler died in 1945. By portraying Hitler as alive and well—even healthier than his much younger captors—Steiner and later Hampton have created a fantastic scenario, "a direct reversal of ground rules" because the audience comes to the play believing that the former German dictator is dead but finds to their surprise that the archvillain is alive and healthy: the "[p]olar opposite is Reality."[14]

Hitler was a living person, of course, but what happened to his body, the mystery that shrouded his death, and whether he could have possibly escaped, have been the object of much speculation. And although the Holocaust was obviously a genuine historical tragedy, it is bizarre that one man, with the help of some cronies, could employ language, rhetoric, national pride, and ethnic hatred to transform a nation, to incite millions to violence in an epic destruction that led to the deaths of eleven million people, including six million innocent Jewish civilians, during World War II. It is fantastical, beyond human reason, that a man who clearly did not possess Nordic looks could, using his power of speech and influence, transform a nation and in the process convince a people to slay millions of Jews, Gypsies, homosexuals, Jehovah's Witnesses, disabled human beings, Communists and other political prisoners because they were not considered Aryans or members of "The Master Race." Yet it happened from 1933 to 1945 in Germany, a modern and civilized nation that elected Adolf Hitler, considered the architect of perhaps the most heinous genocide in world history, in a democratically-held national election. These events rival Hitler's fantastic escape to the Amazon in their defiance of logic and credibility. Given that Hitler was successful in transforming and brainwashing an entire nation, is his fantastic escape to the Amazon really so far-fetched?

Can we truly ascertain the truth—beyond the shadow of a doubt—

about Hitler's demise when his body was burned beyond recognition and the Russian government has been far less than forthcoming about what they found upon reaching the bunker? Holocaust drama has evolved from plausible situations toward more fantastical and experimental plots, such as the idea posited by Steiner that Hitler's double, not the Führer himself, perished in the bunker, and that the Nazi dictator escaped to South America on the last plane out of Germany before the Russians arrived. Hitler's body was recovered and examined, but in the play, British agent Ryder says with uncertainty that the German dictator's escape is "just possible. Just. Million to one. I don't think that plane could possibly have got out. Those last days the sky was like a furnace."[15] But the slightest doubt, like the one that Ryder feels, is all that it takes for the fantastic to work effectively. The creation of fantastic, conjectural, and implausible situations permits audiences to ponder what could have happened or even how they would have comported themselves in such scenarios. Steiner and Hampton employ great detail to describe how Hitler could have survived his bunker in Berlin (mentioning the dental plate, the Russian cover-up, the broken bone, and the possibility of a double) in order to create a sense of verisimilitude. Steiner's premise of the discovery of Hitler in 1979 at the age of ninety is also possible given that Adolf Eichmann was captured in 1960. In addition, Nazi collaborator Paul Touvier was recaptured in Nice, France in 1989; Nazi perpetrator Klaas Carel Faber, convicted of murdering twenty-two Jews in the Westerbork concentration camp in the Netherlands, died at the age of ninety in 2012, with the Dutch never able to capture him after his escape from a prison in the Netherlands; Hungarian Nazi Sándor Képíró died in 2011 at the age of ninety-seven, while under house arrest; and Hungarian Nazi László Csizsik-Csatáry, who allegedly deported almost 16,000 Jews from Hungary to Auschwitz, was captured in 2012. Since Nazi collaborators are still being captured in the twenty-first century, audiences can intellectually accept the plot of a Nazi being found alive in 1979—except that this prisoner is, fantastically, the most infamous and sought after of all, Adolf Hitler himself.

The fantastic story of Hitler's escape to South America might be troubling to those who believe that literature and other forms of art that deal with the Holocaust must be historically accurate for the sake of the millions who tragically lost their lives—that the deviation from historical truth could trivialize the suffering of the victims or embolden deniers of the Shoah. With this taboo in place against creating non-historical works about the Holocaust, it is quite conceivable that some people would find fantastical works about the Shoah offensive, particularly when it involves such a heinous villain as Adolf Hitler, the architect of arguably the most horrific genocide in world history.

Berel Lang, for instance, considers the Shoah to be "an event as close to sacred, after all, as anything in a secular world is likely to be."[16] Lang's point is that the Holocaust tragedy is so horrific, and destroyed so many innocent lives, that it is sacred and deserving of unmitigated respect; conversely, irreverence, or the clearly ahistorical (or the fantastic as in *The Portage to San Cristóbal of A.H.*), is essentially sacrilegious. Such treatments, Lang suggests, could be hurtful to the memories of those who suffered during the Holocaust. Lawrence L. Langer respects and sympathizes with Lang's concern (and that of others who consider the Holocaust to be sacred and untouchable), yet he is cautious, nonetheless, because this belief "sets limits on the range of language and imagery that is appropriate to its subject. A sacred topic demands restraint and respect in verbal approach that an unholy one might not, and this in turn raises the question of fundamental differences between historical and artistic truth."[17] However, these limits on expression should be a concern because fantastic literature can find new avenues for investigation and critical thought. *The Portage to San Cristóbal of A.H.*, for instance, can show audiences the obsession of Nazi hunters, the understandable but sometimes excessive thirst for vengeance, the political ramifications of capturing another high-level Nazi official, and the power of rhetoric and language in regard to persuasion and mind control—all of which are integral themes in Genocide Studies. Because it is highly unlikely that a high-ranking Nazi officer will ever be captured again, it takes a fantastical and imaginative work of literature to create a scenario in which this situation could occur again and be thoroughly investigated. Fantastical literary works can be created by authors to place people, both historical and fictional, in situations that shed light on truth, interrogate moral and human decisions, and teach audiences about history and the human condition.

The Capture of Hitler

The plot of *The Portage to San Cristóbal of A.H.* is fantastical and the audience knows before the play begins that Hitler is dead. So, despite some doubts and hesitance, the audience recognizes that the premise is untrue but agrees to accept it, adhering to Samuel Taylor Coleridge's concept of "that willing suspension of disbelief for the moment, which constitutes poetic faith."[18] As Gary K. Wolfe suggests, "contemporary fantasy must engage in an implied compact between author and reader—an agreement that whatever impossibilities we encounter will be made significant to us, but will retain enough of their idiosyncratic nature that we still recognize them to be impossible."[19] Nikolai Maximovitch Gruzdev, the Russian doctor in the play who inspected the purported body of Hitler, says that he believed the body was not that of the Führer but rather of a double, yet that he was forced to admit it was Hitler after the KGB pulled out his fingernails to coerce him.[20] The plot is rendered more confusing by Gruzdev's suggestion that the Nazi hunters are foolishly chasing the double, even though he asserts that it was the double who was murdered in the bunker. In fact, it cannot be fully proven whether the Nazi hunters have caught the actual dictator or his double. Thirty four years have passed since Hitler was seen in civilization. Steiner and later Hampton leave open the possibility that the man giving the fiery defense at the end is the double. How else can it be explained that the man changes from speaking German to English and talks fluently in English while the historical Hitler could not?[21] Yet the stage directions clearly state that the captured man is "unmistakably, ADOLF HITLER."[22] *The Portage to San Cristóbal of A.H.* provides a credible explanation of how Hitler could have survived and escaped Berlin, thus blurring the demarcation between truth and fantasy. Steiner and Hampton thus explore an idea that fascinates many: What would have happened if Hitler had survived the war?

Such a creative and fantastical story is crucial because it allows readers to explore significant aspects of history, art, and ethics without being limited by historical fact. Sometimes fiction is more fascinating and meaningful than historical fact. Hitler alive and defending himself is much more intriguing than a dead, decomposed, and burned body that yields no answers or defense. Early Holocaust drama consisted largely of melodramatic, fictional theatre that pretended to be factual. Fantastic theatre, however, does not pretend to be truthful but instead is openly truthful about not being factual. The fantastic plot of Steiner's and Hampton's work is important not only for its entertainment value but also because it enables the authors and the audience to explore meaningful concepts, such as the limits of vengeance and the power of language.

Obsessive revenge is represented in *The Portage to San Cristóbal of A.H.* in the character of Lieber. For decades Lieber has been pursuing leads about Hitler's whereabouts. In order to inspire the Nazi hunters to continue their mission in the unforgiving Amazon jungle, Lieber constantly reminds his Nazi hunters about the former German Chancellor's heinous crimes by listing them as a litany of evil:

At Maidanek ten thousand a day, unimaginable because innumerable, in
one
   corner of Treblinka seven hundred thousand bodies.
I will count them now.
Aaron, Aaronowitch, Aaronson, Abilech, Abraham. I will count seven
hundred
   thousand names and you must listen, I will say Kaddish till the end of
time and
   still not reach the millionth name, at Belzec three hundred thousand
[....]
Names gone in fire and gas, ash on the wind at Chelmno, the long black
wind at
   Chelmno, Israel Meyer, Ida Meyer [....]
Four hundred and eleven thousand three hundred and eighty-one in section three
   at Belsen [....]
The one being Belin the tanner whose face they sprinkled with acid and
who was
   dragged through the streets of Kershon behind a dung cart but sang
[....]
The one being all because unnumbered hence unrememberable.[23]

Vivian M. Patraka claims that "Lieber's language represents an attempt to
construct not metaphors or examples but an unending, memorializing
litany to the dead that is all encompassing."[24] Lieber has been obsessed
with the capture of Hitler for many years and wants him punished for the
Führer's innumerable crimes that cost people their lives. Millions of people
were murdered, and their bodies and their identities have been lost forever,
so Lieber recites the names of the victims to honor them and to show his
hunters the need for revenge. Perhaps Steiner, whose family was fortunate
to escape the Holocaust, agrees with Lieber to some extent; in 1940, the
Steiners happened to take a trip from their home in France to New York
shortly before the Nazi occupation of Paris. Steiner was one of only two
Jewish students in his class who survived the war. He felt lucky to have
survived while his classmates perished, but his guilt in having survived,
while his friends did not, resulted in his need to sustain the memories of
Holocaust victims. Steiner asked himself, "'Why me? Why did I deserve
to get away?' Part of the legacy was a sense of obligation. 'My whole life
has been about death, remembering and the Holocaust,' he says. 'Name-
lessness' was Hitler's taunt—'Who remembers the Armenians?' I've had
to be a 'remembrancer.'"[25] Steiner's desire to be a "remembrancer" is apparent in his novella and particularly shines through in the character of Lieber.
    Although the Nazi hunters have been ordered by Lieber to capture

Hitler unharmed and bring him back to Israel for trial, the impetuous Amsel wants to kill him right away out of revenge because of the Führer's responsibility for the Holocaust and because Amsel's father died while searching for Hitler after the war. After capturing Hitler, Amsel declares triumphantly, "You're ours. You know that, don't you? The living God. Delivered you into our hands."[26] Amsel asserts that God has placed Hitler into his grasp because the Lord sanctions revenge against him, implying that by capturing the former Führer, he is God's instrument. Amsel is so excited about revenge that he speaks haltingly in short, staccato fragments. Himmler, Goebbels, Göring, and many other Nazis are already dead, but the fantastic element in the play is that Hitler remains alive thirty-four years later, thus allowing the writer, audience, and characters to ponder at least two questions: When does justice transform into vengeance; and When is vengeance worthwhile?

In the swamps of the Amazon, the Nazi hunters start to have second thoughts about their role in the capture of Hitler. They begin to distinguish between justice and vengeance, wondering what good would result from putting Hitler on trial in Israel or from killing him. When Amsel tells Gideon that he has joined the mission because "I want vengeance, just the same as you," Gideon responds sardonically:

> Vengeance? There can be no vengeance. Why should history apologize to the Jews? ... You think the dead will sit up just because we've got Hitler? They won't. You can dip him in boiling oil six million times. What's that going to mean to a man who's seen his six-year-old daughter so terrified she dirtied herself before they killed her? You think that can be made good?[27]

Gideon brings up a significant point: the capture and ultimate killing of Hitler cannot undo the atrocities of the past. What is the value, Gideon ponders, of capturing Hitler thirty-four years after his escape, when the former Nazi leader is ninety? Killing him now or bringing him to trial will not redeem the victims. Gideon also distinguishes between revenge and refusal to forgive, suggesting that he can never forgive Hitler for the atrocities but that the failure to exact vengeance does not constitute forgiveness. Holocaust survivor Jean Améry wrote this message to Nazi hunter and Shoah survivor Simon Wiesenthal: "What you and I went through ... must *not happen again, never, nowhere.* Therefore ... I refuse any reconciliation with the criminals and with those who only by accident did not happen to commit atrocities, and finally, all those who helped prepare the unspeakable acts with their words."[28] A man who willingly murdered innocent people, such as the SS soldier who asked Wiesenthal's forgiveness, "permanently cut himself off from the possibility of forgiveness."[29] Lawrence Langer calls the genocide "an unforgivable crime." Roth adds that although forgiveness is necessary, it is also

> dangerous because it can minimize accountability, trivialize suffering, and condone injustice, if only inadvertently.... Many deeds and events, including the Holocaust, are unforgivable ... because they involve persons whose lives have been taken from them, and they are in no position to forgive, at least not in any way of which we have knowledge in our current times and places.[30]

Gideon has no intention of forgiving Hitler, and such forgiveness would prove a meaningless gesture. Yet the Nazi hunter discerns no value in killing Hitler thirty-four years after the war. Steiner/Hampton distinguish between Gideon and Lieber who, by virtue of pursuing Hitler incessantly for thirty-four years, goes beyond the refusal to forgive into the realm of monomaniacal vengeance, finally capturing him at the point at which Hitler is now, according to the stage directions of the play, *"pale and shriveled."*[31] Furthermore, bringing Hitler to justice could not prevent future genocides from occurring (as we know from the mass murders in Cambodia, Bosnia, Rwanda, and Sudan), so the destruction of the German dictator would not serve as a deterrent to future genocidal maniacs. Is there a certain point at which the past, no matter how disturbing, should be left alone, or should Hitler, had he survived the bunker, been hunted down and put on trial regardless of time, place, and cost? Steiner/Hampton seems to use Gideon as a *raisonneur*, for the work does not demonstrate any good that comes from the capture of Hitler. Only in a fantastic work of literature, as in one in which Hitler remains alive, is such a moral question possible.

The Trial

When the captors find themselves unable to take Hitler out of the Amazon because of the swamps and their lack of adequate equipment, they decide to hold a makeshift trial of Hitler in the Amazon for his war crimes and genocide. When they put Hitler on trial, they fail to heed the stern warning of their leader (Lieber) not to let the former Nazi dictator speak: "You must not let him speak. Gag him if necessary or stop your ears.... His tongue is like no other" (268). Dazed initially by his capture, the ninety-year-old Hitler becomes animated when put on trial and allowed to talk, as Lieber anticipated, and mesmerizes his captors. Robert

Skloot points out that trials in Holocaust literature have the ability to illuminate "the mind of the Nazi perpetrators, and the way in which this inquiry into the Nazi mind has, over the last decade or more, revealed deep and lasting changes in the way we think of the issue of justice when it is placed in the context of postmodern culture."[32]

Yet another aspect of the fantastic in this work is that the trial and the stage play merge into one, as if Hitler is not on trial but rather playing a part in a play—which he actually is. Hannah Arendt says, in a relevant comment, that "[i]t was precisely the play aspect of the [Eichmann] trial that collapsed under the weight of the hair-raising atrocities. A trial resembles a play in that both begin and end with the doer, not with the victim."[33] In *The Portage to San Cristóbal of A.H.*, this tribunal stage does not scare Hitler because it is exactly what he craves.

To the dismay of Steiner's readers and Hampton's audiences, the trial invigorates Hitler, for it provides the charismatic speaker with his own platform. Hitler passionately defends his actions during the Holocaust in a series of four claims: he borrowed the idea of the Master Race and genocide from the Jews; the Jews deserved to be destroyed because they created conscience through their belief in an omnipresent and omniscient God; the Nazi genocide pales in comparison to other mass murders; and he is responsible for the creation of Israel. Hitler's defense statements are problematic and complex in part because some truth lies behind his sophistry.[34] Although Robert Skloot dismisses the former German dictator's defense as a "profoundly anti–Semitic, rhetorical onslaught,"[35] that is too simple. Propaganda confuses and hoodwinks those it influences because falsehoods, illogical statements, and rationalizations are intertwined with facts as well to deceive the pliant and those who, by virtue of sharing the same or similar values, are made vulnerable to deception.

Hitler's first claim to the makeshift tribunal is that he derived his theory of the "Master Race" from the Jews' concept of "The Chosen People." He declares to the Jewish tribunal, "*Your* teaching. A chosen people. Chosen by God for His own. The only race on earth chosen, exalted, made singular among Mankind.... Moses, Joshua, the anointed king who has slain his thousands, no his ten thousands, and dances now before the ark.... To set a race apart.... To hold before it a promised land. To scour that land of its inhabitants or place them in servitude."[36] Audiences are disturbed by this excuse because Hitler likens himself to the Jews, claiming that by creating his separate and pure nation, he was copying the Jews, his own victims. He claims to have borrowed the idea of genocide to purify a homeland from the Old Testament, implying that his victims used to be the perpetrators in genocide. Hitler's claim is disturbing because genocide occurs throughout the Old Testament, and it is, as he claims, divinely sanctioned. What follow are some of the examples that support the Führer's contention[37]: The Lord orders Saul to "'attack Amalek, and proscribe all that belongs to him. Spare no one, but kill alike men and women, infants and sucklings, oxen and sheep, camels and asses!'" Saul is then punished by God for disobeying orders when he spares the lives of King Agag and cattle. God rejects Saul as King of Israel because he failed to "'make war on them until you have exterminated them.'"[38] God tells Joshua to destroy all the people of Jericho: "They exterminated everything in the city with the sword: Man and woman, young and old, ox and sheep and ass."[39] God tells Moses to destroy the people of Heshbon and allows the Israelites to destroy all the Amorites ("we doomed every town—men, women, and children—leaving no survivor"[40] and then the Bashanites ("we dealt them such a blow that no survivor was left."[41] The mass murder of Jews and other victims during the Holocaust was tragic and unconscionable, but what about the Amaleks, Amorites, and Bashanites? To justify genocide, Hitler once asked if anyone remembered the Armenians. Can the same question be asked about the Amaleks, Amorites, and Bashanites? Perhaps no one cares because they are all gone, while millions of Jews remain. Hitler's argument seems to sway members of the tribunal, but it should not. Even though Hitler is correct that the Jews set their people apart and the Bible sanctions genocide, the existence of previous actions and atrocities in no way justifies genocide. Indeed, there is *no* way to justify the murder of millions of innocent people, under any circumstances. Yet no one refutes his deceitful argument.

Hitler's second argument blames the Jews for creating the belief in an all-powerful God that causes people to feel guilty and have a conscience. He claims that they deserve punishment for this "crime." It is the weakest of the four arguments and does not merit as much attention as the others.

The former Führer's third argument is that he could not have murdered millions by himself and that Stalin and others killed more than he did. He declares:

I was only a man of my time.... Had I been the singular demon of your fantasies, how could millions of ordinary men and women have found in me the mirror, the plain mirror of their appetites?.... Stalin slaughtered thirty million.... He perfected genocide when I was still a nameless scribbler in Munich.... How many Jews did Stalin kill? Answer me that. Had he not died when he did, there wouldn't have been one of you left alive between

Berlin and Vladivostok. Yet when Stalin died in bed, the world stood hushed before the tiger's rest. Whereas you hunt me down like a rabid dog, drag me through the swamps, tie me up at night.[42]

Hitler is correct on both points. It is true that he did not commit genocide by himself. He was elected into office, and it took millions of German soldiers as well as ordinary citizens in Germany and Nazi-occupied Europe to enact "The Final Solution." Hitler succeeded in his evil actions because he enjoyed widespread support. He is also correct that he is responsible for fewer murders than Stalin and other dictators. These points seem to convince the Israelis on the tribunal, which makes them silent. Hypnotized by Hitler's rhetoric and charisma, they fail to realize that his defense in no way justifies his actions. Although it is true that millions supported his actions, that does not mitigate his murders; millions of innocent people died because Adolf Hitler paved the road for genocide and incited people to kill. That Stalin and others were responsible for more murders than Hitler does not make the German dictator any less of a genocidal maniac.

Hitler's fourth and final argument in his defense is that by inspiring the Holocaust, he is indirectly responsible for the creation of the nation of Israel. Again, there is some truth in Hitler's words that obfuscate a greater truth. He adds that he should be thanked by the Jews: "Perhaps I am the Messiah, the true Messiah, the new Sabbatai, whose infamous deeds were allowed by God in order to bring his people home."[43] Tragedies and mass murders during the Holocaust led the world to decide that the Jews needed their own homeland. During his trial, Hitler states that his actions led to the creation of the state of Israel, so he accepts credit for the Jewish homeland. Although he is correct that the destruction of the European Jews led indirectly to the establishment of Israel, he omits that he is responsible for the deaths of six million innocent Jews. In this point the former dictator again uses sophistry in an effort to mitigate his horrendous crimes—atrocities that should allow no defense. Skloot labels Hitler's defense in the play "a mixture of confused history and self-promotion that is intended to confuse the documented facts of genocide and their commonly agreed-upon interpretation[, and] that is based less on fact than on cruel fantasy."[44] Yet the same rhetoric that inspired people to hate and murder has now left the Nazi hunters on the tribunal spellbound and speechless. They expected Adolf Hitler to be a monster, but he turned out to be merely a human being. To the horror of some audiences and critics, Hitler is quite eloquent and has the last word, with his captors being so mesmerized and awed that they do not challenge him as the novella/play concludes.

A major complaint about the work is that Hitler speaks last, as if to say that his defense is justified and beyond refutation; even Teku, their Indian guide, bows in submission to Hitler after the dictator is done speaking. Perhaps Steiner/Hampton wish to show that when one employs rhetoric and propaganda masterfully, many people are hoodwinked, which is one reason why the Nazis came into power initially. Ironically, while living in poverty in the Amazon jungle, Hitler is harmless, but now that he has been captured and will be brought to civilization to stand trial for his crimes against humanity, he will become dangerous again because he will be forced to have an audience. The tribunal remains quiet just as Germans sympathetic to the plight of the Jews during the Shoah also stood meekly and silently. The silence of the tribunal could happen in an unusual, fantastic work but not in a traditional, melodramatic literary piece. As Skloot correctly observes, Steiner/Hampton require that the "audience provide the refutation of Hitler's appalling conclusion that the Jews' 'blackmail of transcendence' [and other crimes] caused their own deserved destruction. By doing so Steiner [and Hampton] insist that the inheritors of the post–Shoah world are responsible for confronting the wrongful and catastrophic lies that history can be distorted to support."[45]

With many Holocaust survivors now dead, and the rest elderly, it is up to others to speak for them. This, I think, is one of the reasons why Steiner/Hampton choose to let the members of the tribunal remain silent; it is up to us to speak for those who no longer can. And only a play infused with or built upon the fantastic could create an ahistorical situation from which audiences can understand this responsibility.

NOTES

1. George Tabori, "*Die Kannibalen*: Zur europäischen Erstaufführung," in *Unterammergau oder Die guten Deutschen* (Frankfurt am Main: Suhrkamp, 1981), 37. Anat Feinberg, trans., *Embodied Memory: The Theatre of George Tabori* (Iowa City: University of Iowa Press, 1999), 236.

2. Feinberg, 237.

3. Lawrence L. Langer, *Versions of Survival: The Holocaust and the Human Spirit* (Albany: State University of New York Press, 1982), 72.

4. Tabori, "*Die Kannibalen*," 38; Feinberg, *Embodied Memory*, 237.

5. Robert Skloot, ed. *The Theatre of the Holocaust: Four Plays*, vol. 1 (Madison: University of Wisconsin Press, 1982), 117–18.

6. S.C. Fredericks, "Problems of Fantasy," *Science-Fiction Studies* 5 (March 1978): 37.

7. W.R. Irwin, *The Game of the Impossible: A Rhetoric of Fantasy* (Urbana: University of Illinois Press, 1976), 4.

8. Tzvetan Todorov, *The Fantastic: A Structural Approach to a Literary Genre* (Ithaca, NY: Cornell University Press, 1975), 25

9. Freddie Rokem, *Performing History: Theatrical Representations of the Past in Contemporary Theatre* (Iowa City: University of Iowa Press, 2000), 36.

10. George Steiner, *Language and Silence: Essays on Language, Literature, and the Inhuman* (New York: Atheneum, 1967), 123.

11. Lawrence L. Langer, *The Holocaust and the Literary Imagination* (New Haven, CT: Yale University Press, 1977), 15.

12. Because Hampton's play is so faithful to Steiner's novella, for the purposes of this paper, I will refer to the work as being written by Steiner/Hampton.

13. Robert Skloot, Introduction to *The Theatre of the Holocaust: Six Plays*, vol. 2 (Madison: University of Wisconsin Press, 1999), 29.

14. Eric S. Rabkin, *The Fantastic in Literature* (Princeton, NJ: Princeton University Press, 1976), 14–15.

15. Christopher Hampton, *The Portage to San Cristóbal of A.H.*, in *The Theatre of the Holocaust: Six Plays*, vol. 2., ed. Robert Skloot (Madison: University of Wisconsin Press, 1999), 273. All quotations from the play *The Portage to San Cristóbal of A.H.* are from this edition.

16. Berel Lang, *Holocaust Representation: Art Within the Limits of History and Ethics* (Baltimore, MD: Johns Hopkins University Press, 2000), 17–18.

17. Lawrence L. Langer, *The Holocaust and the Literary Imagination* (New Haven, CT: Yale University Press, 1977), 72.

18. Samuel Coleridge, Chapter XIV of *Biographia Literaria*, in *The Collected Works of Samuel Taylor Coleridge: Sketches of My Literary Life & Opinions*, vol. 7, Bollingen Series LXXV, ed. James Engell and W. Jackson Bate, (Princeton, NJ: Princeton University Press, 1983), 6.

19. Gary K. Wolfe, *Evaporating Genres: Essays on Fantastic Literature* (Middletown, CT: Wesleyan University Press, 2011), 70.

20. Hampton, *The Portage to San Cristóbal of A.H.*, 280.

21. One must consider the possibility that Hitler can speak English eloquently; if he can't address the other characters in English—in front of an English-speaking audience—the play becomes ineffective because Hitler cannot be understood.

22. Hampton, *The Portage to San Cristóbal of A.H.*, 269.

23. Ibid., 295–96.

24. Vivian M. Patraka, *Spectacular Suffering: Theatre, Fascism, and the Holocaust* (Bloomington: Indiana University Press, 1999), 33.

25. Maya Jaggi, "George and His Dragons," *The Guardian*, 16 March 2001, accessed 15 September 2012, http://www.guardian.co.uk/books/2001/mar/17/arts.highereducation.

26. Hampton, *The Portage to San Cristóbal of A.H.*, 269.

27. Ibid., 288.

28. John K. Roth, *Ethics During and After the Holocaust: In the Shadow of Birkenau* (Basingstoke, England: Palgrave Macmillan, 2005), 129.

29. Quoted in Roth, *Ethics During and After the Holocaust*, 130.

30. Ibid., 135.

31. Hampton, *The Portage to San Cristóbal of A.H.*, 267.

32. Robert Skloot, "Holocaust Theatre and the Problem of Justice," in *Staging the Holocaust: The Shoah in Drama and Performance (Cambridge Studies in Modern Theatre)*, ed. Claude Schumacher (Cambridge: Cambridge University Press, 1998), 10–11.

33. Hannah Arendt, *Eichmann in Jerusalem: A Report on the Banality of Evil* (New York: Viking Press, 1964), 3

34. I want to be very clear that even though some of Hitler's statements are true, I am definitely not defending his words or actions. Genocide is always a horrible and cruel act—and never justified.

35. Robert Skloot, Introduction to *The Theatre of the Holocaust: Six Plays*, vol. 2, ed. Robert Skloot (Madison: University of Wisconsin Press), p. 29.

36. Hampton, *The Portage to San Cristóbal of A.H.*, 322–23.

37. *1 Samuel* 15: 3. All Biblical quotations are from, *The Jewish Study Bible*, ed. Adele Berlin, and Marc Zvi Brettler (Oxford: Oxford University Press, 2004).

38. *1 Samuel* 15: 18

39. *Joshua* 6: 21

40. *Deuteronomy* 2: 34

41. *Deuteronomy* 3: 3

42. Hampton, *The Portage to San Cristóbal of A.H.*, 327–28.

43. Hampton, *The Portage to San Cristóbal of A.H.*, 328.

44. Skloot, Introduction, 21.

45. Ibid., 31.

"Hidden in Plain Sight"

On Holocaust Fantasy in the Metaphysical Detective Story

Patricia Merivale

I take "fantasy," as applied to Holocaust fiction, to be a generous umbrella term for non-"realistic" fictional strategies, such as magic realism, myth, and parable, based in such genres as fantasy (Narnian), folk- and fairy tale, horror stories, science fiction, and its flourishing stepchild, alternate history (in which "Hitler won the war," is by far the most common "alternative"). And also, I shall argue, in the "metaphysical" or "postmodern" detective story. Numerous Holocaust police procedurals, spy stories, political and other thrillers, and even most Holocaust detective stories, whether "cozy," like those featuring Agatha Christie's Miss Marple, or "mean," like those with Raymond Chandler's Philip Marlowe, need not, on the whole, apply. But the generic conventions derived from each main type of detective fiction, Marple and Marlowe, by their "metaphysical"/ postmodern/"anti-detective" successors, key, in turn, to their Holocaust variants, are deployed from the beginning of the genre: four tales by Edgar Allan Poe in the 1840s. His strategies were developed by Arthur Conan Doyle (largely 1890s), were made metafictional, paradoxical, and "metaphysical," i.e., of philosophical (and religious) import, by G.K. Chesterton (early–20th century), then secularized by Jorge Luis Borges (mid–20th century).

This is the metaphysical detective story (so named in tribute to Chesterton), which has yielded, in recent years, oblique ("postmodern") ways of writing about the "unrepresentable" Holocaust: absent/invisible presences, traces, silence, omissions, negations, and, significantly, arbitrary rules resulting in ludic constraints: for *"the game is a world apart with distinct boundaries."*[1] We find various admixtures of the detective story's generic conventions with the ludic constraints of some late- or post-modernist "experiments." And detective stories made by such strategies tend to provide a great many clues and few, if any, solutions.

As missing persons feature almost oftener than "murderees" in the private eye novels, so do missing persons in the metaphysical mysteries (not quite detective stories) of the displaced and "disappeared" of the Holocaust. W.G. Sebald (*Austerlitz*, 2001), Aharon Appelfeld (*Badenheim*, 1979 [1939]), Imre Kertész (*Liquidation*, 2003) and many others, have also left a black "hole at the centre" of such stories—the unrepresentable represented by an absence, or by the "invisibility" of something you know is there, but can't see, the unspeakable spoken of by—pointedly—never mentioning it, and other such strategies of displacement. These books are all metaphysical mysteries, written in the form of "riddles, to which the solution is 'Auschwitz'" (to borrow Borges's formulation, that the word "chess" must not appear in a riddle, to which the solution is "chess"). And of course the "solution" never, or hardly ever, or only cunningly disguised, appears within the riddle that it solves.

The "tail job," as in Poe's "Man of the Crowd" (1840) and in Chandler, Hammett and their hard-boiled and/or "noir" heirs, lends its structure to (post)-modern identity quests, which constitute the largest single group of what I call "Holocaust mysteries," rather than Holocaust detective stories: A.M. Klein's *The Second Scroll* (1951), Jonathan Safran Foer's *Everything Is Illuminated* (2002), Art Spiegelman's *Maus* (1986; 1991), Robert Majzels's *Hellman's Scrapbook* (1992) and a great many others. They are commonly second-generation seekers after "truth" (their parents') and "identity" (their own), and investigative skills, if not usually "detection" as such, are essential to their searches.

Patrick Modiano suggests one such strategy, in a novel on the generic borderline between detective story and "mystery." In *Rue des Boutiques Obscures* (appropriately translated as *Missing Person*, 1978/2004), a detective, and amnesiac Jewish survivor, is lost in the labyrinthine city of his own supposed guilt. He seeks futilely for his past, and with it, his identity, following faint clues to a doubly "difficult time"—of the Occupation, of the Holocaust—clues that keep breaking the surface of the present: a faint memory of attempting to cross the Swiss border, of sentries, of a faked "diplomatic" status, nothing solid, only nuances of what might be recollection. But no one will identify him positively, though some will not dispute an identity that he himself, however tentatively, claims. He is caught up in a tail job, trying to follow "himself," to find the "missing person" who *is*, in fact, himself, through the amnesiac clouds of negative memory.[2]

There tends to be a crucial amalgamation and reduction of roles and/or identities in such stories. While the detective, as in Modiano's novel, can himself be or become the "missing person," slippage from detective to criminal (Robbe-Grillet's *Les Gommes*, 1953), or from detective to victim (Borges's "Death and the Compass" [1942]) is more typical. And as such narratives become more explicitly metafictional, they become more postmodern. The role of detective-as-writer alternates in Paul Auster's work, say, with that of writer-as-detective (employed, like Samuel Beckett's Moran, to report on the man pursued), or becomes detective-as-author (in "scenes of writing"), or even detective-as-reader: "This [last function] was called exegesis and any sleuth is fond of it," said Robert Majzels's narrator, the Heretic Sleuth (see below: Majzels, 44a).

This metaphysical tail job story, which Poe's "gumshoe Gothic" "The Man of the Crowd" inaugurates (1840), is the most successful branch of the metaphysical detective story, both in quantity and quality.[3] Note the stark simplicity of its basic plot: One man follows another, in order to "understand" him or to write a (potentially metafictional) report on him, or both, and finds in the end that he has, to some degree, become that man, or, as Kobo Abe put it, "No matter how I follow myself around, I will never see anything but my own backside."[4] But the metaphysical detective story is a very large genre, and its "Holocaust" variant is a very small one.

Beckett's *Molloy* (1955) is sometimes spotted as a detective story of that very kind. As early as 1961, Hugh Kenner neatly and quotably, if parenthetically, summarizes, "(unless a Molloy is simply what a Moran turns into when he goes looking for a Molloy)"[5]—a plausible quick definition for this major class of metaphysical detective stories—from Poe to Paul Auster (his New York *Trilogy* is a notable beneficiary of Beckett, of course),[6] and beyond.

Agent Moran's not wholly tangible employers seem to be mere bargain-basement "Sundays," poor imitations of the Chestertonian quasi-divinity, and so his tail job fails. On both grounds, however, not to mention the several "scenes of writing" and an abundance of what Arthur Saltzman would call "epistemological errands and metafictional tangles,"[7] Molloy is a metaphysical tail job, which gives structure to its metaphysical identity-quest, while its parodic wartime spy story supplies details and atmosphere: Agent Moran pursues ... whom? And at whose command? The novel is, as Jonathan Boulter puts it, "a parody and critique of the epistemological assumptions of the detective novel,"[8] and thus eminently qualified to count, in this context, among the "metaphysicals."

The problem is not with the metaphysical detective story tag, but with the other part of my brief. Is *anything* by Beckett, master of the abstract and the minimal, the "universal" writer of the "existential" gloom of the "human condition," to be tainted with historical specificity? It is tempting to claim, as Gary Adelman does in the strongest terms, that Beckett is "haunted by the ghosts of Auschwitz." For instance, in post-trilogy Beckett, "We live in a world of matter and pain, all Inferno, or, rather, *more specific to Beckett, the world of the concentration camp.* The metaphor of the writer as a condemned Jew ... [is] implicit everywhere" (my italics).[9] And *The Unnamable* (1953) has more than enough of the Holocaust "trace" images Adelman cites—"pits, fires, furnaces, ashes, and the implements of torture"[10]: "the distant gleams of pity's fires biding their hour to promote us to ashes."[11]

But it is harder, on Adelman's evidence, to *prove* the "haunting": the Holocaust is far more visible in his programmatic statements than in the specifics of his readings. The closer one moves into Beckett's texts, the further—always just out of reach—historical specificity seems to retreat, as several critics have noted: "[T]he difficult relation between Beckett and the Holocaust [is one] that has long been recognized by Beckett's readers, but [it] has proven troublingly resistant to critical articulation."[12]

Similarly, something that Rosette Lamont "*sensed rather than reflected upon ...* [was] that Samuel Beckett is one of the great Holocaust writers" (my italics).[13] "Representing" the Holocaust provides special challenges for the "acknowledged subtraction.... The loss of all qualities" that Theodor Adorno notes as a chief element in Beckett's style.[14] He sees Beckett, for that very reason (in *Waiting for Godot* [1953] and *Endgame* [1957]), as the key writer for the "corpsed" post–Holocaust world: "Beckett's trashcans are the emblem of a culture restored after Auschwitz."[15] "[H]istory is cancelled out,"[16] and Beckett's barely surviving beings are the last men on earth.

Marjorie Perloff, in her definitive article, "In Love with Hiding": Beckett's War" (2005), both appreciates and critiques Adorno's readings of Beckett,[17] clarifies the politically convenient reasons that post-war, especially French, critics had for finding Beckett "existential," "universal,"[18] and so forth, and provides a brilliant account of Beckett's 1946 trilogy, "The Expelled," "The Calmative," and "The End,"[19] as, collectively, a moving report on Beckett's war: "A nightmare Beckett never wrote about directly, although allusions to it are ... everywhere in the texts of the post-war decade."[20] She gives examples of Beckett's characteristic removal of specificity from his texts, noting, for instance, that "Ariège," the escape route to Spain, becomes the less historically specific "Pyrenees' in *Godot*,[21] and that the explicitly Jewish name "Lévy" is changed to Estragon—a bitter herb, thus a different *kind* of specificity.[22]

In addition to Perloff, Jonathan Greenberg ("Moran as Authoritarian Personality") and Julie Campbell ("Moran as Secret Agent") make a case for *Molloy*—or Moran at least —as Holocaust-inflected.

By now much of Beckett's oeuvre, for instance his early play *Eleutheria* (McMullan, Blackman, 2008), *Waiting for Godot* (Lamont), *The Lost Ones* (McHale), *How It Is* and *The Unnamable* (Adelman), has been seen as shadowed by Vichy and the Gestapo, by the sheer physical and mental circumstances of the writer's life in wartime, and by "Auschwitz," the most powerful of Holocaust synecdoches.

But, counter-intuitively, *The Unnamable*, the third, and by far the least "referential" of the *Three Novels*, has attracted more critical interest for being "haunted by the ghosts of Auschwitz" than either *Molloy* or *Malone Dies*: Lisbeth Gronbaek allows for the possibility[23]; Gary Adelman (see above) and Alysia Garrison provide substantial accounts, with Garrison speaking of "[*The Unnamable*'s] situated allusions to a damaged time" and "an oblique, alien, and disquieting subtext in ... a novel which functions as an *effect* of these atrocities."[24] And David Houston Jones, in his intriguing account of Beckett and the Holocaust, sees him not as representing, or even attempting to represent it in his fictions, but as wrestling with that second-order "witnessing" that constitutes "testimony," at least two removes from the "event," thus giving a new twist to the Adornian description of Beckett as writer of the post–Holocaust. Jones attempts to solve this dilemma by moving Beckett's subject from the historical events, widely seen as "unrepresentable," in any case, to the transmission of those events by "witnesses" in the form of "testimony."

That "relentless process of negation" that S.E. Gontarski, Wolfgang Iser, Shira Wolosky, Adorno, and numerous others have seen as a hallmark of Beckett's fictions is exemplified by Iser's image, "a poster stamped 'performance cancelled' is still a poster."[25] Or it is exemplified by an "invisible" item, which should not be confused with an "absent" or "non-existent" one; or by the negative imagery of an absence which leaves *traces*: like Iser's "poster," or like the warmth of a recently vacated seat, or that staple of detection, footprints, or a "d" and an "f" in close textual proximity (Perec), where the missing "e" is alluded to in its very absence, or like "the presence of the absence of a letter in Owley's [formerly Howley's] name."[26]

Here Perec and Majzels employ an expressly "literal" form of that strategy of negative traces employed in Holocaust fiction from start to (not-yet) finish: less is often more, and "nothing" may be everything—even as Beckett makes manifest: "nothing is more real than nothing."[27]

Four notable authors, while equally given to negative traces, shape their Holocaust detective fictions, however, as "whodunits" rather than tail jobs. The Chilean, Ariel Dorfman, the Brazilian, Luis Fernando Verissimo, the Canadian, Robert Majzels, and the Frenchman, Georges Perec, have written strikingly "metaphysical" Holocaust detective stories, not by following Poe's "Man of the Crowd," or Moran tailing Molloy, but by accepting Poe's three great paradoxical conventions: "purloined letters ... hiding in plain sight," "least likely suspects," and "locked rooms" (see Chesterton's "The Invisible Man" [1911] for all three in one story), and thus finding themselves closer to Christie and Borges than to Chandler and Beckett.

Ariel Dorfman's Chestertonian parable of murder in Auschwitz constitutes the seventeen-page introductory section of *Hard Rain* (1972; tr. 1990), his political and ethical allegory of "los desaparecidos," in country after country around the globe. But "Auschwitz," as template or originary paradigm, has pride of place, for "los desaparecidos" are, as Dorfman makes clear, Latin America's historical analogue to the "disappeared" of Auschwitz.

A murder is committed in an Auschwitz prison block. Why, when the victim would have been gassed in a few days anyway? The Germans, even more oddly, set in place a thorough investigation, even hiring Christie's Hercule Poirot to conduct it, in order to solve the murder in the classical, conventional, and, above all, rationalist way. But it's useless: he's not a metaphysical detective. And, in any case, why bother? The murderer is also going to be gassed within the week. Reading Chesterton's "The Sign of the Broken Sword" (1911)—i.e., "Where do you hide a leaf? In a forest...," "Where do you hide a body? On a battlefield..."—illuminates Dorfman's ingenious inversion of the "hiding in plain sight" of classical detection.[28]

For Father Brown would have spotted at once both the foregrounding of an individual life in the context of mass anonymous murder and the tiny moral victory achieved in forcing the mass murderers themselves to take seriously an individual death and assign an individual responsibility for it. Majzels (see below) might find a partial answer to his anguished question: "Shall we solve this death, or that one?" Perhaps Dorfman noticed the arrival of Poe's Dupin to deal with a "stolen letter" in chapter 4 of Perec's *La Disparition* (1969), and similarly set up a "classical" detective (Poirot) to fail miserably.

In Luis F. Verissimo's *Borges and the Eternal Orang-utans* (2000), a rather Chestertonian "Borges" character deploys Poe's three "classical" tropes to find that the Holocaust has reached across time and space, and echoed, quite recently, in Buenos Aires.

"Vogelstein," Verissimo's crypto–Borgesian unreliable narrator, presents a darkly comic homage, ultimately to Christie (see her classy variant of the "least likely suspect" in *The Murder of Roger Ackroyd*), but more immediately to "Borges," who is not only a character in the story, but, *faute de mieux*, the "detective"—and one keenly interested, both fictionally, as here, and in biographical fact, in its Jewish themes, central to both identity and motive. "Hidden in plain sight" at the very beginning is Verissimo's epigraph, taken from Borges's story "Abenjacán el Bojari, Dead in his Labyrinth" (1949): "Remember Poe's stolen letter, remember Zangwill's locked room." The by now suitably hackneyed solution to that first locked room novel, Israel Zangwill's *The Big Bow Mystery* (1891), indeed elucidates Verissimo's. Zangwill provides the *modus operandi*: the person who breaks down the locked door enters first, "finds" the (drugged) victim, kills him, and then declares him to have been already dead. Vogelstein skillfully plants "red herrings" (false clues), to distract both reader and the other characters.

The story is set at an international Poe conference in Buenos Aires, with "Borges" in attendance, along with rival professors of murky academic character: one is named "Cuervo," or Raven, to honor Poe, while the villain/victim's name, "Rotkopf," surely echoes Borges's "Red Scharlach," from "Death and the Compass." Distractions of (David) Lodge-like academic satire mingle with even more distracting Borgesian cabalistic clues and occult hypotheses. Clues to a different *kind* of motive are thus rendered invisible. But Vogelstein's own cunningly understated back-story, about a mother left behind in France in 1940, under the protection of a German officer who betrays her, provides ample motive for an implicitly parricidal revenge killing many years later. Our narrator gets away with murder and lives to write a story that (almost) out–Borges's his great hero, Borges. "Borges" writes him afterwards with the solution outlined above, which serves as the book's Afterword—or does he? Our narrator has already admitted to writing under Borges's name on an earlier occasion (writing pseudonymously is something the "historical" Borges was also well known for).

The Jewish occult adumbrated here, however, may have still more to offer. Borges employed Cabala in "The Secret Miracle" (1943) in his astonishing poem, "The Golem" (1964), in essays like "A Vindication of Kabala"

(1931), and, as detective coding, in "Death and the Compass." Perec, in *La Disparition*, his lengthy "e"-less novel—deftly highlights Oulipian constraints with numerous Cabalistic ones; and, in *Apikoros Sleuth* (2004), Robert Majzels sees Holocaust through the double focus of detective story and his own pseudo–Talmudic commentary upon it.

The individual typography of each page of *Apikoros Sleuth* proclaims this strategy: the central text is surrounded, as in the Talmud, by marginal texts which constitute the commentary upon it.[29] Of Majzels's two metaphysical detective stories, the relatively accessible *Humbugs Diet* (2007), although written later, should probably be read first, since its ingredients are familiar: a guilty, albeit (unlike Vogelstein) well-intentioned, narrator, a detective-story plot, a moral focus, and adequate elucidation of highly technical Talmudic terms and situations, which are more complex and far thicker on the ground in *Apikoros Sleuth*, where they receive very little explication. Kitty Millet provides some welcome assistance on *Sleuth*'s Talmudic and Cabalistic elements: "Apikoros" means "heretic," for instance.[30] Introducing our detective's internal debate about his Talmudic obligations to the victims of murder, which seem to need qualifying in the present world, Millet briefly explains the role of Gemara and Mishnah in the typographical format, along with other similarly material matters. But she also alludes to *"an unarticulated narrative happening beyond the margins of the page"* (my italics), suggesting (along with many explicit echoes) significant parallels to Beckett: I incline to think of *Sleuth* as constituting, similarly, an oblique, but not wholly inaccessible, Holocaust text.

Apikoros Sleuth is a complex marvel of typography and erudition, ingenious and funny, in which plot and character are shadowy, to say the least: there are a lot of gaps for the reader/ interpreter to fill in. But Majzels is willing to help. He quotes extensively, for instance, Gertrude Stein's *Blood on the Dining Room Floor* (1933; the title suggests a detective-story cliché, like Christie's *The Body in the Library*, 1942) in his pseudo–Talmudic side notes, and follows Stein's proto-metaphysical lead: "[O]n the whole a detective story does have to have an ending and my detective story did not have any" (says Stein with uncharacteristic modesty, in "Why I Like Detective Stories," 1937).[31] The whole metaphysical genre prides itself, as I have said, on having too many clues and, if at all possible, no solutions, and Majzels's book, casting off Stein's quasi-retraction, is a model in that respect.

In the course of a series of murders, however, metaphysical traits, requiring metaphysical detection, leap to the eye:

The blackened mirror of his own proleptic guilt sketched on the front page of murder, mystery and the news of the day (20b);
In this way we learn that we are the suspect and not the intended victim (29a);
A footprint of blood in the hallway between mind and body. Redhanded (33a);
But that grimace is always already precisely the face of a murderer (45a);
A face, bloodless, but still recognizable. My own (47b);
[event]: his painful lack of a right hand... [marginal commentary]: Let us say, he sought to keep his pain at arm's length (49a).

The detective-exegete, our narrator, tries to at least name, if he cannot shake off, the burden of exegesis, and clearly the modest number of murders in his detective story point clearly, as in Perec, toward the Holocaust of multitudes:

Shall we solve this death or that one? Having failed to solve, or represent, or think those millions.... Shall we testify to the limits of what can be said, knowing *there is something which cannot be said, but is trying to be said?* (compare to Millett's comment, above; my italics, 19a);
He sought the absent letter in an alphabet of names.... Death lay in wait in that space between letters.... What can be the source of so much death? (34b);
Shall we compose a musical accompaniment to drown out the screams of the victims?.... War becomes the conduct of a postmortem operation upon millions.... After murder, why won't language vanish? (26a)[32]

Majzels's missing letter, both "purloined" as in the case of Poe and "disappeared" as in the case of Perec, could well be "H" (for "Holocaust"). "Howley," a recurring minor character, loses his "H" and must henceforth answer to "Owley" (17a). Howley exists, insofar as he does, in the Golem-like disappearing letters of his name: "that missing letter pulled a long tongue after it" (32a). Such somber word-play deprives even "Auschwitz" of its "A" and "W," we are told, in Majzels's sole reference to this iconic synecdoche (34b).[33]

Majzels's work further resembles Perec's, although he gives Talmudic constraints priority over Oulipian ones. We may note considerable resemblance in practice, however, between privileging a letter by removing it wherever found, as Perec does, and privileging it with a heavy, but (by definition) unstated, cabalistic significance. Majzels shares with Perec a cabalistic sense of truth coded into letters—that is, seemingly uninterpretable letters coding inaccessible truths.

Not unlike Majzels, Perec makes only two explicit, but similarly random-seeming and non-contextualized, Holocaust references: first, in his Avant-Propos, to "a pogrom at Drancy,"[34] the notorious Parisian staging post for deportations to the death camps, and then, near the end of the book, to "a day on which Auschwitz would turn up its gas."[35] These shadows pull above their weight in Perec's seemingly playful obliquity—in not quite giving us glimpses of the "black hole" of the Holocaust, at the beginning and near the end of his work.

Perec's *La Disparition* (1969) is a lipogrammatic masterpiece, perhaps the only one, and certainly the longest of any significance. This three-hundred page novel without a single "e" in it silently conveys its purpose by means of a purely arbitrary constraint, like the rules in a game; for the lipogram is perhaps OuLiPo's most experimental, challenging, and profoundly playful constraint—or at least, thanks to Perec, by far its best known.[36]

A strong link emerges between Perec's dedication to his *W: Memories of a Childhood* (1974), in many ways a companion volume, and the typographical constraint of *La Disparition*. If "e" = "eux" (the French pronunciation of the letter), as most critics believe, the dedication of his *W* (perhaps the richest and most complex of what I call the Holocaust mysteries) to "E," signifies Perec's lost parents (the word "eux" meaning "them"). In *La Disparition*, the "e(s)" missing from all those individual words hide like ghosts, invisible but not absent, on every page. Perec liked the shapes and sounds of letters, too. An "E" is a "W," turned sideways; they are forms of each other. The letter "W" (an unusual initial in French), by analogy with the "e" = "eux," is pronounced "double vay," which I take to signify the double sorrow in the German words, "Weh! Weh!" ("Woe! Woe!").

Perec's "purloined" letter happens to be the *fifth*, and most often used, letter of both the French and English alphabets, the letter "e"—an even more formidable generative constraint in French than in English. His title, *La Disparition*, becomes, in Gilbert Adair's *tour de force* translation, similarly e-less, *A Void*. We forgive Adair of his occasional freedoms, given the strenuousness of this constraint,[37] but he loses thereby the legal significance of "disparition," a word used of French Holocaust victims "missing" and never found.[38] A numerical leitmotif, 25/26, recurs, where the unnamable (because "missing") item in each series of twenty-six is invariably the fifth. Notably, of the twenty-six chapters in the book itself, the *fifth* is the missing one. And curious objects appear, which cannot be named, although they can be described: objects made up, for instance, of three horizontal lines of which the middle one is shorter,[39] or "a logo, so to say, of a 3 as shown in a mirror."[40]

Impassioned frustrations color Perec's versions of "in plain sight": Amaury "wholly fails to grasp that staring at him, in print, is a solution to that conundrum that is haunting him, consuming him" (i.e., in an ordinary book, full of "e[s]"[41]). Anton Vowl ("Voyl," in the French text), perhaps the protagonist, becomes the first missing person, as if sucked out of life by approaching too closely the quicksand of a "castoff vacuum thirstily sucking us into this thing unsaid,"[42] the "black hole," as we might now say, which *is constituted by* each missing "e." For the characters themselves, the situation is an enigma, a conundrum, a mechanism for concealing an absence that is staring them in the face, and the source of their ever-increasing bafflement and terror. Person after person goes missing, all members, it turns out, of the same extended family. It is brought to the brink of extinction, for reasons its members cannot fathom, to expiate a guilt that is never clarified, in the course of "a gradual invasion of words by margins,"[43] from beginning to end.

It seems odd, reading *La Disparition* now, that this, and much else in the book (see Lisbeth Gronbaek for a particularly good account of the Holocaust elements) could ever have been read as "outside" the Holocaust; it seemed even odder, when the book first came out, that a reader could fail to take note of the absence of "e(s)." But Heather Mawhinney[44] cites Perec's reproach (1981) of René-Marill Albérès, an early reviewer (1969), for not spotting (as it were), the missing "e(s)," while she herself makes not a single, even parenthetic, Holocaust reference.

Perec chided some of his critics for their critical strategy of "eeny, meeny, miny, mo"—for working out, that is, the *details* of the constraints, while missing the *point* of them. Voyl, his protagonist, like most of Perec's critics, is seeking the (literal) "figure in the carpet,"[45] which will clarify his situation, when he, and they (or we), should be attending to the silent prowling of the "Beast in the Jungle," which we could, perhaps, designate as the invisible and (almost) never mentioned Holocaust. This metaphor suggests something like Beckett's own (non-figurative) formula: "in my work there is consternation behind the form, not in the form."[46]

The last remaining characters discuss a document they have just received, one even more lipogrammatic, lacking "a(s)" and short on "y(s)," than *A Void* itself: "—it hasn't got a solitary 'a!'" notes one, "just a solitary 'y,'" adds another. But the third, "finding it impossibly difficult to say what's on his mind," makes a (fatal) mistake: "[He] murmurs in a dying fall: Nor has it got a solitary."[47]

So almost the last "character" disappears both typographically and narratively into the blank on the page. Soon thereafter, at the end of the

English text, those few remaining characters, at the climax of their own baffled terror, disappear into "*A void* rubbing out its own inscription,"[48] not, as in the French, "*la mort*, où va s'abîmant l'inscription" (my italics),[49] for obvious reasons. This game is, after all, a matter of lif*E* or—d*E*ath.

The Holocaust is a verbal presence, as I have said, in only two uncontextualized references, but it is implicit in the gap in almost every word. There is "a hole in the fabric of language," through which may be drawn the "nothing" behind it, said Beckett. Charlotte Delbo's "gaps and empty places on the page,"[50] like Elana Gomel's images of ellipses (...), and (astrophysical) "black holes,"[51] like "silence" and many other tropes of negation in earlier Holocriticism, trenchantly convey the disappearances of all those tiny individual "e(s)" from Perec's text, and the world's.

And it is the finest example, of the many in Holocaust fiction, of how the arbitrary rules of a game—its "constraints"—like the marginally less arbitrary conventions of a genre, may achieve something of what only "survivors" were once thought able to do: if representation is no longer possible, the serious play of the imagination is left to "by indirection find direction out."

CODA

While conventions and constraints are by no means mutually exclusive, and all the texts I've discussed, like most of the world's texts, should—and do—employ both, some of these "conventions" rather than "constraints" seem primary. Modiano is writing a book recognizable as a mystery/identity quest, having employed its generic conventions, rather than detective story ones, whereas Dorfman and Verissimo employ detective story conventions in the excessive mode of parody: neither story would succeed as a Holocaust parable in the form of a detective story, were it not plainly—in these two variants—to be read parodically. Such exaggerated foregrounding resembles conventions familiar in Chesterton, Christie, and Borges, and flamboyantly highlights such metafictional jests as bringing Poirot (Dorfman), Borges (Verissimo) and Dupin (Perec, in parodic mode), not to mention the authors themselves, as characters, into their own stories. Verissimo and Dorfman, whose wonderfully shaped, and (also) blackly humorous contributions to the Chesterton/Borges tradition of the metaphysical detective story, are, at best, "minor" masterpieces, if placed in the company of Beckett and Perec.

Now Beckett, Majzels, and Perec do plenty of parody as well; I may have found Beckett to be parodying Poe's "Man of the Crowd,"[52] but the particular force of their representation of the notoriously unrepresentable Holocaust comes through the deployment of chiefly ludic constraints: arbitrary restrictions, chosen as the rules of their particular textual games. Cabalistic and Talmudic elements are "red herrings" in Verissimo, having borrowed them from Borges, who took them, in his own witty way, rather more seriously. They are central in Majzels, though he is by no means averse to adding some Oulipian and metafictional frolicking, albeit tangential, and contrapuntal. While Oulipian constraints, and one such constraint in particular—the lipogrammatic—forms the substance of the "figure in the (perecquian) carpet," it points to the invisible—but not absent—Beast called Holocaust, patrolling quietly in the Jungle, who is also the "black hole" into which, one after another, Perec's characters fall.

The Beckettian texts most shaped by the constraints of formal pattern, mathematics, and the constant cancelings out of "meaning," from *The Unnamable* on, are of course the least likely to rely on the "conventions" of the detective story, or, for that matter, of any other fictional genre. Beckett's increasingly abstract, musical, mathematical, geometrical, measuring and minimalizing procedures, dominant in his later prose, include, for instance, a piece of mirror-prose that Iser points out (forty sentences, then repeated, but in an order determined by chance). Perec and Beckett are found to share a taste for such "ludic" constraints, as Beckett comes to seem a closet quasi–Oulipian.

It is another trait serving to bring him and Perec closer together—though they seem, oddly, never to have met. The only recorded statement either made about the other appears to be Perec's: hostile to the nouveau roman, and to Beckett, seemingly its successor ("Enfin Beckett vint").[53]

The conventions of the (metaphysical) detective story, the arbitrary rules of Oulipo and Cabala, with the most strenuous "constraints" on language to be found in the modern novel, add up to a picture (too strong a word; it implies representation, which we have not got) of the Holocaust as a present absence, only to be seen indirectly, in "traces" of various kinds, in shadows, in those cosmological processes only measurable by their effects, stars that we know are there because they bend the light of other stars.

Perec's baroque excess of words distracts us, throughout the story, from the concealed "letter," "hiding in plain sight," for both readers and characters; it contrasts with Beckett's strategy of using a restricted vocabulary in as few words as possible, with those few arguing each other into the black humor of *Molloy* or the linguistic standstills of *The Unnamable*.

They are opposites so extreme that perhaps as Gronbaek (astonishingly, the only critic I have found to have written a substantial comparative study of them) maintains, they have come to resemble each other.

Beckett, Perec, and Majzels share a strong ludic streak, propelled, in all three, by a very black sense of humor; they share a tendency, to put it mildly, towards the Oulipian and the cabalistic, in various proportions, in order to suggest an overarching, interpenetrating Holocaust narrative, when (as it were), in the usual "fictional" sense, there isn't one.

These books are *all* metaphysical mysteries, *all* written in the form of "riddles, to which solution is Auschwitz."

But some of them are detective stories as well.

Notes

1. Kimberley Bohman-Kajala, *Reading Games: An Aesthetics of Play in Flann O'Brien, Samuel Beckett, & Georges Perec* (Chicago: Dalkey Archive Press, 2007), 25.

2. See Jeanne C. Ewert, "'A Thousand Other Mysteries': Metaphysical Detection, Ontological Quests," in *Detecting Texts: the Metaphysical Detective Story from Poe to Postmodernism*, ed. Patricia Merivale and Susan Elizabeth Sweeney (Philadelphia: University of Pennsylvania Press, 1999), 179–98.

3. Notable examples include the Québécois Hubert Aquin's *Neige noire* (1974) and *Trou de mémoire* (1968) (tr. as *Hamlet's Twin* [1979], and *Blackout* [1974]), and Graham Greene's (atypical) story, "A Day Saved" (1935). Four Nobel Prize winners are among its practitioners—José Saramago, Orhan Pamuk (*Snow* 2002), Samuel Beckett and J.M. Coetzee, with Kobo Abe as a near miss (of the Prize, that is, not of the story line). See Patricia Merivale and Susan Elizabeth Sweeney, "The Game's Afoot!: On the Trail of the Metaphysical Detective Story," in *Detecting Texts: The Metaphysical Detective Story from Poe to Postmodernism*, ed. Patricia Merivale and Susan Elizabeth Sweeney (Philadelphia: University of Pennsylvania Press, 1999), 1–24.

4. Kobo Abe, *Secret Rendezvous*, trans. Juliet Carpenter (New York: Knopf, 1977/1979), 37.

5. Hugh Kenner, *Samuel Beckett: A Critical Study* (London: Calder, 1962), 65.

6. Stephen Bernstein, "'The Question Is the Story Itself': Postmodernism and Intertextuality in Auster's New York Trilogy," in *Detecting Texts: The Metaphysical Detective Story from Poe to Postmodernism*, ed. Patricia Merivale and Susan Elizabeth Sweeney (Philadelphia: University of Pennsylvania Press, 1999), 134–53; and Julie Campbell, "Moran as Secret Agent," *Samuel Beckett Today 12* (2002): 81–92. For Beckett's "send-up" of the truth-discovering claims of the traditional, rationalist detective story, see Jonathan Boulter, *Beckett: A Guide for the Perplexed* (New York and London: Continuum, 2008), 109–18. Boulter provides a reasonably detailed account of *Molloy*'s detective elements, and their "metaphysical" nature, although he does not employ that term; like several critics working this territory, he might prefer "anti-detective story."

7. Arthur M. Saltzman, *Designs of Darkness in Contemporary American Fiction* (Philadelphia: University of Pennsylvania Press, 1990), 56.

8. Jonathan Boulter, *Beckett: A Guide for the Perplexed* (New York and London: Continuum, 2008), 109.

9. Gary Adelman, *Naming Beckett's Unnamable* (Lewisburg, PA: Bucknell University Press, 2004), 16.

10. Ibid., 79.

11. Samuel Beckett, *The Unnamable*, in *Three Novels: Molloy, Malone Dies, and The Unnamable* (New York: Grove Press, 1995), 300.

12. Peter Boxall, *Since Beckett: Contemporary Writing in the Wake of Modernism* (New York and London: Continuum, 2009), 86.

13. Rosette C. Lamont, "Beckett's Wandering Jew," in *Reflections of the Holocaust in Art and Literature*, ed. Randolph L. Braham (New York: Columbia University Press, 1990), 36. And, more broadly, Shira Wolosky, who wrote: "[Beckett's] intertextual gestures thus remain suspended, seeming to intend some prior text yet never fully pointing to any single one" or "entic[ing] the reader into similar intertextual quicksand." See Shira Wolosky, "Samuel Beckett's Figural Evasions," in *Languages of the Unsayable*, ed. Sanford Budick and Wolfgang Iser (New York: Columbia University Press, 1986), 173, 175.

14. See Theodor Adorno, "Trying to Understand Endgame," in *Samuel Beckett: Modern Critical Views*, ed. Harold Bloom (New York: Chelsea House, 1985), 51–81.

15. Ibid.

16. Ibid.

17. Marjorie Perloff, "'In Love with Hiding': Samuel Beckett's War," *Iowa Review* 35, no. 2 (2005): 79.

18. Ibid., 77.

19. Ibid., 85–86. See also Jackie Blackman, "Beckett's Theatre 'After Auschwitz,'" in *Samuel Beckett: History, Memory, Archive*, ed. Seàn Kennedy and Katherine Weiss (New York: Palgrave Macmillan, 2009), 71–88.

20. Perloff, "'In Love with Hiding,'" 77.

21. Ibid., 76.

22. See Blackman, "Beckett's Theatre 'After Auschwitz,'" 331–33.

23. Lisbeth Gronbaek, "Writing and Reading Beyond the Wordable: Beckett's L'Innommable and Perec's La Disparition" (Ph.D. dissertation, Victoria University of Wellington, 2006), 169–70.

24. Alysia Garrison, "'Faintly Struggling Things': Trauma, Testimony, and Inscrutable Life in Beckett's The Unnamable," in in *Samuel Beckett: History, Memory, Archive*, ed. Seàn Kennedy and Katherine Weiss (New York: Palgrave Macmillan, 2009), 89, 93.

25. Wolfgang Iser, "The Pattern of Negativity in Beckett's Prose," in *Samuel Beckett: Modern Critical Views*, ed. Harold Bloom (New York: Chelsea House, 1985), 126.

26. Robert Majzels, *Apikoros Sleuth* (Toronto: Mercury Press, 2004), 29a.

27. Samuel Beckett, *Malone Dies*, in *Three Novels: Molloy, Malone Dies, and The Unnamable* (New York: Grove Press, 1995), 86.

28. I met Ariel Dorfman at a reading and took the liberty of asking him about the Chesterton connection in this episode. He replied that he had not been aware of it, and then, seeing my faint look of dismay, said, very kindly, "But of course we all read Chesterton as children...."

29. An enterprising reviewer (Emmet Cole) followed this format in his own page-long review of *Apikoros Sleuth*; it would make an ingenious illustration for this account of the book, as well as an introduction to *Apikoros Sleuth* that is both

amusing and useful. See Emmet Cole, review of *Apikoros Sleuth*, by Robert Majzels, *Movable Type* 2 (2006): ucl.uk/graduate/issue/2/Apikoros.

30. Kitty Millet, "Halakhah and the Jewish Detective's Obligations," in *Questions of Identity in Detective Fiction*, ed. Linda Martz and Anita Higgie (Newcastle: Cambridge Scholars Press, 2007), 65.

31. Majzels, *Apikoros Sleuth*, 25b.

32. This last sentence is an Adorno-like marginal note, in the vein of his oft-quoted "to write poetry after Auschwitz is barbaric."

33. Majzels himself sees this as more to do with the stripping of "letters" from a golemic inscription, as in "emet—>met" ("truth"—>"death") in the Golem stories (a major repertory for Holocaust fantasy, of course, and for Borges), than with providing a word "inside" the word "Auschwitz" to serve as a meaningful qualifier of it: private communication. The same presumably applies to "[H]owley."

34. Georges Perec, *A Void*, trans. Gilbert Adair (London: Harvill, 1994), viii. French edition: *La Disparition* (Paris: Denoël, 1969), 11.

35. Perec, *A Void*, 269; *La Disparition*, 284.

36. "OuLiPo" stands for "Ouvroir de littérature potentielle," an *avant-garde* French literary group founded in 1960, much given to textual and linguistic games largely in the form of seemingly random rules and constraints; the "lipogram" and the jig-saw puzzle were Perec's special favorites—along with detective stories, like his *53 Days* and parts of *Life: A User's Manual*, as well as the amazing *W*, the best of the "Holocaust mysteries." There is a good discussion of Borges, OuLiPo and Perec in Pablo Martin Ruiz, "Four Cold Chapters: On the Possibility of Literature Leading Mostly to Borges and Oulipo" (Ph.D. dissertation, Princeton, 2009).

37. On the two texts, Perec's and Adair's English translation, finding the latter, for all its merits, to be a "neo-liberal," somewhat flattened and anachronistic reshaping of the original, see Mireille Ribiére, "La Disparition/ A Void: deux temps, deux histoires?" in *Georges Perec et l'Histoire* (*Études Romanes 46*), ed. Carsten Sestoft and Steen Bille Jørgensen (Copenhagen: Museum Tusculanum Press, 2000), 143–57. Another translation of *La Disparition*, by Ian Monk (unpublished), is called (perhaps a better title?) *The Vanishing*.

38. Ewert, "'A Thousand Other Mysteries,'" 194.

39. Perec, *A Void*, 39; *La Disparition*, 55.

40. Ibid., 201; Ibid., 220.

41. Ibid., 84; Ibid., 100.

42. Ibid., 111; Ibid., 128.

43. Ibid., 16; Ibid., 32.

44. Heather Mawhinney, "'Vol de Bourdon': The Purloined Letter in Perec's *La Disparition*," *Modern Language Review* 97, part 1 (Jan. 2002): 49–50.

45. Perec, *A Void*, 4–7; *La Disparition*, 18–20.

46. Israel Shenker, Interview with Samuel Beckett *New York Times*, May 5, 1956, in *Samuel Beckett: Critical Heritage*, ed. Lawrence Graver, Raymond Federman (New York: Routledge, 1979/1999), 146ff.

47. Perec, *A Void*, 271–72; *La Disparition*, 296–97.

48. Perec, *A Void*, 278.

49. Perec, *La Disparition*, 305.

50. Charlotte Delbo, *Auschwitz and After*, trans. Rosette C. Lamont (Newport, CT: Yale University Press, 1995), 132.

51. Ibid., 131, 163.

52. Samuel Beckett, *Malone Dies*, in *The Unnamable,* in *Three Novels: Molloy, Malone Dies, and The Unnamable* (New York: Grove Press, 1995), 222–23.

53. In Georges Perec, "Le Nouveau Roman et le refus du réel," [1962] *L.G.: Une aventure des années soixantes* (Paris: Éditions du Seuil, 1992): "Enfin Beckett vint. *Puis le Degré zéro de l'écriture...*" (29). A translation, by Rob Halpern, "The Nouveau Roman and the Refusal of the Real," is available on the Internet.

The Summons of Freedom
Fantastic History in Jonathan Safran Foer's Everything Is Illuminated
Paul Eisenstein

Introduction

The bifurcated form of Jonathan Safran Foer's *Everything Is Illuminated* confronts readers almost immediately with a dizzying and potentially disquieting novelistic treatment of the Holocaust. Foer's novel, of course, contains—and alternates between—two radically distinct narratives. The first is a serious, first-person, realist account written by the Ukrainian guide Alexander Perchov that chronicles his efforts to help a twenty-one year old American named Jonathan Safran Foer to find Augustine, the woman who Jonathan believes saved his grandfather Safran from a Nazi massacre. The second is an exceedingly fantastical and comically irreverent history written by Jonathan of his grandfather's and Augustine's hometown, Trachimbrod, from the years 1791–1941. Whereas Alex's account records an earnest search for the past and recovers in the process two very powerful Holocaust testimonies—one by Lista, the last remaining survivor of Trachimbrod; the other by Alex's own grandfather, who accompanies Alex and Jonathan on their search for Augustine—Jonathan's fantastical history of Trachimbrod is wildly and sacrilegiously inventive, appearing at times to be interested in testifying only to the marvelous textual forms that an imaginative rendering of history can take.[1] These two narratives are, moreover, interrupted by a third discourse that only deepens the formal variety and self-referential dimension of *Everything Is Illu-*

minated. This discourse consists of a series of Alex's letters to Jonathan, written in the aftermath of their parting, in which Alex comments directly on the difficulty of writing his own narrative and voices some ethical concerns regarding the inventive liberties Jonathan is taking in his history of Trachimbrod (whose installments Jonathan is sending with some regularity to Alex).

For some readers, such multiple discourses might smack of a solipsistic language game that unjustly usurps the place of the actual memories of survivors.[2] In what follows, however, I want to argue that the novels and letters that Alex and Jonathan are exchanging converge powerfully on the issue of the writer's, and our own, radical freedom to believe (or not) in the impossible and indecent truths of the past. Foer isolates the precise moment at which this radical freedom emerges at roughly the halfway point of the novel, when Jonathan and Alex fail to find Augustine—the survivor-witness who would possess and be able to relate information crucial to the construction of a sequential, value-securing and all-illuminative narrative.[3] It is at this juncture that *Everything Is Illuminated* writes in its own point of origin. By withholding from Jonathan the witness and archival materials required for the narrative that might illuminate everything for him—and that would vindicate Alex's naïvely credulous belief in the recoverability of the past and its affirmative telos—Foer creates a moment in which both Jonathan and Alex become aware of how completely free they are to write, remember, and believe as they wish. This awareness regarding freedom is of a piece with the power of its exercise when it comes to encountering and involving ourselves in the traumatic events of history. If we see the form of Foer's novel as bound up with freedom and the vicissitudes of its exercise, the punctuation of Alex's Holocaust narrative by Jonathan's fantastical historiography does much more than provide intermittent, comic relief from Lista's and Alex's grandfather's traumatizing revelations. Instead, we might see Jonathan's own unreserved exercise of freedom as speaking directly and ethically to the power that Alex has to remain faithful (or not) to the sorrowful Holocaust testimonies of Lista and his grandfather that he encounters. In the end, Foer positions this power as inseparable from Alex's own freedom to reconsider what it means to be human, and ultimately, to change his life—to see all of the signifiers that name his identity as chosen (and thus capable of being revised or discarded), and to see himself and others, via the Holocaust, as bound by a common vulnerability.

The Productive Paradoxes of Holocaust Freedom

This notion of Holocaust freedom, of course, is a thorny one when it comes to discussing the way the Holocaust should be depicted, since some of the most controversial representations of the Holocaust have, in the exercise of a kind of imaginative freedom, been said to cross an important moral limit. The result is that sometimes imaginative freedom itself, in the context of the Holocaust, has come to appear dubious. In his critique of literary and cinematic texts that evince a "surge of the imagination" and "a demonstration of literary brilliance and the power of one's intellect,"[4] Saul Friedländer has pointed to this source of ethical disquiet by asking, "There may be no rules, but doesn't one feel the urge for some kind of parsimony?"[5] We might recall here the arraignment of texts such as Paul Celan's "Todesfugue," Jerzy Kosinski's *The Painted Bird*, William Styron's *Sophie's Choice*, and Binjamin Wilkomirski's *Fragments*. These works (and others) have prompted a great deal of worry about the way figurative language and imagined representations can profane or falsify history and even play into the hands of Holocaust denial. Celan's beautifully lyrical poem, of course, occasioned Adorno's claim that "to write poetry after Auschwitz is barbaric,"[6] that "[t]hrough the aesthetic principle of stylization an unimaginable fate still seems as if it had some meaning: it becomes transfigured, something of the horror is removed."[7] Elie Wiesel has famously claimed that the Holocaust can neither be the source of "literary inspiration" nor be used "for literary purposes," since to use it as such would "mean, then, that Treblinka and Belzec, Ponar and Babi Yar all ended in fantasy, in words, in beauty, that it was simply a matter of literature."[8] Cynthia Ozick, noting the way the imagination's freedom has resulted in "fraud, hoax, or delusion," asserts categorically that what was perhaps permissible to Daniel Defoe ("fiction masking as chronicle") "is not permitted to those who touch on the destruction of six million souls, and on the extirpation of their millennial civilization in Europe."[9] And in a similar vein, Berel Lang has argued for the primacy of historical chronicle over literary rendering, since it is the former's "narrow, prosaic, nonironic, nonfigurative foundation" that guarantees a level of authenticity.[10]

Lang's four adjectives—narrow, prosaic, nonironic, and nonfigurative—function almost as ethical criteria for Holocaust writing as a whole. In the name of a sober, terrible accuracy, the aforesaid critiques argue for the curtailment of the literary imagination's freedom and/or the use of literary language in the representation of the Holocaust. In the process, however, such critiques police generic and aesthetic boundaries within Holocaust literature, since they privilege, sometimes quite explicitly, traditional historiography and survivor testimony over anything explicitly invented or fictionalized, and a spare and solemn realism over anything evincing literary adornment or stylization. A moral injunction of sorts clearly motivates the privileges and prohibitions voiced in this critical discourse: to pay proper respect to the Holocaust's victims and to avoid giving any ammunition to Holocaust deniers.[11] Traditional historiography and survivor testimony, moreover, are believed to be capable, on their own, of teaching the lessons of the Holocaust, of making the biggest or most authentic impact on readers.

As Geoffrey Hartman has suggested, however, what criteria of this kind end up contesting is the very capacity of art as "a performative medium" to provide "a counterforce to manufactured and monolithic memory"—to memorial narratives that consolidate "the identity of nation or group," that limit "subversive or heterogeneous facts," and that "nationalize consensus by suggesting a uniform or heroic past."[12] For Hartman, the art produced via this performativity can in some cases be troublesome, but because a discourse (i.e., literary criticism) exists that can capture the source of the trouble, even the most problematic of fictions helps to keep the memory of the Holocaust alive.[13] To take the defense of imaginative Holocaust literature even further, we might ask whether the textual styles involved in historiography and survivor testimony do not themselves remain the product of stylistic choices. Ruth Franklin asks a version of this question when she notes how so many Holocaust memoirs have been understood as novels as well: "Every canonical work of Holocaust literature," she writes, "involves some graying of the line between fiction and reality."[14] This is perhaps to make an obvious point—that historians and survivors choose their styles, just as 21st century subjects who are reading and learning and perhaps writing about the Holocaust must choose to linger and be touched by its terrible and traumatic dimension, must elect to embrace and to be sorrowed by and to learn from the Holocaust.

Whereas these choices are normally concealed, the form of Foer's novel works to reveal them. It does this in the juxtaposition of two distinct modes of narrating history—one operating within the parameters of realistic representation, the other flying above and beyond such parameters—and in the way that the second mode *summons the freedom of* those ignorant of, indifferent to, or otherwise defensive vis-à-vis the traumatic dimension of history. What Foer aims to show is how the radical power to imagine writ large in Jonathan's fantastical history of Trachimbrod is part of the same human power in Alex to choose a truthful version of history that fully avows the enormity of its sorrow and loss. This human power, moreover, is not just ours to exercise in matters of historical truth or falsity. On the contrary, this is the very same power to share in the suffering of others, the power to empathize, to feel sorrow, and to act in order to arrest intergenerational cycles of violence. It is, in short, a moral and political power, and what is to be learned from the Holocaust has everything to do with its exercise.

The point at issue, then, in the pitting of parsimonious, nonfigurative history and testimony against the inventions of the imagination (in the manner of Adorno, Wiesel, Ozick, and Lang) is that all of the freedom appears to rest with the latter. Freedom appears to be the source of all of the trouble, whereas history and survivor testimony are positioned simply as reasonably compelling rational belief in something authentic and true.[15] Shortchanged in this portrayal of things is the basic ethical wager of the Enlightenment—the notion that the guarantor of truth and ethics lies not in the texts that discursively and intelligibly set forth this or that historical truth or ethical maxim, but rests, instead, in the freedom of human beings to believe a truth or follow a moral law simply because *they can*. This is, in many ways, the gauntlet thrown down by Immanuel Kant, for whom freedom is the ultimate idea against which reason runs aground. If we follow Kant, this means in the last instance that one cannot give a reason for accepting a truth as true or for following a moral law: ultimately, we must believe in such a truth or follow a moral imperative because we are free to do so.

This modern way of conceiving ethics and truth carries with it obvious risks. As Kant himself was forced to concede, it is entirely possible that an individual or individuals might elect *not* to follow the moral law—an unsettling choice that Kant dubbed "radical" or "inextirpable" evil.[16] Nonetheless the notion of freedom remains unavoidably central to our encounters with what transpired during the Holocaust, and to the productive lessons we might take from such encounters. To bite the bullet of Kantian ethics is to regard the Holocaust as very possibly the object of disbelief or indifference, to see that while there are certainly reasons for believing in and being touched by an event like the Holocaust, we must embrace and affirm that the reasons for embracing these reasons cannot themselves be specified: they must, in the last instance, be chosen.

Revaluing the Fantastic

At first glance, the fantastic history of Trachimbrod that Jonathan authors might appear unsettlingly frivolous when juxtaposed with the serious and ultimately catastrophic past recovered and recounted in Alex's story. While it is no doubt the case that Jonathan has failed to find the witness (Augustine) who would enable him to write a realistic book about his grandfather and his village, we might ask whether the failure of his documentary project had to give way so completely to a history that is so false, so lewd, and so full of risible caricatures and absurdities. His grandfather's one hundred and thirty-two mistresses, his twenty-seven hundred sexual encounters, his first orgasm with German bombs exploding audibly in the distance—these features of the portrait of Safran imagined by Jonathan would seem enough to elicit the rebuke that Foer has violated the propriety and decorum we might believe is owed to pre-war inhabitants of an Eastern European Jewish *shtetl*.

To read Jonathan's story is not just to question repeatedly the ethical implications of the imaginative license he is taking at the level of plot and character, but to question also the ontological status of the text itself. This is because Jonathan's narrative of Trachimbrod frequently resorts to non-narrative methods of communication that take a host of shapes on the page, calling attention to the story's excessive textuality. At times, Jonathan's narrative reads like a *tour de force* that seems to symbolize nothing but the nonsensical gesture of symbolization itself: we enjoy (or do not) the dazzling imaginative turns of his story in a manner akin to enjoying the sound of words apart from their sense or meaning.[17]

This feature of fantastical narratives explains why, in the case of the Holocaust, they are so rare, why so few works have chanced to approach in such a lively and stylized way an all too solemn historical event. If, as Berel Lang has argued, literature must "aspire to historical authenticity,"[18] what then is to be done with works which so flagrantly cast aside that aspiration, which court laughter and/or disbelief in their reliance on the fantastic?[19] When a writer imagines sexual liaisons between his dead grandfather and a traumatized Holocaust survivor he has recently met, when this writer juxtaposes seismic orgasms and German bombs, we may have every right to ask after a writer's responsibility to history, and after what constitutes that responsibility's betrayal. If, for Lang, narratives such as George Steiner's *The Portage to San Cristóbal of A.H.* and Philip Roth's *The Ghost Writer* "tread on dangerous ground,"[20] because they stray so clearly from a recognizably factual world, surely the same danger accompanies the handful of other texts that so dramatically (and often comically) challenge known historical facts and even the very laws of the physical world—from Romain Gary's *The Dance of Genghis Cohn* (1968) to Joseph Skibell's *A Blessing on the Moon* (1997).[21]

Like these stories, Jonathan's history of Trachimbrod confronts us with the writer's radical freedom to invent without concern for truth and accuracy, to revel in the power of the imagination to spin magical and marvelous stories. By making this history something overtly presented to Alex, however, and even juxtaposing it formally with Alex's much more serious story, Foer makes explicit the implicit memorial wager of every fantastical Holocaust narrative—the way each one asks us to inhabit the "duration of uncertainty" that Tzvetan Todorov, more than thirty-five years ago, placed at the heart of the fantastic as a literary genre.[22] Such uncertainty is linked directly to Holocaust remembrance because so many of the Holocaust's aspects strike us initially (as they do Alex) as impossible and thus possibly false, as unbelievable and thus possibly not to be believed. What fantastic stories isolate, however, is precisely the moment at which we must choose between being engaged by or indifferent to (to believe or disbelieve) disturbing and unbelievable events.[23] The more excessively false and fantastic the story, the more this choice is fore-grounded, and the more we are being summoned, as it were, to choose historical truth as disquieting and sorrowful—and to elect to undergo the sort of subjective destitution this entails. For this reason, those of who read about and study the Holocaust today should perhaps think twice about the critique of imaginative freedom voiced by Adorno, Wiesel, Friedländer, Ozick, and Lang, and see instead how literary or figurative language is the ally of historical truth and not its unsettling falsifier. Because truth does not magically compel belief, because sorrow is not an involuntary emotion, and because the values and fantasies that motivated the Holocaust are ones we must genuinely elect to analyze and avoid, we cannot do without fantastical texts that foreground and summon the free-dom we must exercise so as to choose truth, sorrow, and an ethic of shared vulnerability. Ultimately, the semi-epistolary dimension of the bifurcated form of Foer's novel is what saves it from the charge that Jonathan's history is a disquietingly indecorous instance of falsification: written explicitly for someone who is actively in the process of choosing the historical nar-rative in which he will believe, Jonathan's story might be seen as enjoining Alex (and other readers born more than forty or fifty years after the Holo-caust) to remain faithful to the shattering testimonies of Lista and Alex's grandfather—to see, in the end, how the departure from accuracy is fundamentally of a piece with the creation and productive impact of accuracy itself.

Making the Choice

The first-person account of Alex's that we read in *Everything Is Illuminated* is the work of an aspiring author who is struggling with the national and familial history he has encountered on the failed search for Augustine. The fact that Lista (and not Augustine) is the last remaining survivor of Trachimbrod is decisive for Alex, since it confronts him with the fact that the national and familial history that he has been taught is incomplete, or that history itself might run up against something that resists recovery and/or narration. Up until the encounter with Lista, Alex has treated his commission as Jonathan's guide largely as a job. Early on, he confesses to never having met a Jewish person and to "the opinion that Jewish people were having shit between their brains" for spending large sums of money "to unearth places where their families once existed."[24] His idealized version of Ukrainian history is of a piece with this perception. There is, for him, nothing disquieting about Ukrainian history because he has taken as self-evident the scholastic, post–Cold War, nation-affirming myth continuous with the anti-fascist histories of the Soviet period—that Ukrainians saved Jews.[25] His master-narrative of history is essentially a sunny one, bearing no material remnants of what got destroyed in the Holocaust and no sense that linear, progressive historical narratives miss or overlook something important about the past.[26]

At the outset of his narrative, Alex is not at all aware of the struggle that will soon consume him. Much of this has to do with the sort of person he was prior to his journey, a person without inwardness who takes literally the images of wealth and virility he encounters on American television and in American movies, music, and magazines. Living with his abusive father, his dream is to emigrate to America with his little brother Igor, and to live in Times Square.[27] As we read of his being hired as Jonathan's guide, Alex's story appears simply to grant him the chance to present himself as the bearer of a manhood he has to this point merely fantasized about. Indeed, writing without any seriousness about the job for which he has been hired, Alex seems more interested in conveying his essential and desirable masculinity: he invokes repeatedly the "currency" he "dig[s] to disseminate ... at famous nightclubs in Odessa,"[28] and reports that his "eyes are blue and resplendent," that he is "unequivocally tall," and that "many girls want to be carnal with me in many good arrangements."[29]

Foer undercuts Alex's story in one obvious way by having him narrate in English. In addition, there are places in Alex's text that contain details that disturb the idealized version he is presenting. These details begin as brief parenthetical asides and later become fuller digressions, but in both cases, their inclusion is accompanied frequently by Alex's insistence that Jonathan share such details with no one, or by his claim that he will later cut from the story he is writing that which he is presently divulging. Where Alex's investment in a certain fantasy of himself (and his family and his country) collides most clearly with the traumatic history of the Holocaust, however, is in the letters that he posts to Jonathan. These letters come just before installments of his story.[30] In the first letter, we see Alex clinging prosaically to the fantasy that if they had just had more time, they might have found Augustine. Subsequent letters, however, show him struggling, with increased desperation, with the freedom bequeathed to him by Augustine's absence. This desperation is spurred by the fact that his own narrative is moving toward his grandfather's traumatic revelation regarding the role the grandfather played in the death of a Jewish friend, and by the pronounced melancholia he sees in his grandfather. Averring to Jonathan in one of his letters that "[w]ith writing, we have second chances,"[31] Alex sees one possible remedy in the kind of story that partakes of what Eric Santner calls "narrative fetishism"—in a story "consciously or unconsciously designed to expunge the traces of the trauma or loss that called that narrative into being in the first place."[32]

The beauty of Foer's formal set up is that even as it gives voice to the writer's desire and freedom to craft a fetishistic narrative, it shows us Alex choosing not to do so. In one of the novel's most salient passages, Alex entertains the notion that Jonathan's fantastical history of Trachimbrod provides tacit permission for his own realist travelogue to become, untruthfully, much more heroic, sentimental, and affirmative—in his words, "high fidelity."[33] That is to say, Alex entertains the notion that since he and Jonathan are free to be "nomadic with the truth," they can make their stories "more premium than life."[34] In one of his letters to Jonathan, Alex outlines several possible plot directions he is free to pursue in his novel. He imagines, for instance, that he and Jonathan might find Augustine; or that Jonathan's grandmother could be written into the story; or that Alex's grandfather could be written in as Safran's savior. As Alex puts it, describing this last scenario, "He [Alex's grandfather] could be Augustine. August, perhaps. Or just Alex, if that is satisfactory to you. I do not think there are any limits to how excellent we could make life seem."[35]

Here, we are faced precisely with the vexing feature of freedom against which traditional historiography and survivor testimony attempt to guard. That is to say, the instant we say that Holocaust representation is always the result of choices that are free, we risk opening the floodgates to all sorts of sentimental or literary-brilliant exaggerations and falsifications. Alex makes plain the warrant for this worry: if the unrecoverable aspect of the Holocaust indeed recalls to us our insuperable freedom and means that any Holocaust writing is the product of a chosen style, then there may indeed be no limit to "how excellent we could make life seem." Why not write stories that are always "more premium than life?" This is linked, too, to what I called earlier the bullet of Kantian ethics: if historical truth and ethical conduct depend ultimately on a subjective exercise of freedom, then we cannot rule out the exercise of that freedom in the direction of the literary or behavioral evils of sentimentalism or disbelief, of indifference or cruelty.

My claim nonetheless is that we who teach and write about the Holocaust must frame the choice as a choice. This is the lesson of the fantastical story that Jonathan writes to Alex, which precisely in its excessive imaginative license, is enjoining Alex to choose to avow the truth of the Holocaust and what it means for the views he holds of himself, his family, his country, and others. What Foer makes plain here is that any hope we have that the effects of confronting and learning about the Holocaust will be lasting—that this hope is linked entirely to a free and entirely elective embrace of its disturbingly sorrowful truths and ethical lessons.

Foer delivers on this hope by having Alex exercise his freedom precisely in this direction. That is to say, rather than pen a narrative that fetishistically works over the revelations involved in his trip, Foer gives us Alex choosing to remain faithful to objects and episodes that cannot be fully redeemed. The reality of this choice, for me, is enough to make Foer's novel forward-looking and even propitious. In so saying, I do not want to minimize how sad and burdensome the past appears in the novel's testimonial scenes. Indeed, the exercise of freedom, as I have been saying, sometimes entails electing to be bound to grave and calamitous and impossibly true events. Thus in his writing of the episode involving Lista, for example, Alex turns his story into a kind of transcription of Lista's testimony—into a form of narration that freely repeats the words of survivors in order to keep them alive.[36] And when it comes to the testimony of his grandfather—the story of how, in a lineup in front of Trachimbrod's synagogue of all its inhabitants, his grandfather had to choose between identifying his best friend as a Jew or else being shot in the head—Alex's own voice is present only in the form of occasional questions (e.g., "What did they do? What happened next?"[37]). To the extent that authorial artifice is present in the transcription of the grandfather's testimony, such artifice appears in Alex's decision to stretch language to the point of communicating only the terror of Nazi violence and the unspeakable grief of a survivor. The entirety of his grandfather's testimony is rendered without paragraph breaks, and as its substance becomes more horrible and chaotic, it is written without periods; in some cases, many words are run together. Among other things, what this testimony makes clear is the ongoing corrosive guilt bequeathed to those who survived the Holocaust's impossibly traumatic moments. As Alex's grandfather puts it regarding his friend, "Herschel would have been murdered with or without me, but it is still as if I murdered him."[38]

Clearly, these testimonies—especially the grandfather's, which plays a direct role in his expiatory suicide at novel's end—darken the horizon of Foer's novel. Christoph Ribbat, for instance, has argued that in the grandfather's revelation, we (and Jonathan and Alex) are confronted with "the destructive force of a much more painful, much more direct form of memory as it destroys another person."[39] According to Ribbat, "There is no coming to terms with the past in Foer's novel," only the emergence of hidden truths that announce "the impossibility of a sane, harmonious learning process."[40] For Mechachem Feuer, the form of the novel contributes to its darker or more pessimistic overtones, since Alex's final letter ends with a plea for forgiveness that the novel's final thirty-three pages leave unaddressed, and the novel itself ends with a suicide note of sorts. For Feuer, the absence of any reply by Jonathan to Alex's plea, combined with the suicide, is a sign of Jonathan's inescapably difficult position—a position that points up the impossibility of post–Holocaust friendship or reconciliation between perpetrator and victim.[41]

But in exercising his freedom in the service of a sad and burdensome past, Alex is also gaining a capacity to use this power to imagine anew his relationships to others, and to change the very life-world in which he exists. That is to say, even as he relates his grandfather's dreadful, distressful confession, he understands it to have implications for the present and future. These implications are made explicit in Alex's direct address to Jonathan at the end of Alex's telling of his grandfather's story: "he said these things to us and Jonathan where do we go now what do we do what with what we know."[42] Part of what Alex does is to set about writing the serious travelogue that makes up one half of *Everything Is Illuminated*. The other part, glimpsed in his letters to Jonathan, is to take up a way of being and a kind of conduct that rejects an idealized fantasy about himself and his family and the legitimacy of pre-given truths in a post–Holocaust world.

When his grandfather asks to borrow his money in order to find Augustine, for example, Alex chooses not to give him the money, claiming that he (Alex) no longer believes in "the Augustine that Grandfather was searching for."[43] Who is this Augustine for whom his grandfather wants to continue searching? In an exchange between the two of them, the grandfather says that love, goodness or God are not to be believed in, and confesses to dreaming that the discovery of Augustine would permit reasonable or intelligent belief.

Clearly, the grandfather has run squarely up against the philosophical truth that I have said lies at the heart of the Enlightenment and that the Holocaust lays bare—that there is no intelligible Other capable of making a belief necessary or compulsory, of guaranteeing the meaning of historical truths or moral maxims. Alex's grandfather, we might say, is incapable of the faith-based dimension of modern, post–Kantian truth and ethics. He cannot see how our belief in a moral Law, in love, in goodness, in God— whatever it is that we embrace to motivate our ethical conduct, to lend meaning to the world—is always chosen. As Kant made clear, these beliefs are never intelligent or reasonable, never made completely on the basis of transparent knowledge. On the contrary, they are free. By having the grandfather commit suicide, Foer explores a canonical Existentialist motif—the fact that our freedom confronts us with the fundamental choice of whether or not to go on living. In the case of the grandfather, however, the nature and terms of this choice are deepened. Bereft of a divine guarantor of love or goodness, the grandfather carries out an act of self-punishment that seeks itself to bring into existence the Other with the capacity to expiate, or to stand itself as a meaningful, empirical sacrifice capable of brokering forgiveness, friendship, and reconciliation.

For some readers, the grandfather's suicide is an indication that Foer "does not want the grandfather to get away with his crime unscarred."[44] And it is perhaps a plausibly just, almost talionic act: having pointed out his friend to the Nazis, the grandfather will give his own life to balance things out. But given the near-total destitution bound up in his confession, Alex's grandfather is clearly already scarred by the very telling of his tale. Moreover, his suicide risks giving far too much away to the perfidious dimension of Nazi violence, which sought precisely to degrade its victims by placing them in situations designed to induce their complicity and guilt. As an attempt to help Alex and Jonathan (and us) to break an intergenerational cycle of suspicion and enmity, of violence and reprisal, the grandfather's suicide is totally poignant but ultimately superfluous. What the suicide attempts to represent is an empirical foundation for moving forward that neither Alex nor Jonathan really needs. I say this because we know that Jonathan is sending installments of his novel to Alex, even after learning of Alex's grandfather's guilt-inducing act. And because Alex—before his grandfather's suicide—*already* sees how the basis of belief (or truth) cannot be entirely empirical: "We could not find her," he says of Augustine to his grandfather, "but that does not signify anything about whether you should believe in her."[45]

It is perhaps telling that at this very moment where belief is linked most explicitly to freedom, Alex confesses to being an entirely different person, to having eclipsed entirely his social identity and the empirical reasons he had for clinging to the values and truths to which he has clung. This power to choose a good because we are fundamentally free to do so is evinced as well in the novel's final letter, the grandfather's suicide note, which is addressed to Jonathan. In this note, we learn that Alex has challenged and dismissed and forgiven his own abusive father in a radical attempt to break an intergenerational cycle of familial violence rooted in the secret and shameful stories of the past. To do this, he abandons the fantasy of his and Igor's escape to America and gives his father all of the money that he had been saving for that purpose. In his gloss on this act, Alex's grandfather sees it as conveying the possibility of a life without violence. He writes that if Alex and Igor "cut all of the strings,"[46] they might live a life without violence. At first glance, this cutting of the strings might appear to evoke the myth of self-invention, where human freedom is exercised in the forgetting or banishing the past. But because Foer has so clearly made Alex the author of one half of *Everything Is Illuminated*, because he has so clearly foregrounded the extent to which choice and freedom are indispensable for an encounter with a sorrowful history and for the recognition of a common vulnerability, we see Alex's cutting of the strings as in fact a gesture that enables the free act of taking them up again.

All of this is to suggest that Jonathan's fantastical history has been successful in summoning Alex's freedom. Herein lies, as I have suggested, the ethically auspicious import of the novelistic form of *Everything Is Illuminated*, which shows us how imaginative freedom can lead to an embrace of a sorrowful truth we might prefer to avoid or deny, and to a more honest and vulnerable way of living—without concealing how such freedom contains opposite and less positive outcomes as well. What Foer lets us glimpse is that the freedom bequeathed to us by the unsymbolizable aspect of the past can enable us to be sorrowed and burdened by it, but also not to repeat or be completely ensnared by it. Though there is a way that generations twice or thrice removed from the Holocaust can come to think that their freedom has been taken from them—*Nothing Makes You Free* is the title of a recent collection, edited by Melvin Jules Bukiet, of "writings by descendants of Jewish Holocaust survivors"[47]—we see in Foer's novel how a genuine confrontation with the traumatic events of the Holocaust can also be liberating or empowering. These traumatic events call forth and depend upon our freedom to write about, believe in, and engage with them. And this freedom extends to acts of writing, belief, and engagement that go beyond the Holocaust as well.[48]

By presenting freedom's difficult exercise in such a positive light, Foer leads us to the operating and unavoidable paradox of Holocaust representation wherein if we try to get rid in advance of all of the potentially unsettling representations—versions that are trite or sentimental or just plain false—we get rid, too, of the ones whose fantastical quality confronts us with the power to choose that is crucial to any Holocaust representation and the impact it seeks to make. Whereas imaginative freedom occasions a great deal of worry today, Foer's novel lets us glimpse how a meaningful engagement with history and the type of individual and social change that Holocaust histories and survivor testimonies aim to produce cannot be separated from it. The exercise of this freedom—writ large in the wildly stylized history of Trachimbrod that is sent by one of the novel's narrators (Jonathan) to the other (Alex)—renders visible a dynamic that is just as present in the writing and reading of Holocaust histories and testimonies, and that is, as the case of Alex makes plain, critical to the changing of one's life. We are thus perhaps at a moment in the discourse of the Holocaust in which the most wildly inventive and imaginative of its representations have a key role to play in forging its legacy—in summoning the freedom required for us not just to confront terrible scenes of devastation but to achieve, even if only one person at a time, the miraculous dream, espoused by Alex's grandfather, of a life without violence.

Author's Note: I am grateful to the students in my ENGL 400 seminar, in particular Teresa Moore Saxton, Alison Barrett, and Mary Irvin, for their help in sharpening my thinking about Foer's novel, and to the

Otterbein University Humanities Advisory Committee (HAC) for a summer writing award that made completion of the essay possible.

Notes

1. Jonathan's history of Trachimbrod includes transcriptions from a communally-held book of recurrent dreams, transcriptions from a history of Trachimbrod that is being written by the town's inhabitants in the form of an encyclopedia, songs, diary entries, memorial plaques, dramatic interludes, family tree-like charts, and lines upon lines of ellipses.

2. Brooke Allen, for instance, has termed Foer's imagining of the traumatic past of his grandfather's village "the height of callowness," claiming that for the survivors (and the children) the Holocaust has been "a real, solid, ugly fact of all our lives," whereas for Foer, "born more than thirty years after Auschwitz, it is merely the unremembered past, ripe for reinvention and reinterpretation by the artist." See Brooke Allen, "Solipsism," review of *Everything Is Illuminated*, by Jonathan Safran Foer, *Atlantic Monthly* (April 2002): 141.

3. When Jonathan imagines first meeting Augustine, he asks her to tell him everything. According to Alex, Jonathan asks "to hear about how she met my grandfather, and why she decided to save him, and what happened to her family, and if she ever talked to my grandfather after the war." See Jonathan Safran Foer, *Everything Is Illuminated* (Boston: Houghton Mifflin, 2002), 148. And to give this imagined story its proper (and redemptive) pathos, Jonathan even wants to know if Augustine and his grandfather were in love. In many respects, Jonathan's search for Augustine shares affinities with the growing ethnography of Holocaust rescue, which has tried to capture and recover the moral values—typically distilled into an ethical maxim—that motivated the act of saving Jews. For this ethnography, see Eva Fogelman, *Conscience and Courage: Rescuers of Jews During the Holocaust* (New York: Anchor, 1995); Ellen Land-Weber, *To Save a Life: Stories of Holocaust Rescue* (Urbana: University of Illinois Press, 2000); Hillel Levine, *In Search of Sugihara: The Elusive Japanese Diplomat Who Risked His Life to Rescue 10,000 Jews from the Holocaust* (New York: The Free Press, 1996); Samuel P. and Pearl M. Oliner, *The Altruistic Personality: Rescuers of Jews in Nazi Europe* (New York: The Free Press, 1988); and Nechama Tec, *When Light Pierced the Darkness: Christian Rescue of Jews in Nazi-Occupied Poland* (New York: Oxford University Press, 1986).

4. Saul Friedländer, *Reflections on Nazism: An Essay on Kitsch and Death* (Bloomington: Indiana University Press, 1984), 20.

5. Ibid., 98. For Friedländer, "the only open avenue [for those trying to represent the Holocaust] may well be that of quietness, simplicity, of the constant presence of the unsaid, and of the constant temptation of silence" (Ibid., 97–98). The notion of disrespected moral limits explored in Friedländer's *Reflections on Nazism* telegraph the central concept in the edited book of his that appeared ten years later—*Probing the Limits of Representation: Nazism and the "Final Solution"* (the expanded proceedings of a conference convened in 1990 at UCLA and a canonical book in Holocaust Studies). In his introduction to this collection, Friedländer argues on moral grounds for a certain limit to representation, insisting that because "the perpetrators invested considerable effort not only in camouflage, but in effacement of all traces of their deeds," the Holocaust "should not be distorted or banalized by grossly inadequate representations." See Saul Friedländer,

Introduction to *Probing the Limits of Representation: Nazism and the "Final Solution,"* ed. Saul Friedländer (Cambridge: Harvard University Press, 1984), 3. As Friedländer puts it, "Some claim to 'truth' appears particularly imperative" (Ibid).

6. Theodor Adorno, "Cultural Criticism and Society," in *Prisms*, trans. Samuel and Shierry Weber (Cambridge: MIT Press, 1981), 34.

7. Theodor Adorno, *Notes to Literature*, trans. Samuel and Shierry Weber (New York: Columbia University Press, 1991), 171.

8. Elie Wiesel, "The Holocaust as Literary Inspiration," in *Dimensions of the Holocaust*, ed. Elliot Lefkowitz (Evanston, IL: University of Northwestern Press, 1977), 7.

9. Cynthia Ozick, "The Rights of History and the Rights of the Imagination," in *Quarrel and Quandary* (New York: Knopf, 2000), 111.

10. Berel Lang, *Holocaust Representation: Art Within the Limits of History and Ethics* (Baltimore, MD: Johns Hopkins University Press, 2000), 34. For Lang, the chronicle is "the zero-point of historiography" (Ibid., 59), the bearer of an authenticity that literary texts, on moral grounds, ought always to keep before them. The problem with imagined representations, for Lang, is the contention implicit in all of them that historical facts "*do not* speak for themselves, that figurative condensation and displacement and the authorial presence they articulate will turn or supplement the historical subject, whatever it is, in a way that represents the subject more compellingly or effectively—in the end, more truly—than would be the case without them" (Ibid., 69). To follow this line of thinking is to see figurative language as hopelessly caught up in the dangers of *mis*representation, and this is an outcome all the more exacerbated by the passing of time and the deaths of direct material witnesses.

11. The link between invention and denial is manifest in the rift between Elie Wiesel and Alfred Kazin over the latter's questioning of whether or not a particular scene in *Night* actually happened—a questioning Wiesel saw as tantamount to support for Holocaust denial. For a fascinating account of this rift, see Gary Weissman, *Fantasies of Witnessing: The Postwar Effort to Experience the Holocaust* (Ithaca, NY: Cornell University Press, 2004). Also relevant in this context is the fake memoir phenomenon, to which belong not only Wilkomirski's *Fragments*, but also, in just the past few years, Bernard Holstein's *Stolen Soul*, Misha Defonseca's *Misha: A Memoir of the Holocaust Years*, and Herman Rosenblat's *Angel at the Fence*. What is unsettling about Wiesel's linking of invention and denial is the way it partakes of an approach used by Holocaust deniers themselves—what Susan Rubin Suleiman has characterized as "the familiar negationist device of reasoning by synecdoche." See Susan Rubin Suleiman, *Crises of Witnessing and the Second World War* (Cambridge: Harvard University Press, 2006), 166. Suleiman distills this method in her discussion of the way French Holocaust denier Serge Thion used Wilkomirski's invented memoir to dispute the Holocaust: "If a single detail in a testimony if false, that renders the whole thing false; if a single testimony is a fake, that renders all testimonies fake" (Ibid.)

12. Geoffrey Hartman, *The Longest Shadow: In the Aftermath of the Holocaust* (New York: Palgrave, 2002), 104.

13. As Hartman puts it, "Fiction is, no doubt, an image maker today, and open to popular misuse, especially in the form of televised simplification. But that is why, first of all, we have literary criticism, a hygiene of reading with iconoclastic overtones" (Ibid. 30).

14. Ruth Franklin, *A Thousand Darknesses: Lies and Truth in Holocaust Fiction* (New York: Oxford University Press, 2011), 11.

15. The absolute truth or authenticity of survivor testimonies is, of course, far from self-evident. Michael-André Bernstein has argued that all eyewitness testimony is "touched by figuration and by shaping." See Michael-André Bernstein, *Foregone Conclusions: Against Apocalyptic History* (Berkeley: University of California Press, 1994), 47. Lawrence Langer, on the other hand, has suggested that oral testimonies escape the kind of manipulative shaping that transpires with written testimonies, and are thus more truthful and authentic. For Langer, when it comes to written testimonies, the very "*appearance* of form is reassuring" (Lawrence Langer, *Holocaust Testimonies: The Ruins of Memory* [New Haven, CT: Yale University Press, 1991], 17). Finally, Kate McLoughlin has also shown how first-person testimony can have no absolute authority because sometimes the same witness can, at different times, give radically divergent testimony. McLoughlin's exploration of this challenge comes in a reading of Philip Roth's fictional portrayal of the Demjanjuk trial, wherein she sees Roth deploy a representational tactic that shares affinities with my analysis of the function of the Trachimbrod section in Foer's novel. Faced with an unrecoverable Truth, "Roth's tactic," McLoughlin writes, "is only to increase the preposterousness, as though, paradoxically, it is only in the face of particularly blatant breaches of consistency and verisimilitude that belief has a chance." See Kate McLoughlin, "'Dispute Incarnate': Philip Roth's *Operation Shylock*, the Demjanjuk Trial, and Eyewitness Testimony," *Philip Roth Studies* 3, no. 2 (Fall 2007): 127.

16. Immanuel Kant, *Religion Within the Limits of Reason Alone*, trans. Theodore M. Greene and Hoyt Hudson (New York: Harper and Row, 1960), 32.

17. At one point in the novel, Jonathan remembers himself and his grandmother shouting words off her back porch at night. He'd shout words like phantasmagoria and antediluvian; she'd shout Yiddish words he did not know the meaning of. See Foer, *Everything Is Illuminated*, 159. This scene is meant to convey the way words have a material dimension that is not entirely absorbed by their meaning or by the things to which they are believed to correspond. The utility of this insight is suggested in the encyclopedia section of Jonathan's story, which contains an entry for the neologism "Ifactiface" (Ibid., 203). Here, Jonathan proposes that one propaedeutic for anti–Semitic violence might rest in the recognition that there is something in the words that structure our identities and our world that resists understanding—or that corresponds to nothing. As he puts it, "[U]ntil we can find a nonapproximate vocabulary, nonsense words are the best thing we've got" (Ibid.)

18. Lang, *Holocaust Representation*, 28.

19. On the subject of Holocaust laughter, see Terrence Des Pres, "Holocaust Laughter?" in *Writing and the Holocaust*, ed. Berel Lang (New York: Holmes and Meier, 1988), 216–33; Sander Gillman, "Is Life Beautiful? Can the Shoah Be Funny?: Some Thoughts on Recent and Older Films," *Critical Inquiry* 26 (Winter 2000), 279–308; and Shai Oster, "Holocaust Humor," *The Utne Reader* 95 (Sept.-Oct. 1999), 82–86.

20. Lang, *Holocaust Representation*, 30.

21. See Romain Gary, *The Dance of Genghis Cohn* (New York: Signet, 1968) and Joseph Skibell, *A Blessing on the Moon* (New York: Berkeley, 1997). Set in 1968, Gary's comical novel is narrated by the Yiddish vaudevillian spirit of a murdered Jew (Moishe Cohn) who haunts—in the manner of a *dybbuk*—the body of the SS Officer (Hans Schatz) who killed him twenty-four years earlier. Skibell's novel records the story of Reb Chaim Skilbelski, who, after being shot and cast into a mass grave, climbs out and commences a journey through a moonless world

that takes him, among other places, to a mythical resort where he is reunited with his entire family and ultimately back to his hometown where he must help to excavate and raise the moon. The most well known, deliberately non-mimetic representation of late is perhaps a cinematic one—Roberto Benigni's *Life Is Beautiful*. For views critical of the falsification and denial inherent in the film's fabular approach, see David Denby, "Darkness Out of Light," *The New Yorker*, November 16, 1998, 114–16, and Thane Rosenbaum, "With the Shoah, Can Tragedy Become Farce?: Considering an Italian Funnyman's Concentration Camp Comedy," *Forward*, October 23, 1998, http://www.forward.com/issues/1998/98.12.23/arts.html.

22. Tzvetan Todorov, *The Fantastic: A Structural Approach to a Literary Genre*, trans. Richard Howard (Ithaca: Cornell University Press, 1975), 25.

23. This point is made explicitly in Nathan Englander's story "The Tumblers," in which a group of Hasidic Jews from Chelm en route to a death camp find themselves mistaken for circus performers and is shown attempting to practice acrobatic routines on their train. This is, the narrator tells us, clearly "an absurd undertaking. But then again ... no more unbelievable than the reality from which they'd escaped, no more unfathomable than the magic of disappearing Jews." See Nathan Englander, *For the Relief of Unbearable Urges* (New York: Random House, 1999), 42–43.

24. Jonathan Safran Foer, *Everything Is Illuminated* (Boston: Houghton Mifflin, 2002), 3.

25. When Jonathan reports that his grandmother's entire family was killed by the Nazis a few kilometers from Trachimbrod, Alex asks, "Did a Ukrainian save her?" and is surprised that no one saved her family (Ibid., 61). When Jonathan says that it's not all that surprising given the fact that Ukrainians were "almost as bad as the Nazis," Alex adamantly rejects this. Jonathan tells him to "look it up in the history books." Alex replies by saying that "[i]t does not say this in the history books" (Ibid., 62) and insists that Jonathan admit that he is mistaken. According to Zvi Gitelman, though Soviet historiography clearly minimized the fact that Jews were the Holocaust's primary victims and that many living in the Soviet Union's western republics (Ukraine and Belorussia) often collaborated with the Nazis, there was no "uniform, universally applied party line on the issue." See Zvi Gitelman, "The Soviet Union," in *The World Reacts to the Holocaust*, ed. David Wyman (Baltimore, MD: Johns Hopkins University Press, 1996), 312. Gitelman suggests, moreover, that part of Khrushchev's attempt to countervail Western charges of official anti–Semitism involved the promulgation of the idea that "gentiles frequently saved Jews in occupied territories" (Ibid.) On the vexed issue of Ukrainian complicity in the Holocaust—an issue only now beginning to be avowed and addressed—see Martin Dean, *Collaboration in the Holocaust: Crimes of the Local Police in Belorussia and Ukraine, 1941–44* (New York: St. Martin's Press, 2000); Rebecca Golbert, "'Neighbors' and the Ukrainian Jewish Experience of the Holocaust," in *Lessons and Legacies, Volume VII: The Holocaust in International Perspective*, ed. Dagmar Herzog (Evanston, IL: Northwestern University Press, 2006), 233–52; and Boris Zabarko, ed. *Holocaust in the Ukraine*, trans. Marina Guba (Portland: Vallentine Mitchell, 2005).

26. At first glance, Alex's initial mistaking of Lista for Augustine is perhaps innocent enough: having seen Jonathan's photograph of Augustine, he believes Lista's eyes are identical to the eyes shown in the photograph. But his subsequent comment allows us to see how a certain vision of history might be behind this mistake: "And I was certain, looking at her eyes, that she had saved the hero's grandfather, and probably many others. I could imagine in my brain how the days

connected the girl in the photograph to the woman who was in the room with us. Each day was like another photograph. Her life was a book of photographs. One was with the hero's grandfather, and now one was with us." See Foer, *Everything Is Illuminated*, 148. Imagining Lista's present almost as the culmination of a montage sequence in a sentimental film, Alex's lines here recall the historicism excoriated by Walter Benjamin. That is to say, according to Walter Benjamin, Alex sees Lista's history as a sequence of photographed moments—in Benjamin's terms, "like the beads of a rosary" through "homogeneous, empty time." See Walter Benjamin, "Theses on the Philosophy of History," in *Illuminations*, trans. Harry Zohn (New York: Schocken, 1985), 263, 261.

27. In one letter to Jonathan, Alex speaks of the money he is saving to emigrate to America and he imagines himself and his younger brother residing in a "luxurious apartment in Times Square" complete with "a large screen television to watch basketball, a jacuzzi, and a hi-fi to write home about." See Foer, *Everything Is Illuminated*, 101.

28. Foer, *Everything Is Illuminated*, 2

29. Ibid.

30. There are seven such letters included in the novel, with the first one dated three weeks after the trip (September 23, 1997) and the last coming about four months later (January 26, 1998, written four days after Alex's grandfather's suicide).

31. Foer, *Everything Is Illuminated*, 144.

32. Eric Santner, "History Beyond the Pleasure Principle: Some Thoughts on the Representation of Trauma," in *Probing the Limits of Representation: Nazism and the "Final Solution,"* ed. Saul Friedländer (Cambridge: Harvard University Press, 1992), 144.

33. Ibid., 179.

34. Ibid.

35. Ibid., 180.

36. Alex writes, "You cannot know how it felt to have to hear those things and then repeat them, because when I repeated them, I felt like I was making them new again" (185). It may be tempting to see Alex's unique position as a translator as authorizing the repetition of a survivor's testimony, but Foer appears to suggest here that there might be a non-appropriative way for nonwitnesses—or members of the second and third generation—to repeat via speech (to themselves or to others) the testimony of Holocaust survivors.

37. Ibid., 248.

38. Ibid., 247.

39. Christoph Ribbat, "'Nomadic with the Truth': Holocaust Representation in Michael Chabon, James McBride, and Jonathan Safran Foer," *Anglistik und Englischunterricht* 66 (2005), 213.

40. Ibid. Though Ribbat does see a hopeful opening in the way Foer's novel's "pastiche of styles" enacts a coexistence of representational or aesthetic strategies, he writes that "[e]ven in the richest literary collage, a sense of insecurity refuses to disappear" (Ibid., 214).

41. Menachem Feuer, "Almost Friends: Post-Holocaust Comedy, Tragedy, and Friendship in Jonathan Safran Foer's *Everything Is Illuminated*," *Shofar: An Interdisciplinary Journal of Jewish Studies* 25, no. 2 (Winter 2007), 24–48.

42. Foer, *Everything Is Illuminated*, 252.

43. Ibid. 241.

44. I thank an anonymous reader of this essay for confronting me with this notion.

45. Foer, *Everything Is Illuminated*, 245.

46. Foer, *Everything Is Illuminated*, 275.

47. Melvin Jules Bukiet, ed., *Nothing Makes You Free: Writings by Descendants of Jewish Holocaust Survivors* (New York: W.W. Norton, 2002).

48. In his survey of Jewish American Fiction from 1977 to 2002, Adam Meyer traces one direction for the exercise of this freedom on the part of contemporary Jewish-American writers—toward explicitly religious, Jewish themes in their work. See Adam Meyer, "Putting the 'Jewish' Back in 'Jewish American Fiction': A Look at Jewish American Fiction from 1977 to 2002 and an Allegorical Reading of Nathan Englander's 'The Gilgul of Park Avenue,'" *Shofar: An Interdisciplinary Journal of Jewish Studies* 22, no. 3 (Spring 2004), 104–20.

The Last of the Just
Lifting Moloch to Heaven
JULES ZANGER

There are privileged areas, literary works that conventionally resist being treated or regarded as fantasies in spite of their internal characteristics, of those moments of hesitation, or their supernatural contents, of those ground-rule reversals which academics critics have employed to define the fantasy. There are clear areas of societal reluctance to acknowledge the fantastic—most obviously those having to do with the Old and new Testaments, though Jacob wrestling with the angel or Christ blasting the fig tree are intrinsically neither more nor less fantastic than Conan battling the "devil from the Outer Dark." The intensely mixed reception of Salman Rushdie's *Satanic Verses* suggests another level, a split level, of this resistance; one community's fantasy is another community's blasphemy. Milton's *Paradise Lost* and Shakespeare's *Hamlet* represent an additional locus of conventional unwillingness, not because of the sacredness of the texts (though *Paradise Lost* bridges these classifications), but rather because of their traditional literary status as complex masterpieces which could be diminished by a formulaic reductivism to fantasy.

There is another area of literary concern in which texts possessing those internal characteristics which define the fantastic are not usually regarded as fantasies. These are those concerning themselves with powerful and immediate social issues whose contemporary significance overrides the formal mode that embodies them. So, as a minor example, it was more appropriate and useful in 1966 to regard Barbara Garson's *MacBird* as a political satire than as a fantasy. There was no objection raised to Garson's use of fantasy to attack Lyndon Johnson's very real political ambitions. Robert Coover's *The Public Burning*, which treated Richard Nixon

103

with the same contemptuous irreverence, was equally fantastic and equally immune to the criticism that the use of fantasy somehow diminished the significance of its subject. To my knowledge, only the Holocaust has been singled out as a secular and contemporary subject which would be inappropriate to treat fictionally, let alone fantastically. This position would appear to be based on the apprehension that such treatments of the Holocaust would be trivialized or distancing or, possibly worse, exploitive and consolatory. In any case, we must agree that any fiction or fantasy will finally be inadequate to record that tragedy, as it must be inadequate to record the death of a single beloved child.

On the other hand, such works, however inadequate, may serve to memorialize that which grows increasingly ephemeral, the past itself. *The Last of the Just* is such a memorializing work, recording not so much that Holocaust itself, but rather the intellectual and spiritual crises suffered by those Jewish survivors in the wake of the Holocaust. In *The Purposes of Writing*, Jean-Paul Sartre called the novel, "a thoughtful, relentless, profound work, an attempt devoid of any illusions to recover all of the dead we have killed."[1] I would argue that in addition to being an attempt to recover to memory those dead, it is an agonized attempt to re-examine God's covenant with the Jews in the light of immediate history.

The Last of the Just, by André Schwarz-Bart, was published in 1959 in France where it won the Prix Goncourt. Swarz-Bart, a French Jew of Polish descent, lost both his parents in the death camps in 1939 and subsequently fought with the Maquis till the end of the war. This was his first novel and one of the earliest fictional treatments of the Holocaust. As a Holocaust novel, it is committed to the gross data of history; at the same time, it is a peculiarly poetic, visionary, even ecstatic account of human suffering and barbarism which takes as its controlling postulate a premise that is classically fantastic: supernatural and oneiric. This premise, the Legend of the Just Men, is that there are, in Martin Buber's account, "in each generation, thirty-sex 'hidden' *zaddikim* who secretly do their good deeds. These deeds constitute the true foundation of the created world."[2] It was to these Just Men that Allen Ginsberg alluded when he wrote in *Howl*, "They broke their backs lifting Moloch to Heaven!"

The legend has its roots in ancient Jewish traditions, in folk, and Hasidic belief going back possibly to the "suffering servant" in the Book of Isaiah. Its more immediate analog is to be found in the debate in Genesis XVIII between Abraham and the Lord as to the fate of Sodom and Gomorrah. Abraham demands of God, "Wilt though also destroy the righteous with the wicked?" and the Lord responds, "If I find in Sodom fifty righteous within the city, than I will spare all the place for their sakes." Abraham, before the debate is over convinces God (dare I say, "Jews Him down?") to save the city if there are only ten righteous men to be found. However, only one, Lot, can be found and the Cities of the Plain are destroyed. This story has a number of significant implications, but central to it is the idea of a divine wrath restrained by a divine unwillingness to act unjustly. "Shall not the judge of all the world do right?" asks Abraham, and the Lord agrees, but only conditionally. This conditionally restraint is echoed in the Hasidic Legend of the Just Men in which thirty-six Just Men must exist to support the whole world. According to the legend, as Schwarz-Bart expands upon it,

> the world reposes upon thirty-six Just Men, the Lamed-Vov, indistinguishable from simple mortals; often they are unaware of their station. But if just one of them were lacking, the sufferings of mankind would poison even the souls of the newborn, and humanity would suffocate with a single cry.[3]

Offered in the opening pages of the novel, this statement provides its central fantastic premise—that thirty-six men embody the indwelling divine presence in the created world, and that the world's continued existence is conditional and contingent upon their existence. It provides as well the novel's dominant imagery—images of suffocations, of air made unbreathable and poisonous.

To this legend, Schwarz-Bart links the historical reality of the martyrdom of the Rabbi Yom Tov Levy in York in England in 1185 where the "gentle and very luminous" Rabbi cuts the throats of the willing members of his congregation to save them from the mob, before cutting his own throat. Schwarz-Bart compounds this amalgam of fact and legend with an additional fantastic premise—that following the massacre and suicide, God promised the soul of the martyred rabbi that "to all his line, and for all the centuries is given the grace of one Lamed Vovnik to each generation."[4] The novel begins with the burning of Rabbi Levy's body, traces the generations and martyrdoms of the Rabbi's descendents, and then focuses on the life of Ernie Levy, the Last of the Just, who dies without issue in Auschwitz.

The central argument dramatized by the novel is suggested in the tension between, on the one hand, the promise of God—that "for all the centuries" there shall be Just Men to intercede for suffering humanity—and on the other, Schwarz-Bart's title *The Last of the Just*, which announces that the divine presence in the world has finally withdrawn under the press of human evil. Schwarz-Bart's title postulates the need of the supernatural resistance, of a divine check, the brutal natural order. The argument of the novel is then eschatological—a novel of what may be the last days, and more specifically, of what may be the Death of God in the world.

Though in the last century the Death of God was a central theme in the philosophy of Friedrich Nietzsche, in the period following World War II the idea re-emerged in France with particular force as a tenet of the Existentialist movement articulated by Jean-Paul Sartre in his *Existentialism* in 1947, and opposed by Gabriel Marcel in *The Mystery of God* in 1951. Martin Buber published *The Eclipse of God* in 1952, opposing Sartre as well. It is in the context of this debate, stimulated in part at least by the war, that Schwarz-Bart's novel was written. I would contend, further, that the conflict between the belief in the Death of God and the belief in the Eclipse of God provides the central conflict of the novel.

Significantly, it was in this period that more conventional fantasy fiction took as major theme the withdrawal Faerie, of the supernatural, under the pressure of technology or cold iron or human beastliness, from the affairs of mankind. This was, most influentially, a premise of Tolkien's *Lord of the Rings* trilogy, published in the 1950s, and was followed by Lloyd Alexander's Prydain series, Susan Cooper's *The Dark Is Rising* novels, and, with modifications, by writers as various as Michael Moorcock and James Blish.

In *The Last of the Just*, this divine withdrawal is revealed as a progressive unfolding in time, in the diminishing deaths and lives of the generations of Just Men descendent from the Rabbi Yom Tov. From the first of these descendants, Solomon Levy, who is miraculously reborn in a York charnel house swarming with flies to the tenth generation, all of these Just Men die martyrs' death. They are burned alive, impaled, drowned, racked, dragged by wild horses, and hacked apart. In their lives, they were leaders of their communities, defenders of the Jews, poets, theologians, great doctors. Their wanderings had an awesome magnitude, bringing them from York, to Paris, to Moscow, to Vilna, to Kiev to meet their deaths. but after the tenth generation, we see a diminishment.

From wandering the world, the Levy family settles down in Zamyock, a Polish *shtetl*. Instead of poets and doctors, they have become peddlers, leather workers, peasants, and with a marvelous irony, crystal trimmers. Most significantly, these last generations of Levys are denied the crown and confirmation of martyrdom; they die in their own beds. Further, with the settling of the Levy family in Zamyock, the clear line of descent is broken: Brother Beast, the last direct descendent of the Rabbi Yom Tov and an idiot, has no issue, and the identity of the Just Man becomes impossible to establish.

The unfortunate Levys sought vainly to identify the signs by which God made his choice? Was it necessary to engulf oneself in prayer? To work in the field? To love animals, men? To accomplish high deeds? To simply live out the miserable but so sweet existence of Zemyock? Who will be the Chosen One?[5]

In a sense, these successive Levys devalue their predecessors, reducing them to legend. In doing so, they appear to devalue the divine promise.

It is only with the last three generations of Levys—Grandfather Mordecai, Father Benjamin, and Ernie, all of whom die at the hands of the Nazis—that the confirmation of identity by martyrdom appears to be restored to the line of the Just Men. Ernie's brief life would appear to be a recapitulation of the history of the Just Men: as child-scholar, mystic, vain defender of the Jews until his suicide, his "first death," covered with buzzing flies like those in the charnel house in York, from which he miraculously survives. Following that "death," Ernie, after serving in the French army, degenerates into a "dog," a "Brother Best," surviving in unoccupied France by gobbling up raw scraps of meat, sexually servicing a French farm-wife, and denying he is Jewish. It is only when he is recognized as a Jew that he is born a third time, and accepts his destiny as a Just Man. This destiny brings him to German-occupied Paris where he meets and falls in love with Golda who he voluntarily follows into Auschwitz to their deaths in the gas chamber surrounded by the children they will never have.

Certainly this pattern of repetitions and echoing images might imply that the history of the Just Men is cyclical rather than cataclysmic. Ernie dies in Auschwitz, crying to the children clinging to him "Breathe deeply, my lambs, and quickly,"[6] points him back to the death of Rabbi Yom Tov at the beginning of the novel. In the same way, the crematorium smokes in which the "Luftmenschen" turn "into Luft" at the end of the novel mirrors the opening image of the smoke of the great pyre upon which the Rabbi's body was thrown. It, in turn, looks forward to the Cyclon B gas billowing down in the concluding section. All of these images recall the novel's epigraph:

> How am I to toll your death,
> How may I mark your obsequies,
> Vagabond handful of ashes
> Between heaven and earth?

All of these have as their antecedent that passage in Genesis in which Abraham looked down towards Sodom and Gomorrah, "and there he saw thick smoke rising high from the earth like the smoke of a lime-kiln."

The problem the novel posits for the reader is how this symmetrical structure of imagery is to be read. Does that last pillar of smoke from the chimneys of Auschwitz, referring us back to the smoking pyre of Rabbi Yom Tov in the Eleventh Century, imply an eternal return, still another miraculous rebirth in the charnel house? On the other hand (and this is the appropriate Talmudic mode of inquiry), might not rather be evidence of a completed pattern, of the end of the divine hypostasis in the world, as the novel's title states? Certainly, there are details that seem to support a despairing, cataclysmic reading. Unlike Rabbi Yom Tov, Ernie has not child to be miraculously resurrected. Further, when the Rabbi's body was burned in York, the pious Benedictine who witnessed the burning worried, "His body was thrown upon a great pyre, and unfortunately his ashes were cast to the wind, so that we breathe it and so that, by agency of mean spirits, some poisonous humors will fall upon us, which will confound us entirely."[7] When Ernie is burned, however, we are told, "the smoke that rises from the crematoriums obeys physical laws like any other; the particles come together and disperse according to the wind that propels them."[8] Whatever metaphysical properties the Rabbi's ashes might have possessed in the eleventh century, they are denied to the physical smoke of the twentieth century ovens. In additional support of the cataclysmic position, it can be argued that Ernie's deliberate martyrdom is significantly different from that of the Rabbi Yom Tov who cuts the throats of his congregations and his own so that in the face of torture and "the seduction of the Vulgate" they may die spiritually intact. "Brothers," he said to them, "God gave us life. Let us return it to him ourselves by our own hands..."[9] Ernie's decision to enter the death camp is precipitated by the arrest of Golda whom he has met in Paris and whom he loves, and when he is in the camp, all of this energy is devoted to finding her. Ernie, the last of the just, appears to be a romantic hero, not a religious one, and his death, as Gatsby might have said, only personal. In a sense, he is closer to Puccini's Des Grieux following Manon Lescault to her doom than his to Yom Tov. Finally, in arguing for cataclysm, it should be noted, however pedantically, that the word Holocaust signifies a total sacrifice, as opposed to the partial sacrifices of the past which always left at least a remnant of the Just Men to sustain the world. It would certainly seem that Ernie's last prayer on his way to the gas chamber is a plea for cataclysm, a plea to end the cycle of pain and sacrifice that the Just Men appear committed to:

> It seems to him that an eternal silence was closing down upon the Jewish breed marching to slaughter—that no heir, no memory would supervene to prolong the silent parade of victims ... "O God," the Just Man Ernie Levy

said to himself as bloody tears of pity streamed from his eyes again, "O Lord, we went forth like this thousands of years ago. We walked across arid deserts and the blood-red Red Sea in a flood of salt, bitter tears. We are very old. We are still walking. Oh, let us arrive finally."[10]

On this issue of how the reader is to understand the implication of the death of the last Just Man, and by extension the Death of God in the world, Schwarz-Bart refuses any resolution. The last scene of the novel appears only to confirm the deliberate ambiguity of its stand. On the one hand, in Ernie's last conscious moment he recalls the legend of Rabbi Chanina ben Taradion:

When the gentle rabbi, wrapped in the scrolls of the Torah, was flung upon the pyre by the Romans for having taught the Law, and when they lit the fagots, the branches still green to make his torture last, his pupils said, "Master, what do you see?" And Rabbi Chanina answered, "I see the parchment burning, but the letters are taking wing".... "Ah, yes, surely, the letters are taking wing," Ernie repeated....[11]

This last vision, and Ernie's affirmation of it, would appear to deny any cataclysmic interpretation of the novel, suggesting as it does a survival of the "letters" of the Law, and of the whole cluster of values they represent, including reflexively, this novel itself. On the other hand, "to take wing" is itself an ambiguous idiom, meaning, perhaps, to fly, or, perhaps, to fly away.

Equally ambiguous is the significance of the prayer that concludes the book:

And praised. *Auschwitz.* Be. *Maidenek.* The Lord. *Treblinka.* And praised. *Buchenwald.* Be. *Mauthausen.* The Lord. *Belezec.* And praised. *Sorbibor.* Be. *Chelmno.* The Lord. *Ponary.* And praised. *Theresienstadt.* Be. *Warsaw.* The Lord. *Vilna.* And praised. *Skarysko.* Be. *Bergen-Belsen.* The Lord. *Janow.* And praised. *Dora.* Be. *Neuengamme.* The Lord. *Putskow.* And praised....[12]

From one point of view, it might be concluded that the prayer of praise envelopes and transcends the tally of death camps. From another, we hear not one voice, but two, the second intruding, rebutting, insisting on its litany of murders, refusing to be silenced by the ancient prayer.

The novel denies resolution to the reader; it denies it equally to its narrator, the biographer of "my friend Ernie," who concludes the novel telling us, "Yesterday, as I stood in the street trembling in despair, rooted to the spot, as drop of pity fell from above upon my face. But there was no breeze in the air, not cloud in the sky.... There was only a presence."[13]

This presence is, of course, finally equivocal, offering neither renewal nor an active instrumentality, only "a drop of pity." It is here, in this agonized resolution between the vision of the Death of God and the Eclipse of God, between cataclysmic and cyclical visions of human and divine history, that the novel ends.

NOTES

1. Jean-Paul Sartre, *Between Existentialism and Marxism* (London: New Left Books, 1974), 21.

2. Martin Buber, *Tales of the Hasidim: The Early Masters* (New York: Schocken Books, 1947), 319.

3. André Schwarz-Bart, *The Last of the Just* (New York: Bantam, 1960), 5.

4. Ibid., 6.

5. Ibid., 37.

6. Ibid., 420.

7. Ibid., 4.

8. Ibid., 422.

9. Ibid., 3.

10. Ibid., 419.

11. Ibid., 422.

12. Ibid., 422.

13. Ibid.

The Door to Lilith's Cave

Memory and Imagination in Jane Yolen's Holocaust Novels

Ellen R. Weil

Once upon a time, the writer imagined things that were not here. He imagined one's own death, for instance. What are the obsessions in literature: death, childhood, solitude, anger, madness. Once upon a time, we had to invent all these concepts, give them life and then they emerged.

Today it's just the opposite.... Whatever takes place today is beyond our imagination. This is rooted in our own experience during the Holocaust; the unimaginable become true and therefore became imaginable later. Even today we cannot imagine the past. Even today it's hard for us to grasp, with our fantasy, with our imagination, that the past really took place there. So, rather than imagine the future, we try to imagine the past. Again, the terms of reference are those of the Holocaust.
—Elie Wiesel[1]

"To write poetry after Auschwitz is barbaric," wrote Theodor Adorno, in what is probably the most widely quoted statement about the Holocaust as a theme in imaginative literature.[2] Echoing this, Elie Wiesel has written, "Auschwitz negates all literature.... Holocaust literature? The very term is a contradiction."[3] In one sense, these statements of Adorno and Weisel are unanswerable, and the argument might be made that only the available documentary evidence—the words of witnesses and survivors, together with the ghoulishly meticulous records of the Nazis themselves—can ever speak with authority on the subject. Yet Wiesel, in the passage quoted at the beginning of this essay, also points out an apparent flaw in this argument: while on the one hand the historical Holocaust seems almost beyond the scope of the imagination, beyond the range of acceptable subject matter for the storyteller, on the other it seems to *demand* the exercise of the imagination in order to make it comprehensible in anything resembling human terms.

Even when we read the accounts of actual survivors and witnesses, we encounter them imaginatively as stories, and the ancient voice of the storyteller—in particular, the storyteller of Jewish tradition—has begun to emerge as one of the most effective devices for providing us with access to the Holocaust as a human experience. Wiesel's own voice—almost universally counted as among the most definitive of Holocaust voices—has been identified with that of the storyteller by Robert McAfee Brown, who writes that "the story teller creates a *bridge between two worlds.* His story beings us into contact with a world to which access is otherwise denied us."[4] The Israeli novelist and survivor Aharon Appelfeld, whose novels almost all deal with Holocaust themes, has said of his own work that his goal is to bring the Holocaust

> down to the human realm ... to attempt to make the events speak through the individual and in his language, to rescue the suffering from huge numbers, from dreadful anonymity, and to restore the person's given and family name, to give the tortured person back his human form, which was snatched away from him.[5]

For the imaginative writer, then, the risk involved in dealing with the Holocaust is not so much the risk of telling a fictional story about a real event—which is one of literature's oldest techniques—but rather of telling a story which does not violate the historical experience of that event, as preserved in the memories of survivors and their descendants. The danger of being accused of trivialization is an ever-present and legitimate concern—a concern which is multiplied greatly if one's intended audience is young people, if one employs fantastic devices within the story, or if one relates the story in terms of such notably "unrealistic" modes as the fairy tale. Jane Yolen, in her two novels with Holocaust themes, has faced all these risks, and in so doing has explored significant new ways of approaching the Holocaust by means of the fantastic.

Yolen's award-winning young adult fantasy *The Devil's Arithmetic*, concerning a modern Jewish girl transported back in time to the period of the Holocaust, was published in 1998 to extraordinary acclaim. Cynthia Samuels in *The New York Times* described is as "a brave and moving book";

Kirkus reviews said it was "triumphantly moving"; *School Library Journal* said Yolen "adds much to children's understanding of the effects of the Holocaust." The book went on to receive the National Book Award for Children's Literature and the Sidney Taylor Children's Book Award from the Association of Jewish Libraries, was listed as an honor book by the Women's National Book Association and the Parent's Choice Awards, was cited as a notable children's trade book in social studies, and was even a finalist for the Science Fiction Writers of America's Nebula Award. *Briar Rose*, published in 1992 as part of a series of adult retellings of fairy tales from Tor Books, has not yet been reviewed at the time of this writing.

Despite the considerable praise heaped on *The Devil's Arithmetic*, the novel has not escaped controversy. One editor of a children's book journal even attacked the novel publicly at a young adult librarians' convention in Texas, objecting to the ideas of using time travel to place a modern Jewish girl in the midst of the Holocaust. "Why," he asked, "when we have a *real* account like *The Diary of Anne Frank*, should we waste time with Yolen's 'less real' story?" This "seemed to him to trivialize the Holocaust," according to science fiction writer Orson Scott Card, who was present at the convention. Card later took the unusual step of defending the novel in print, however, in his review column for *The Magazine of Fantasy and Science Fiction*, writing, "It infuriates me that because of an elitist critic, there may be thousands of children who cannot find this book in their library."[6] Though Card does not name Roger Sutton, associate editor of the *Bulletin of the Center for Children's Books*, who had taken the equally unusual step of making his review of the novel a full-scale editorial in the October 1988 issue of that journal, it is obviously him. While praising the story as powerful and memorable, Sutton argues that "the horror—and the history—are betrayed by the essentially comforting vision of the story and its time-travel form." He expresses concern that the depiction of the Holocaust is "more graphic than any we've seen in Holocaust fiction for children before," objects to the "sensational twist" of using the gas chambers (called "Lilith's Cave" by the prisoners in the novel) as a source of suspence, and feels that the heroine's comment of "Ready or not, here we come!" is "a flip Americanism that serves as epitaph" for the other victims. Most of all, he seems to object to the safe return of the heroine.[7]

In several particulars, Sutton is simply wrong. Anyone who can claim that time travel is an "essentially comforting" form of narrative must draw his notion of this tradition more from *Bill and Ted's Excellent Adventure* than the actual literature of time travel, starting with H.G. Wells's *The Time Machine* and including such disturbing texts as Octavia Butler's

Kindred, about a modern black woman transported back to the early days of slavery. When Sutton objects to Hannah's saying "Ready or not, here we come!" he overlooks the fact that this comment serves as a framing device for the time-travel portion of the narrative, and that the same comment early in the novel accompanies Hannah's magical transportation back into the past. He also ignores another, more crucial framing device which Yolen herself points out in a paper in *Language Arts:* namely, that the novel "begins with the sentence 'I'm tired of remembering' and ends with the words 'I remember, I remember.'"[8] By the careful use of such framing and structuring techniques as these, Yolen is able to take advantage of the strengths of both fantasy and the personal historical narrative—but it is precisely the combination of these two narrative modes that seems to lie at the heart of Sutton's objections to the book. Paradoxically, he is concerned that the book is too real—"more graphic" than any previous Holocaust fiction for children—and not real enough—it is after all a fantasy. Perhaps inadvertently, Sutton has identified the central narrative problem that Yolen faced in setting out to write this novel—how to preserve the integrity of real historical experience in a novel whose very premise asks us to believe the impossible.

Yolen's first and most important tool in solving this problem is her own storyteller's voice. One of the legitimate resources available to the storyteller is the fantastic, and Yolen is far from being the first author to use fantastic events in the context of a Holocaust narrative. Even Wiesel's autobiographical *Night* includes an unexplained incident in which a character experiences a prefiguring vision of death in the ovens; and other authors, from André Schwarz-Bart to David Grossman, have made fantastic conceits central to their novels. Sometimes this fantasy is legitimized by appeal to Jewish traditions—such as that of the thirty-six just men in Schwarz-Bart's *The Last of the Just* (1961) or the *dybbuk* who occupies a ex–Nazi's mind in Romain Gary's *The Dance of Genghis Cohn* (1968). Sometimes, as in the work of Jakov Lind or Jerzy Kosinski, the "fantastic" primarily takes the form of breaking the narrative into surrealistic or phantasmagorical episodes which suggest the nightmarish fragmentation of consciousness in the victims.

Nor is Yolen the first author to treat the Holocaust in the context of young adult literature. The most familiar "Classic" in young adult literature, even though it was never originally intended for such an audience, is of course *The Diary of Anne Frank*, which Sutton cites in his attack on *The Devil's Arithmetic.* But as Orson Scott Card points out, "Frank's account ends where the true horror begins."[9] A more telling criticism of the way the Frank diaries have been used comes from Bruno Bettelheim, who argues that "the world-wide acclaim given her story cannot be explained unless we recognize in our wish to forget the gas chambers, and our effort to do so by glorifying the ability to retreat into an extremely private, gentle, sensitive world."[10] More telling is Bettelheim's observation that the often-quoted closing line of the play and movie adapted from the book—"In spite of everything, I still believe that people are really good at heart"—is not supported or justified by anything in the actual diary!

Bettelheim's concern that the Holocaust might become an improbable platform for the glib reassertion of "family values" in face of mortal danger takes on added weight in the context of much more "realistic" Holocaust literature for young people. Reading such novels as Aimee Sommerfelt's *Miriam* (1960: English translation 1963), Hans Peter Richter's *Friedrich* (1970) or Doris Orgel's *The Devil in Vienna* (1978), one might come away with the impression that the Holocaust was primarily a test of the power of childhood friendships to survive under trying circumstances. By far the most bizarre of such works—written for children rather than young adults—is Margaret Will's *Let the Celebrations Begin* (1991), about a family celebration staged against all odds in a concentration camp. All these works resolutely avoid the fantastic, and equally resolutely avoid coming to grips with the real nature of the horror. Apart from *The Devil's Arithmetic*, the only example I could find which extensively uses fantasy in a Holocaust narrative apparently directed at young adults is Lisa Goldstein's *The Red Magician* (1982), and here the fantasy elements are not only rooted in Jewish mystical tradition, but are carefully confined to events before and after the protagonist's internment in a concentration camp, which is described in a single realistic chapter in the center of the narrative.

Yolen, however, takes her narrative directly into the camps, and is unflinching in her portrayal of brutalization, murder, and suicide. Furthermore, she locates all this graphic (and historically sound) detail in the middle of a very traditional kind of literary fantasy. In fact, I think *The Devil's Arithmetic* is better understood if we look at it in terms of literary fantasy rather than as a science fiction time-travel story. (No sort of science fiction rationale is ever offered for the young heroine's magical journey back in time.) In his essay "Symbolic Fantasy," Gary K. Wolfe identifies a number of common characteristics of literary fantasies from George Mac-Donald to C.S. Lewis: an innocent protagonist is magically transported to another world (often through a portal such as a doorway or mirror).[11] He or she must learn the ways of this other world, usually with the aid of a tutelary figure or figures, and eventually gains enough strength and wisdom to be a leader to others. The villain, rather than a simple antagonist, is often the agent of some monstrous evil. This evil may or may not be defeated—what finally enables the protagonist to return is not so much the conquest of evil as the purging of some vice or illusion he or she has labored under in the "real" world. Upon returning to this world, the hero discovers that very little "real" time has passed, and that his or her change in attitudes or belief seems unaccountable to others.

This outline permits us to examine in detail exactly how Yolen has altered the traditional materials of fantasy to accommodate historical knowledge, how she has used the structure of fantasy to frame and distance painful historical reality, and how she has managed this without violating the integrity of either the form of fantasy or the details of the historical record. What Wolfe's outline shows is that, structurally, the historical Holocaust occupies exactly the same position in Yolen's narrative that the magical fantasy worlds of Oz or Narnia occupy in the more traditional fantasies. Like those earlier fantasies, Yolen begins *The Devil's Arithmetic* by firmly grounding the reader in a convincing, and perhaps even autobiographical, account of contemporary Jewish family life—while at the same time introducing the themes of memory and storytelling that will prove central to the larger narrative. Hannah complains not only about how much she has to remember during the ritual of Seder, but also about the stories of the Nazis that her grandparents and great-aunts insist on repeating.

The key fantastic event does not occur until after three chapters, when Hannah, asked to perform the ritual opening of the door for Elijah during Seder, opens it to find herself not in the familiar hallway of her grandparents' apartment building, but rather in a rural Polish village in 1942. In a way, Yolen reverses the polarities of traditional fantasy by transporting her protagonist not to a less real world where magic works, but to a more real world which makes Hannah's own memories of her modern life seem like magical fantasies. It is Hannah (now called Chaya) who speaks of wonders such as America and movies, Hannah who unrealistically argues, "We should go down fighting,"[12] until she is reminded that there are no guns or knives to fight with.

From Hannah's point of view, Poland in 1942 is what Kathryn Hume calls a "subtractive world"—a world from which expected elements are missing—rather than an "additive" or augmented world as in heroic fantasy.[13] Because of her memories of movies and modern life, Hannah brings new knowledge into this world and becomes a popular storyteller among the other girls in the Polish village where she finds herself (Hannah's skill as a storyteller was already established earlier during the narrative's modern sequence, when she entertains her younger brother with a vivid retelling of a horror movie). Yolen takes advantage of this to set up specific contrasts between this world and the expected magical world of fantasies and fairy tales: Hannah muddles up her retelling of "Hansel and Gretel" (with its ominous images of witches, children, and ovens) and notes that the real forest near the *shtetl* is *"even more magical than the forest in Oz."*[14] But her memories also establish another reversal from traditional fantasy: whereas the usual fantasy protagonist is ignorant of the new world, Hannah knows *too much* about it from her study of the Holocaust in school. She uses what she knows (or as much as she can remember) to try to warn the others, but her warnings are treated as yet another of her stories, and her warnings are treated as yet another of her stories, and her "modern" memories disappear suddenly when her head is shaved in the camp: "Her memories became camp memories only."[15] Gradually her memories begin to reappear, but for most of the remainder of the narrative she must act without privileged information; her decision to enter Lilith's Cave in place of her friend Rivkah is her own act of courage, not the act of a time traveler who knows she is safe. Her final comment—"Ready or not, here we come"[16]—is, as we have already noted, an echo of the same comment Hannah had made just before she was transported back in time. As Roger Sutton puts it in his editorial, this "flip Americanism" is usually associated with the game of hide-and-seek; it is the child's formula of discovering what has been hidden, and it reminds us not only that Hannah is still a child, but that her quest has finally led her to the discovery of the greatest of all secrets.

When Hannah returns to her grandparents' apartment, she finds that virtually no time at all has passed. Her newfound awareness reveals itself only when she is able to explain to her Aunt Eva the private meaning Eva had assigned to her number tattoo—an explanation Hannah had never been able to sit still for before. From her own experience of being literally shorn of memory, Hannah has finally come to understand the importance of remembering—but equally important, she has learned why remembering is so important to her Grandpa Will, and why he behaves the way he does at family gatherings—cursing the TV set, droning on at the Seder, recounting his and his family's hardships at every opportunity. Earlier, Hannah had wished that Will were more like her other grandfather, Dan, who was not a survivor, but who—ironically, as it turns out—had the habit of ending every story with "How do I know? I was there!"[17] The importance of personal testimony is a continuing and central theme in the frame story of *The Devil's Arithmetic*, and it introduces an important corollary theme: that of not only learning about the history of the Holocaust, but of understanding the behavior of survivor.

Understanding the behavior of survivors is also a central concern in Yolen's adult Holocaust novel *Briar Rose* and even provides the principal impetus for that novel's action. But here the problem is not that of an aging survivor talking "too much" about the Nazi era, but rather that of a survivor unable to talk about her experiences at all, or at least unable to talk about them directly. Rebecca Berlin (Becca), the story's protagonist, has grown up listening to her grandmother Gemma tell an oddly distorted version of the Sleeping Beauty story, in which Gemma claims that she herself was the princess who lived in a castle. On her deathbed, Gemma extracts a promise from Becca to find the castle, and this sets Becca on a quest to discover her grandmother's true identity and the details of her past, which have never been shared with any family members. Becca's investigation is initially presented as a kind of mystery, the only clues provided by a box of photos and newspaper clippings Gemma had kept throughout her life and what little family history Becca can glean from her parents. Eventually, the clues lead Becca first to Oswego, New York— site of America's only wartime camp for Holocaust survivors and a kind of barbed-wire concentration camp in its own right—and later to the Polish village of Chelmno, site of one of the worst of the Nazi extermination camps. (In an afterword to the novel, Yolen notes that only two men are known to have escaped from Chelmno, and only two others were found alive when the camp was liberated; no woman is known to have survived Chelmno.) Throughout the novel, fragments of Gemma's "Briar Rose" story are interspersed with the tale of Becca's investigation, gaining an edge of horror as their meaning becomes more and more clear.

Despite its title, *Briar Rose* is far from a fairy tale, and is not even a fantasy. Insofar as it functions in the narrative at all, the fantastic is confined to Gemma's strange, transformed version of the fairy tale, which she repeatedly insists is her own story (we eventually learn that the story of Briar Rose was the only memory she retained after he experience at Chelmno). Becca has long been aware that Gemma's version of Briar Rose differs from the famous fairy tale in a number of ominous ways; on more than one occasion during her childhood, friends hearing the story had grown upset and angry over the unfamiliar variations. The evil fairy who places the curse on Briar Rose is described as wearing big black boots and silver eagles on her hat; her curse is that everyone will die when a great mist descends over the castle; the good fairy's ameliorative promise is that a few will not die, but only sleep; and when the prince awakens the princess with a kiss, no one else awakens (in the standard version, of course, everyone in the castle is saved). There is no mention of a spinning wheel or the princess pricking herself with the needle, but much is made of the barblike thorn that grows around the palace and of the fact that no one outside cared to know about the fate of the victims. Reconciling this fantastic, dream-like narrative with the details of her own family history becomes Becca's obsession, and when she finally learns her grandmother's true story, from a homosexual Polish survivor who had helped rescue Gemma from Chelmno, the story she hears is a graphic and credible survivor's tale, involving resistance fighters and Nazi persecution of gays as well as life in the camps.

The key to the novel lies in the relationship between these two narratives, the fairy tale and the survivor's tale, and in Yolen's exploration of fantasy to order experience and make it bearable. It becomes apparent that Gemma's view of herself as Briar Rose, the sleeping princess, has been the only means by which she could come to terms with her tragic history; the fantastic becomes a way of coping with her terrible memories and sharing them with her grandchildren. From the point of view of the novel's realistic framework, certain questions remain unanswered: Why, for example, did Becca's mother never pursue her own mother's history, and why does Becca depend on her father, Dr. Berlin, for the fragmentary details of this history? Why are Becca's sisters—who seem almost borrowed from another fairy tale, "Cinderella"—indifferent and at times almost hostile to her quest? And the series of coincidences that enable Becca to uncover nearly all the sources of Gemma's Briar Rose story in Poland and New York lend a deterministic, almost enchanted aura to her search, as though Becca is enacting her own fairy tale. The power achieved by Yolen's juxtaposition of these various narratives—Gemma's "Briar Rose," Becca's investigation, and Gemma's actual history—is undeniable. Yolen adds to this rich texture of stories by offering us glimpses of still other, thematically related tales, such as the search conducted by Becca's boyfriend, an adoptee, for his natural mother. (In Yolen's other two fantasies for adults, *Sister Light, Sister Dark* [1988] and *White Jenna* [1989], she also explores the varieties of storytelling by juxtaposing alternative versions of the same tale, as recounted in myth, legend, story, song, and academic scholarship.) Like *The Devil's Arithmetic*, *Briar Rose* is really about coming to understand the ways in which remembering is transformed into storytelling, and about the crucial role of storytelling in making sense of our lives.

Jorge Luis Borges, in a brief mediation titled "The Witness" writes,

We may well be astonished by space-filling acts which come to an end when someone dies, and yet something, an infinite number of things, dies in each death.... There was day in time when the last eyes to see Christ were closed forever. The battle of Junin and the love of Helen died with the death of some one man. What will die with me when I die?[18]

This thought, or something very like it, is much on the mind of many Holocaust survivors. They are concerned about self-styled "revisionists" who attempt to deny that the Holocaust ever happened, but they are equally concerned with the preservation of their own personal stories, their lost family history. Many of them are anxious to speak to groups of young people, not merely to confront them with the horrendous statistics, but to tell them their own stories—because they know that this is what young people remember, and because it is a way of keeping those stories alive. Both *The Devil's Arithmetic* and *Briar Rose* address this concern directly, by dramatizing how survivors' tales may be saved from oblivion by capturing the interest of a single younger family member.

When Hannah returns to the present in *The Devil's Arithmetic* and recognizes her Aunt Eva and Grandpa Will, she realizes they are living links with the horror she has just experienced, just as Becca comes to realize that her grandmother connects her to the story she heard from the survivor at Chelmno. As a narrative strategy, this serves to firmly ground Hannah's fantastic experience and Gemma's fantastic fairy tale in historical reality. Aunt Eva provides external validation that the place where Hannah has been is not the product of her own imagination, and the survivor at Chelmno provides external validation that Gemma's version of Briar Rose was not the product of *her* imagination. But more important, both novels establish a link between a younger generation and their family histories through emphasizing the importance of memory and storytelling. For all the well-researched detail about life during the Holocaust, this is what Yolen's Holocaust novels finally achieve. By walking through the door to Lilith's Cave, Hannah becomes her own story, just as Gemma "becomes," in her own mind, the princess of "Briar Rose." When history itself becomes unimaginable, Yolen seems to suggest, it is only through fantasy and imagination that we can make ourselves part of it, and make it real.

NOTES

1. Harry James Cargas, *Harry James Cargas in Conversation with Elie Wiesel* (New York: Paulist Press, 1976), 114–15.
2. Jorge Luis Borges, *A Personal Anthology*, ed. Anthony Kerrigan (New York:

Grove Press, 1967), 23; Lawrence S. Langer, *The Holocaust and the Literary Imagination* (New Haven, CT: Yale University Press, 1975), 1; Sidra DeKoven Ezrahi, *By Words Alone: The Holocaust in Literature* (Chicago: University of Chicago Press, 1980), 6.

    3. Elie Wiesel, *A Jew Today*, trans. Marion Wiesel (New York: Random House, 1978), 197.

    4. Jorge Luis Brown, *A Personal Anthology*, ed. Anthony Kerrigan (New York: Grove Press, 1967), 44.

    5. Quoted in Ellen Weil, *The Holocaust in Literature* (Chicago: Roosevelt University External Studies Program, 1990), 4.

    6. Orson Scott Card, "Books to Look For," *The Magazine of Fantasy and Science Fiction* 76, no. 4 (April 1989): 38.

    7. Roger Sutton, "Editorial," *Bulletin of the Center for Children's Books* (October 1988): 23.

    8. Jane Yolen, "An Experiential Act," *Language Arts* 66, no. 3 (March 1989): 51.

    9. Card, "Books to Look For," 37.

    10. Bruno Bettelhim, *Surviving* (New York: Vintage, 1980), 247.

    11. Gary K. Wolfe, "Symbolic Fantasy," *Genre* 8, no. 3 (September 1975): 194–209.

    12. Jane Yolen, *The Devil's Arithmetic* (New York: Viking Penguin, 1990), 142.

    13. Kathryn Hume, *Fantasy and Mimesis* (New York: Theuen, 1984), 83.

    14. Yolen, *The Devil's Arithmetic*, 52.

    15. Ibid., 135.

    16. Ibid., 160.

    17. Ibid., 14.

    18. Borges, "The Witness," *A Personal Anthology*, ed. Anthony Kerrigan (New York: Grove Press, 1967), 178.

Mother Goose Tales

Intergenerational Storytelling and the Holocaust in Jane Yolen's Briar Rose and Peter Rushforth's Kindergarten

VANDANA SAXENA

That castle is yours. It is all I have to leave you. You must find the castle in the sleeping woods. Promise me.—Jane Yolen, Briar Rose[1]

As Holocaust fiction for young adult readers, Jane Yolen's *Briar Rose* and Peter Rushforth's *Kindergarten* integrate the profound complexities of Holocaust testimony with the concerns of coming of age fiction. The plot development follows the shift of the narrative from the story of the adolescent protagonist to that of the older generation, of the grandmothers who survived the Holocaust and overcome the years of silence to share their memories with the second generation. In both novels the testimony is couched in the form of well known fairy tales, a genre usually associated with young readers. In Yolen's novel, Gemma, Becca's grandmother, tells her story through the fairy tale of the "Sleeping Beauty" who was given a new lease on life by the kiss of the prince. Gemma vehemently insists that she is the Sleeping Beauty of the Woods, forcing Becca to look beyond the surface of the story and decipher its metaphors. Rushforth's *Kindergarten* repeatedly turns to the narratives of abandonment and insecurity told against the backdrop of fairy stories like "Hansel and Gretel," "Bluebeard," and "The Fitcher's Bird." The fairy tales, fractured and twisted in these retellings, become the testimonies of Holocaust survivors, their legacy to the generation whose temporal distance from the event makes them reluctant to bear the burden of the past. This essay explores the intergenerational storytelling in these two texts as it becomes a means to integrate personal memories, a family's past, and traumatic historical events. Through storytelling, this essay contends, the familial relationship between the grandmother and the grandchildren is recast into the relationship between the victim and the listener; the themes of growth and coming of age of the adolescent protagonist are intertwined with the awareness and trauma of the older generation.

The use of fairy tales in two such texts highlights one of the central dilemmas of writing about the Holocaust for children: how to reconcile the humanist resolutions of the coming of age literature with the literature of trauma. While the narratives of coming of age tell the story of growth and integration of a child into the folds of adult society, Holocaust testimonies tell the story of isolation, exile and dehumanization of the victim. At the center lies the trauma of an unspeakable event. The inability to understand, the reluctance to remember and bear witness—these mark the memories of the survivors as well as the witnesses. Holocaust is an event that lies beyond understanding and memory: "a gap that carries the force of the event and does so precisely at the expense of simple knowledge and memory. The force of this experience would appear to arise precisely, in other words, in the collapse of understanding."[2] Such collapse of understanding also signifies a collapse of conventional narrative forms with structures and conventions that are meant to totalize and explicate. Critics like Kenneth Kidd, Hamida Bosmajian, and Adrienne Kertzer have discussed the problems and limitations of children's literature when confronted with the theme of trauma.

In *Briar Rose* and *Kindergarten*, fairy tales offer a medium to narrate events that defy the teller's understanding and comprehension and hence the conventional modes of narration. The ambiguous temporal and spatial dimensions of fairy tales create a space to represent and map the experiences of trauma and exile. The formulaic "once upon a time" indicates a temporal shift to a mythical past or an imaginative time. Similarly a spatial displacement from the realm of the known and familiar to a forest or an enchanted castle signifies displacement, isolation and danger. The stories of "Sleeping Beauty" and "Hansel and Gretel" defamiliarize the conventional association between home, family, and safety. Despite their humanist resolution, at the core of these fairy tales lies a narrative of danger, isolation, and hovering death. The turn of the familiar into the unfamiliar creates an eerie sense of unreality that pervades the Holocaust and now surrounds the traumatic memories of the survivors. Conventional rational understanding collapses in the world of violence and trauma of the Nazi camps.

Feeding on the oral tradition, fairy tales build on modes of storytelling that do not recount first person experiences directly but center on the relationship between the storyteller and the listener. The narrator, often a Mother Hubbard or a Mother Goose–like figure, creates an illusion of intimacy, of home and family; her stories bridge the divisions in time. She is the generic icon of the narrative form, the "frontispiece of fairy tale collections."[3] According to fairy tale theorist Marina Warner, the storytelling sibyl "fulfills a certain function in thinking about forbidden, forgotten, buried even secret matters."[4] As they are passed down from generation to generation, the stories become the repositories of cultural memories which, though muted, are never forgotten.

In *Briar Rose* and *Kindergarten*, the figure of the grandmother, as well as her narrative, preserves the distance between the victim and the listener (and hence the reader) even as the event is integrated into the history of the family. Intergenerational storytelling uses the testimony of the grandmother to bring the past into the present; at the same time, the presence of the third generation listener opens a space for reader identification, not with the victim but with the listener. In the dialogic space between victim and listener—between the grandmother and the third generation listener—history interacts with the present, the traumatic memories of the past come together with the concerns of the present as the memories are reclaimed. As Marianne Hirsch claims, "at stake is precisely the 'guardianship' of a traumatic personal and generational past with which some of us have a 'living connection' and that past's passing into history."[5] Despite their humanist resolutions, fairy tales call for an interpretation and a depth of understanding that lie beyond conventional realism. Their narrative underscores strategies wherein despair, loss, and uncertainty retain their presence despite the life-affirming nature of children's literature.

Fairy Tales and Fractured Memories

In Yolen's novel, the story of Gemma, the grandmother, survivor, and storyteller, is embedded within the story of Becca, her granddaughter. Gemma's version of "Sleeping Beauty" is repeated incrementally in Becca's memory of her grandmother's retellings throughout her childhood. Becca remembers how Gemma's retelling twisted the popular tale in a way that frightened Becca's friends and schoolmates. Gemma's story faltered at the crucial moment when listeners waited for the arrival of the prince to undo the spell: "There had always been something decidedly odd about the whole telling.... In Gemma's story everyone—other than the prince who wakes the princess with a kiss and Briar Rose and afterwards their child— everyone else sleeps on."[6] It leaves the listeners disturbed and upset. The twisted fairy tale, along with Gemma's death-bed insistence "I am Briar Rose,"[7] hints at the "split self"—the presence of the other co-existing along-side the beloved grandmother. The frequent retelling of the story of Briar Rose or the "Sleeping Beauty in the Woods" hints at the presence of an other, an alien within the self who, while distanced by time, space, and memories, constantly haunts the present—the new name, identity and life that Gemma creates for herself in America. The split narrator, the frac-tured fairy tale, Gemma's irritation with the interruptions—these are the real testimonies of trauma. As a victim, Gemma remembers the cata-strophic sequence of events in great detail. At the same time, the nature of the event evades knowledge; it confounds ordinary forms of under-standing. It upsets yet eludes the "I," "here," and "now" of the safe world, where a death camp seems impossible, distant and unreal. Belau claims that the victims of the past are the "ambassadors of an exceptional realm, bearers of a higher (albeit more terrible) knowledge than is available to the rest of us."[8] At the same time, the distance between the victim and "the rest of us" also reflects the split within the psyche of the victim. The response holds together contradictory elements: "One is the traumatic event, registered rather than experienced. It seems to have bypassed per-ception and consciousness and falls directly into the psyche. The other is a kind of memory of the event, in the form of a perpetual troping of it by the bypassed or severely split (dissociated) psyche."[9]

Like Freud's uncanny, Gemma's compulsive repetition is a traumatic expression of the experience that is estranged, alienated, or willfully for-gotten as a strategy of survival. At the same time, it is an uncanny expres-sion of estrangement, of "unreality" and the fragility of the present, with its illusions of contentment and safety. The recurrence of barbed wire, the mist[10] that consumed all her family and citizens, the castle of death— these horrific motifs displace the fairy tale that children are familiar with, the story which Freudian psychologists like Bruno Bettleheim have inter-preted as a case history of latent female sexuality and passive socialization of girls. As photographs, forms, and documents from Gemma's past come to light, the story emerges as a symptom of familial history. The family speculates over Gemma's changing names and identities—from Gemma to Gitl to Genevive to Dawna to Briar Rose. Like memory that is remembered only by being willfully forgotten, the place of origin, the erstwhile home, is scratched off the immigration form. The task of being a witness to such an event haunts Gemma, a task she leaves behind for her Becca. Gemma's fairy story acquires meaning only posthumously as Becca works out the metaphors that drive Gemma's "Sleeping Beauty of the Woods." As the text progresses, Gemma's story, italicized and occupying a distinct space within the narrative, becomes intricately linked with the narrative of Becca's growth.

Unlike *Briar Rose* where a single tale is transformed into the narrative of an individual survivor, in Rushforth's *Kindergarten* the voices from the past resurface in various guises. Corrie, the seventeen year old protagonist, discovers a cache of letters written in the years immediately preceding the Second World War. These are the letters from Jewish students and parents—all fearing the pending catastrophe and pleading for safe passage for their children to England. As Corrie reads the letters, he remembers Grimm's fairy tales—"Hansel and Gretel," "Wolf and the Seven Kids," and "Fitcher Bird"—all brought to life by the pre-war paintings of Lilli, his grandmother. Mingled with these are references to a range of children's books of the pre-war generation—from Kenneth Grahame's *Wind in the Willows* to Eric Kastner's *Emil and the Detectives.* Lilli, whose paintings hang on the walls of the house, tells Grimm's tales to the younger brother Matthias as she bakes cakes "minutely detailed like Hansel and Gretel gingerbread house."[11]

Mingling with the world of the unreal are the terrors and violence of the real world. The story of "Hansel and Gretel" alternates with the news on television about a school under terrorist siege in Berlin. The terrorist group involved in the siege is the same that attacked the airport in Rome years earlier that left Corrie's mother dead. The violence in stories like "Hansel and Gretel" and "The Fitcher Bird" is echoed by the events of the world around the children.

Behind the imaginative fairy tale world and the contemporary world of terrorist attacks lurks a black hole of history—the Holocaust, an event which never surfaces in family talk. Unlike Gemma's attempt to voice her past, Corrie and his family avoid talking about the event. Lilli's family perished in Nazi Germany, though she was able to escape to safety in 1939. The memory of loss haunts her paintings. Corrie can even discern the pain of the past in her visage:

He looked at her face. Physical pain always faded as time passed. The memory of humiliation and mockery never died. Each time the memory was revived, the feelings returned as intense as they had been at the time they were experienced.[12]

Yet as Corrie tells us, "Lilli, like the girl bound to silence in 'The Six Swans,' had never spoken a word about her past, her life in Germany, her family; her books and paintings had remained locked away, from herself, and from everyone else."[13] It is only in her art—in the paintings from before the war, when she was a famous artist; in the illustrations of the Grimm's tales where the characters resemble her dead family—that one can discern Lilli's loss. Her inability to paint after the war, like her silence, is a testimony of loss—her story that is telling in her refusal to tell.

For Corrie, the news of the terrorist siege of the school brings back the memories of the terrorist attack which killed his mother. The image of a suffering mother outside the school conjures, in his mind, the letters of Jewish parents—anxious for their children's safety, ready to abandon them to ensure survival. As he works through the letters from 1934 to 1937, he becomes aware of the impending catastrophe in 1939. Yet, he is also aware these are "a part of the past of Lilli, and of himself"[14]; that "these historical events, these dates, had been a part of her life. She lived through them. She had been there. When she married Grandpa Meeuwissen in 1939, she had been a refugee from Germany."[15]

Corrie's awareness is built not only on textbook history, letters from past, and from discourses across media like television and newspapers, but also through untold stories and silences like that of Lilli. The memory—and the postmemory—of the Holocaust remains surrounded by a silence that is never broken but finds its way into life through the uncanny repetition of the trauma in his family. Hirsch uses the term "postmemory" as a "*structure* of inter-and trans-generational transmission of traumatic knowledge and experience. It is a *consequence* of traumatic recall but at a generational move."[16] Postmemory of an event reflects the coalition between continuity and rupture. While the later generations are deeply connected to the memories of the previous generation, theirs is a received memory, distinct from the recollections of the witnesses and participants who lived the event. Through such postmemory, present tragedies like the siege of the school and the death of his mother become what Dori Laub calls "the second Holocaust" in the family: the loss is relived as haunting memories persist "at once through the actual return of the trauma and through its inadvertent repetition, or transmission, from one generation to another."[17] Hence, Laub claims that

The "second Holocaust" thus turns out to be itself a testimony to a history of repetition. Through its uncanny reoccurrence, the trauma of the second Holocaust bears witness not just to a history that has not ended, but specifically, to the historical occurrence of an event that, in effect, *does not end*.[18]

The silence, the fractured stories of the past and the horror that underlies them—all these signify a moment where human understanding and the search for meaning encounter an insurmountable past. Cathy Caruth refers to the latent memories of the victim as the symptoms of a history that cannot be entirely understood and thus possessed. Fragmented and interrupted fairy tale metaphors become the testimonials of such a past; survivors of trauma, "we might say, carry an impossible history within them, or they become themselves the symptom of a history that they cannot entirely possess."[19]

In Gemma's case, the twisted story of the "Sleeping Beauty" attempts to tell and preserve the memories. For Lilli, the memories are preserved by the very act of silencing. Her silence, along with the paintings that cover the walls of her house, hints at the past that haunts her and the later generation of the family. The grandmothers become one with the sibylline narrator of the fairy tales, Mother Goose, who is exiled, abandoned, and muted, whose stories bridge the divisions in time.

Circle of Listeners

> Fairy tales are stories which, in the earliest mentions of their existence, include that circle of listeners, the audience ... they successfully involve their hearers or readers in identifying with the protagonists, their misfortunes their triumphs.
> —Marina Warner, *From the Beast to the Blonde*[20]

> The emergence of the narrative which is being listened to—and heard—is, therefore, the process and the place where in the cognizance, the "knowing" of the event is given birth to. The listener, therefore, is a party to the creation of knowledge de novo.
> —Dori Laub, "Bearing Witness or the Vicissitudes of Listening"[21]

The presence of a listener, the third generation adolescent, is crucial to the testimonial narratives of survivors. Eaglestone insists that the task of any kind of representation of the Holocaust is to preserve the radical otherness of the event and the victim. Narratives that assimilate by calling for identification with the victim or by providing a humanist resolution are guilty of making the event falsely comprehensible. The violence of the Holocaust was a rupture in the cultural continuum; it demands a retelling that preserves the otherness, the incomprehensibility. Though Yolen's and Rushforth's novels call for identification, the young readers are meant to identify not with the victim but with the listeners, with Becca and Corrie. The presence of a listener also offers a space and time wherein young adult readers can confront the past and share its psychic burden, for as Laub claims, in the testimony of the Holocaust the listener is a participant whose presence enables the narration:

> The listener has to feel the victim's victories, defeats and silences, know them from within, so that they can assume the form of testimony.... The listener, however, is also a separate human being and will experience hazards and struggles of his own, while carrying out this function of a witness to the trauma. While overlapping, to a degree with the experience of the victim, he nonetheless does not become the victim—he preserves his own separate place, position and perspective; a battleground for forces raging in himself, to which he has to pay attention and respect if he is properly carry out his task.[22]

Hence the role of postmemory and witness of the later generation, the witness who did not experience the event first-hand but inherited the narratives of the victims, like Gemma's granddaughters or Lilli's grandsons. The field of Memory Studies, which deals with complex relationship between the past and the present, emphasizes the way this relationship is articulated in the domains of experience. Its focus on the social, political and cultural aspects of the memory, on what and how people and communities try to remember is central to the Holocaust narratives. According to Erin Heather McGlothlin, the engagement of these generations with the past "seeks to artistically restore some of the holes that riddle the memory of the catastrophe, to imagine an event of which one cannot be epistemologically certain, to tell the story to remember what the survivors themselves have forgotten."[23] The stories are necessary precisely because the immediacy with which the first witness experienced the event is incomplete. If the traumatic event lies beyond immediate understanding and knowledge, an event that cannot be known or witnessed as it occurred, then "this notion of trauma also acknowledges," according to Cathy Caruth in *Unclaimed Experience: Trauma, Narrative, and History*, "that perhaps it is not possible for the witnessing of the trauma to occur within the individual at all, that it may only be in future generation that 'cure' or at least witnessing can take place."[24]

Becca is able to understand Gemma's story when she delves into the past, into the collective memories and narratives of her community. She deciphers Gemma's portrayal of the prince's passage through the briar hedge, where on "either side of the path white birch trees gleamed like the souls of the new dead," as she learns of the folk belief that "birch trees housed the souls of the dead." She learns of Gemma, the "Sleeping Beauty," who was housed with several others at a dilapidated castle before being gassed at the Chelmno death camp, and who later was rescued from the mass grave, from the heap of bodies of those who did not survive. The prince who resuscitates her with a life giving kiss is Joseph Potocki, a homosexual, in love with Aron, Becca's grandfather. When the rescued girl does not remember her past, Potocki names her Briar Rose. Later Potocki helps pregnant Gemma immigrate to America.

Gemma's "Sleeping Beauty" debunks conventional fairy tales at various levels, overturning and reconfiguring the stereotypes and expectations associated with popular storytelling. Potocki tells the story of the war and its victims who were thrust into the horrific flow of events that lay beyond their control. It is a story of fear, death, and the gradual dehumanization of the victims. Potocki tells about his younger self who lived in denial even as the others were hunted down by the Nazis, until the misfortune struck him, too. His experience at the Sachenhausen labor camp destroys any other sense of identity except being a homosexual, the "crime" for which he is arrested:

> If you had asked Josef Potocki to describe himself before he entered Sachenhausen, he would have said: "I am a Pole educated in Cambridge, a poet and playwright, a member of the minor aristocracy, a man of literate tastes, master of five languages (Polish, German, English, French and Italian), and a gourmet cook." He would never have mentioned sexual preferences. That was no one's business but his own. Besides, he was quite aware of family honor which demanded an heir, an abstract concept he was prepared to deal with in the future.
>
> After Sachenhausen he would have said, "I am a fag." Not gay—there was nothing gay about being a homosexual in that place. Nothing sexual either. Like the other men, he lost all desire for anything but staying alive.[25]

As a partisan fighter, Potocki is not a warrior-hero. He claims that the partisans were neither romantic nor heroic: "These [partisans] were the flotsam and jetsam of the world, driftwood like Josef, whose victories were sometimes catastrophes, whose defeats were the stuff of legends."[26] Yet, along with other partisan fighters they accomplish a single act of heroism: that of saving one girl among thousands who died at Chelmno—an act that is their single greatest success in the face of the millions being murdered. Though Gemma's marriage to Aron, a fellow partisan, seems to affirm life and resilience in the face of death (like a fairy tale), it is immediately followed by Aron's death. For Magda, Becca's guide, the event, like the other horrors of Holocaust, is subsumed under the narrative of martyrdom and sacrifice: "In the not-so-past history are many tragedies. Every family can recite them. The blood of so many martyrs are still wet on our soil."[27]

Yet, this narrative, one of sacrifice and heroism, is debunked by other narratives. The people of Chelmno hold the memories and horror at bay by a forced insistence that "nothing" happened. The records of more than 300,000 people who were murdered in Chelmno are insistently and violently denied. The event and the accompanying sense of guilt are forcefully buried, surfacing only in the moments of crisis, for instance, told to the priest in confession boxes and on death beds. In Becca's journey to the past, Gemma's twisted and fragmented "Sleeping Beauty" is overlaid with multiple narratives by Potocki, by Magda, and by the people of Chelmno— all in constant dialogue and constant effort to come to terms with the past.

Unlike Becca, who works out the metaphors in her grandmother's story, Corrie in *Kindergarten* actively reworks and reimagines the fairy tales, imbuing them with his own meaning and interpretation. The discovery of the pre-war letters opens the door to the past as does his discovery of his Jewish identity: "Discovering his Jewishness—it couldn't be denied, could it?—Corrie felt as though he had opened some forbidden door, and made some shocking discovery which overturned all the certainties in his life."[28] Corrie connects these doors metaphorically to the doors of the forbidden room in "The Fitcher Bird." Opening the door ushers in terrible knowledge, just as the discovery of the letters and his own Jewish identity make him connect with the fate of the children who are abandoned, first in the English school for safety and survival, and later in the dark, pathless woods, the forests of the concentration camps, where the crematoria await. In his mind, he rewrites the end of "Hansel and Gretel," as it is the two children who perish in the oven. Like the Nazi soldiers, the witch undresses Gretel, cuts off "all of Gretel's hair, close to her skull," and removes her necklace which had a little star at the end of it. It does not free Corrie from the sense of despair. His younger brother, Jo, suffers from a similar depressive state as the news of the school siege and his mother's death become linked in his mind.

It is only at the end, after Lilli opens the channels of communication by returning to her art and talking to her grandsons about her lost family, that the brothers are able to talk about the past. Both brothers recognize the faces in her fairy tale illustrations as she shows them the photograph of her family, all of whom were killed in the war. Lilli does not deny the contempt Corrie and Jo express: "This is what mankind is like."[29] She does not deny her anger and suffering at the loss of all her loved ones. Yet, she offers new insights by remembering the acts of goodness and kindness.

Kindergarten foregrounds the power of dialogue that unfetters the monologic news accounts on television and history at large. The end of Rushforth's novel offers a humanist resolution as Lilli places the future in the hands of the children:

> We *are* wandering, we *are* lost in darkness, perhaps, in England, in Germany, over much of the world, but it is the children who will lead us out of this darkness, who will put an end to our wandering. With each child's birth, they say, the world begins again, and it is you who must use your life in trying to find a way, trying to light that darkness.[30]

At the same time, Lilli also voices the pain of the generation lost in the traumatic memories of the past—memories which can be expressed and externalized in the presence of listeners, the third generation that is willing to share the burden. Both, the young protagonist and the readers, become able to process the profound loss of life as well as the loss of invaluable human narratives. Memories of the past are preserved as they become integrated into the stories of later generations. Denying the illusions of a happy ending that Gemma's survival might create, Yolen insists in the "Author's Note" to *Briar Rose* that "Happy ever-after is a fairy tale notion, not history."[31] For Adrienne Kertzer, "The lesson that emerges in this sophisticated interplay between text and peritext is not the consoling lesson of spiritual triumph but a much harder one about the reality of historical facts and the difficulty such facts pose for representing this particular history for young people."[32] These two young adult novels, with their generic thrust to understand larger social and cultural attitudes, interweave the narrative of growth and future with darker and more complicated questions raised by the traumatic past. The focus on unreality and fragmentation contests not only the official records but also the linear narratives of growth and selfhood. It installs a dialogue in the place of official records and victim's silence—a dialogue where the narrative of the future co-exists with the despair and trauma of the past. Magda's question to Becca at the end sums up the attitude succinctly: "'Let sleeping princesses lie?' Magda laughed. 'We are all sleeping princesses some time. But it is better to be fully awake, don't you think?.'"[33] The fairy tales told by these grandmothers to their grandchildren (and thereby to adolescent readers) develop into bridges between the victims and survivors who directly experienced trauma and the future, preserving their collectivity as the event recedes further and further into the past.

Conclusion

> *The future is when people talk about the past. So if the prince*
> *knows all their past lives and tells all the people who are still*
> *to come, then the princes live again and into the future.*
> —Jane Yolen, *Briar Rose*[34]

Gemma's injunction emphasizes the central impulse of children's and young adult fiction about the Holocaust. Rather than integration within the community which marks the end of a traditional *Bildungsroman*, the sense of loss, rupture, and exile remains integral to the narrative. The stories of survivors which form the core of the narrative move from community to isolation, from a presence to an absence. Hence, Foley suggests that the "survivor narrative" makes up an anti–*Bildungsroman*. The narratives that come after the anti–*Bildungsroman* of the survivors, the stories told by the third generation, are marked with an intense relationship with the traumatic past. Postmemory in these texts emerges as a textual memory which replaces the definitive resolution of young adult fiction with an openness that encourages participation. Becca learns that "Truth is never tidy."[35] Corrie acknowledges traumatic events as "a part of the past of Lilli, and of himself."[36]

Hamida Bosmajian underlines the need to integrate the historical event, howsoever traumatic, with the projects of socialization and acculturation that drive young adult and children's fiction:

> The young reader is to become conscious of the Nazi era and the suffering of its victims and, through the act of reading consciously, critically, and emphatically, appropriate a memory—or rather post-memory—that is not part of his or her experience but is supposed to ensure that "never again" will there be a repetition of such a disaster.[37]

Stories thus become a crucial means to remember, to preserve the memory into the future. Sue Vice, making a case for the legitimization of Holocaust fiction as a genre, argues that "Any new literary perspectives on the Holocaust after the middle of the third millennium can only be written by descendents of survivors or by novelists with no connection to the event."[38] As fiction, these narratives do not appeal to historical truth but to the issues and ethics of representation that surround the literature of Holocaust.[39] They acquire a greater complexity when placed in the context of children's literature: "authors have struggled with the question of how much to reveal and how much to conceal in texts concerned with horrific events. Naturally, it is imperative to be even more mindful of these issues with impressionable young readers than with mature ones ... the stakes are higher in writing for children."[40]

Scholars like Hasse point out how genres like the fairy tale offer a space to reinterpret a child's experience of traumatic environments. Intertextual in its connections to testimony, memoirs, and history museums, a fairy tale, in conjunction with the historical narrative, becomes a dialogic narrative. In addition to *Briar Rose*, Jane Yolen uses the tale of Rumplestiltskin in her story "Granny Rumple" to tell the story of an old Jewish woman. In *Devil's Arithmetic*, the protagonist Hannah, who is embarrassed by the oddities of her grandparents who survived the Holocaust, fantastically travels back in time to a Nazi concentration camp. Her experiences help her to forge a link with her familial past which, until then, was a tiresome burden that she was reluctant to inherit.

Lois Lowry's *Number the Stars* invokes fairy tales and their unreality at the time of a crisis that demands great courage: Annemarie, the young protagonist believes that "It was all imaginary, anyway—not real. It was only in fairy tales that people were called upon to be so brave, to die for one another. Not in real-life Denmark."[41] Yet the story of "Little Red Riding Hood" provides a model to Annemarie to make an active, though small intervention into the events beyond her control. Roberto Innocenti's *Rose Blanche*, a story about a girl who secretly delivers food to the inmates of a concentration camp, also alludes to "Little Red Riding Hood." Louise Murphy's *The True Story of Hansel and Gretel* reconfigures the story of Hansel and Gretel into a narrative of Nazi persecution and the abandonment of children during the Holocaust.

These novels underscore the function of fairy tales as carriers of collective cultural history whose narrative tropes shift and adapt to the changing epochs. The sibylline narrator is a repository of cultural memories sidelined and suppressed by the official narratives. Warner highlights the paradoxical nature of such retellings: "she (the sibyl) is exiled, even abandoned, her voice is muffled, even muted. Yet from inside the 'manacle' of the monument, she goes on speaking ... the blocked-up cave is unblocked in the imaginary world of her story, by the memory of her presence inside, the fantasy of her magic and knowledge."[42]

In Yolen's and Rushforth's texts, the fairy tale and its sibylline narrator not only provide space wherein the traumatic memories of the older generation can be expressed, but also offer a space and time wherein the young adult protagonists can confront the past and share the psychic burden. Postmemory in children's and young adult narrative is tied to ideas of mourning and community: it simultaneously forms and ruptures ideas of community, and it is as oriented to the future as it is to the past. Through the fragmented and repetitive stories told by the grandmother, the children traverse the psychic landscape of the Holocaust victims. The connection established between the generations becomes an injunction to remember, that which must not be forgotten. The multiple layers of storytelling in the two texts negotiate the distance—temporal as well as spatial—between the generations, between the trauma and horror of the past, which frequently resurfaces in the minds of the survivors, and the security and confidence of the younger generation. These intergenerational collaborations make it possible to preserve the individual memory, filling in gaps in history told by the statistics and official documents and safeguarding it from receding into the past.

NOTES

1. Jane Yolen, *Briar Rose* (New York: Tom Doherty, 1992), 25.
2. Cathy Caruth, *Trauma: Explorations in Memory* (Baltimore, MD: Johns Hopkins University Press, 1995), 7.
3. Marina Warner, *From the Beast to the Blonde: On Fairy Tales and Their Tellers* (New York: Farrar, Strauss and Giroux, 1994), 23.
4. Ibid., 11.
5. Marianne Hirsch, "The Generation of Postmemory," *Poetics Today* 29, no. 1 (Spring 2008): 104.
6. Yolen, *Briar Rose*, 42.
7. Ibid., 35.
8. Linda Belau, "Trauma and the Material Signifier," para. 1, *George Washington University*, http://pmc.iath.virginia.edu/text-only/issue.101/11.2belau.txt.
9. Geoffrey H. Hartman, "On Traumatic Knowledge and Literary Studies," *New Literary History* 26, no. 3 (Summer 1995): 537.
10. When Becca asks the meaning of "mist," Gemma seems to flounder at recalling the memory. The mist, for Gemma, is not a weather phenomena. She explains it as "A fog. An exhaust." See Yolen, *Briar Rose*, 43.
11. Peter Rushforth, *Kindergarten* (San Francisco: McAdam/Cage, 2006), 28.
12. Rushforth, *Kindergarten*, 9.
13. Ibid., 33.
14. Ibid., 67.
15. Ibid., 34.
16. Hirsch, "The Generation of Postmemory," 106.
17. Dori Laub, "Bearing Witness or the Vicissitudes of Listening," in *Testimony: Crises of Witnessing in Literature, Psychoanalysis and History*, ed. Shoshana Felman and Dori Laub (New York: Routledge, 1992), 66.
18. Laub, "Bearing Witness or the Vicissitudes of Listening," 67.
19. Caruth, *Trauma*, 5.
20. Warner, *From the Beast to the Blonde*, 23.

21. Laub, "Bearing Witness or the Vicissitudes of Listening," 57.

22. Ibid., 58.

23. Erin Heather McGlothlin, *Second-Generation Holocaust Literature: Legacies of Survival and Perpetration* (New York: Camden House, 2006), 10.

24. Cathy Caruth, *Unclaimed Experience: Trauma, Narrative, and History* (Baltimore, MD: Johns Hopkins University Press, 1996), 136.

25. Yolen, *Briar Rose*,141–42.

26. Ibid., 145.

27. Ibid., 106.

28. Ibid., 35.

29. Ibid., 132.

30. Rushforth, *Kindergarten*, 136.

31. Yolen, *Briar Rose*, 187.

32. Adrienne Kertzer, *My Mother's Voice: Children, Literature, and the Holocaust* (New York: Broadview Press, 2002), 67.

33. Yolen, *Briar Rose*, 182.

34. Ibid., 94.

35. Ibid., 197.

36. Ibid., 67.

37. Hamida Bosmajian, *Sparing the Child: Grief and the Unspeakable in Youth Literature About Nazism and the Holocaust* (New York: Routledge, 2002), xv–xvi.

38. Sue Vice, *Holocaust Fiction* (London and New York: Routledge, 2000), 8.

39. Literary or fictional representations of the Holocaust have evoked complex debates, most prominent being Adorno's insistence on the impossibility of poetry after Auschwitz. Elie Wiesel has famously asserted that "'the Holocaust as Literary Inspiration' is a contradiction in terms." See Elie Wiesel, "The Holocaust as Literary Inspiration," in *Dimensions of the Holocaust: Lectures at the Northwestern University*, by Elie Wiesel, Lucy S. Dawidowic, Dorothy Rabinowitz, and Robert McAfee Brown, anno. Elliot Lefkovitz (Evanston, IL: Northwestern University Press, 1977), 7. Hence, Vice begins her discussion of Holocaust fiction by invoking this notion of fictional narratives of Holocaust as "'scandalous,' an illegitimate supplement to real/valid narratives, the Testimony." See Vice, *Holocaust Fiction*, 1.

40. Naomi B. Sokoloff, review of *Representing the Holocaust in Children's Literature*, by Lydia Kokkola, *The Lion and the Unicorn* 30, no. 1 (Jan. 2006): 139.

41. Lois Lowry, *Number the Stars* (New York: Houghton Mifflin, 1989), 26.

42. Warner, *From the Beast to the Blonde*, 11.

The Devil's Arithmetic
and Time Travel
Truth and Memory
CAROL A. SENF

A relative newcomer to Holocaust studies as well as someone with little personal connection to the events of that period, I immersed myself in the Holocaust several years ago to prepare to teach a couple of classes on the subject. One class explored representations of the Holocaust in American film while the second, part of a Georgia Tech foreign study program in Italy, focused on the Holocaust in European film. Watching seemingly hundreds of films, I wondered about the choice of fantasy elements, most obviously time travel and fairy tale plot lines, in films depicting the real horror of the Holocaust like *Forbidden Games* (1952), *Life Is Beautiful* (1997), *Twilight Zone: The Movie* (1983), *The Devil's Arithmetic* (1999), and *Inglourious Basterds* (2009).

The Devil's Arithmetic is certainly not the only film to use fantasy elements in connection with the Holocaust. Ellen R. Weil, for example, observes in "The Door to Lilith's Cave: Memory and Imagination in Jane Yolen's Holocaust Novels" (an essay reproduced in this volume) that fantasy has often been used in literature about the Holocaust:

> Yolen is far from being the first author to use fantastic events in the context of a Holocaust narrative. Even Wiesel's autobiographical *Night* includes an unexplained incident in which a character experiences a prefiguring vision of death in the ovens; and other authors, from André Schwarz-Bart to David Grossman, have made fantastic conceits central to their novels. Sometimes this fantasy is legitimized by appeal to Jewish traditions— such as that of the thirty-six just men in Schwarz-Bart's *The Last of the Just* (1961) or the *dybbuk* who occupies an ex–Nazi's mind in Romain Gary's

The Dance of Genghis Cohn (1968). Sometimes, as in the work of Jakov Lind or Jerzy Kosinski, the "fantastic" primarily takes the form of breaking the narrative into surrealistic or phantasmagorical episodes which suggest the nightmarish fragmentation of consciousness in the victims.[1]

Even though this essay focuses primarily on the film version of *The Devil's Arithmetic,* the use of fantastic elements in conjunction with the Holocaust comes directly from Jane Yolen's novel of the same name.

While it is not the only film to use fantasy elements in connection with the Holocaust, what makes *The Devil's Arithmetic* so effective as a film designed to introduce children and young adults to the Holocaust is its juxtaposition of fantasy with scenes of realistic violence and horror and its willingness to tackle the fact that indifference to what happened to the Jews in Europe between 1933 and 1945 may be almost as dangerous as Holocaust denial. Unfortunately, indifference to the past—any past—seems to be part of the contemporary American character. Choosing to live in the present, we have also chosen to ignore the lessons of the past. Indeed, ignorance of the Holocaust poses a significant danger, as Alan Mintz, citing John Gross, observes: "Holocaust denial may or may not be a major problem in the future, but Holocaust ignorance, Holocaust forgetfulness, and Holocaust indifference are bound to be."[2]

While Jane Yolen, writer of the award-winning but somewhat controversial 1988 novel of the same name, noted on an earlier version of her personal website that the film was done "on a shoestring budget,"[3] *The Devil's Arithmetic* had the support of some of Hollywood's best talent. Robert Avrech, who wrote the screenplay, won an Emmy for "Outstanding Writing in a Children's Special," and director Donna Deitch won an Emmy for "Outstanding Directing in a Children's Special." Dustin Hoffman, who produced *The Devil's Arithmetic*, along with Mimi Rogers, introduces audiences to the controversial use of fantasy by mentioning the film's "magical elements of fable."[4] He adds immediately, however, that the Holocaust was real, not fantasy, and he carefully distinguishes the violence in this film from violence as entertainment. Most important to me, however, is the strategy of using fantasy to transport both character and audience from one real place and time to another real place and time and the question of how that use of fantasy works on viewers.

In addition to its use of fantasy elements, *The Devil's Arithmetic* also differs from other Holocaust films in its use of a contemporary American setting. While most Holocaust films concentrate on the grim reality of what happened in Europe during the period between roughly 1933 and 1945, *The Devil's Arithmetic* is framed by a present familiar to most American viewers. The tree-lined suburbs of New Rochelle, New York, where the protagonist Hannah Stern and her friends live, lacks the dramatic physical reminders of the Nazi era or of World War II that one might find in Germany, Poland, or even Italy. Therefore, despite the existence of survivors and a school curriculum that now includes the Holocaust as part of the study of World War II, it is possible to ignore the Holocaust as Judith Doneson observes in *The Holocaust in American Film* (1987), noting that Americans "have no tangible understanding of its dimensions because they have not experienced it."[5] Furthermore, as Mintz observes in *Popular Culture and the Shaping of Holocaust Memory in America* (2001), Americans are more likely to identify with the liberators than with the victims of Nazi persecution.

The Devil's Arithmetic further suggests that younger Americans are no longer interested in listening to stories of what happened. Protagonist Hannah Stern, for example, is surrounded by survivors but ignores her relatives who "were there" and confesses that she and her fellow students did not pay attention to a history teacher who wanted to teach them about the Holocaust. Played by Kirsten Dunst, a Christian of Swedish-German heritage who has described her own interest in the Holocaust and enthusiasm for Yolen as a writer,[6] Hannah is actively indifferent to her Jewish heritage. The film's opening shows her in a tattoo parlor, where she is considering getting a butterfly tattoo, and she later whines to her parents that she doesn't want to go to the Seder. The opening scene suggests how distanced Hannah is from her heritage, for, unlike Yolen and the others involved with the film, Hannah is thinking of a butterfly only as a pretty object, not of the connection of butterflies and the Holocaust.[7] Indeed, her desire for a tattoo distances her from her Jewish heritage in at least two ways: the fact that many of the people at her aunt's Seder table (their arms shown in extreme close up) bear the tattoos that had been given them in the camps and the fact that some Orthodox Jews regard tattoos as a mutilation of the body.

Through the spoiled Hannah, the film meets its American audience where we are: ignorant about the historical past, complacent about the present, and possibly numbed to the suffering of others. Casting Dunst and Brittany Murphy, already well known for their roles in *Interview with the Vampire* (Neil Jordan, 1994), *Little Women* (Gillian Armstrong, 1994), and *Clueless* (Amy Heckerling, 1995), also helps to make the film immediate rather than exotic. It appears initially to be a suburban fable of teenage rebellion rather than an exploration of the historical past.

Hannah reluctantly winds up accompanying her parents and younger brother from their very modern suburban home to her grandparents' apartment in the Bronx. The shift in setting and the presence of young Orthodox Jews outside her grandparents' building provide a gradual transition back to a somewhat earlier time, thereby preparing the audience for the more magical element of time travel that transports Hannah back to World War II Poland. In fact, the color palette changes from vivid colors in the tattoo parlor and the stark black and white of the Stern home to sepia tones in the apartment that remind the viewing audience of old photographs.

During the drive into the city, the film introduces an important element in Hannah's character, the fact that she is a storyteller, a skill she will use later to inspire her fellow inmates in the concentration camp. The apartment is also the home of her favorite relative, her Aunt Eva. A survivor, Eva has never talked to Hannah of her experience in the camp, though several other survivors at the Seder try to tell her. In fact, Eva reinforces the difficulty that Hannah and the viewing audience have of coming to terms with the Holocaust by noting, "This experience is so far from your world." The film, however, repeatedly reminds the audience that members of Hannah's family are survivors. As Lawrence Baron observes in "Not in Kansas Anymore: Holocaust Films for Children,"[8] *The Devil's Arithmetic* focuses during the Seder on the tattooed arms of Hannah's relatives and their friends, shots that "serve as a visual link between the slavery of Jews in ancient Egypt and their status as victims of Nazism."

Visibly bored with the ancient ritual of her ancestors' exodus from Egypt that seemingly has nothing to do with her modern life, Hannah disengages from the ceremony. Although her mother warns her not to drink too much Passover wine, the rebellious Hannah doesn't pay attention to her either. Nonetheless, the wine doesn't explain the magical element of time travel that occurs next. Asked to open the door for Elijah the prophet, Hannah steps into a small cottage in Poland. In this alternate reality (the only fantastic element is her mode of transport from one real place to another), she is identified as Chaya and learns that her parents had died of fever and that she had been very ill. Although Hannah initially attributes what happened to a dream or to the Passover wine, her cousin Rivkah says, "This is real." Indeed, despite the fantastic element of time travel, what happens to Hannah and Rivkah later that day is frighteningly real.

Rivkah takes her around the small Polish village and introduces her to the people there, reminding Hannah of names she has heard mentioned before, and the tour of the village reminds the film's audience of an entire culture that had been lost. Toward the end of the day, the girls, who are preparing to attend a wedding, have their picture taken. This photograph, which appears again in the camp and later in Aunt Eva's bedroom back in New York, is a further reminder that Hannah has been transported from one real place to another.

At the wedding, the film's audience is reminded of the date, October 1941. Although Poland fell to the Nazis in September 1939 and ghettos were established shortly thereafter, the full impact of the final solution in Poland began in Autumn 1941 when the Germans introduced mobile gas vans and various killing centers. When Hannah looks around the rural village and notices black-shirted Nazis and their military vehicles, she appears momentarily surprised. Nonetheless, she and her family and their friends proceed complacently to the wedding, which is interrupted by Nazis who collect the participants, force them into trucks, and transport them to a concentration camp. Here Hannah and Rivkah and the others are tattooed, and they and the audience see people wearing clothing that is marked by various symbols (see Figure 2), yellow stars but also red triangles, the film's reminder that, while Jews were singled out for annihilation, other groups, including Communists, were also persecuted during the Holocaust.

Although addressed to a young audience, *The Devil's Arithmetic* minces neither words nor images about the horrors of the camps. Inmates are harassed, starved, overworked, and hanged when they attempt to escape. In the barracks she shares with other women, Hannah comes into her own as a storyteller, sharing stories about superheroes and stories from *The Wizard of Oz* as well as stories about plentiful food and a future in America that seems equally fantastic to her starving and harassed companions. Rivkah reminds Hannah and the others that these stories about the future are important because it means that Jews will survive, go to America, and be safe there, and that "Your stories have been keeping us alive. They give us hope." Indeed the film reinforces the importance of both the memory of what is real, and of the fantastic elements of storytelling. Upon being taken away to the gas for attempting to conceal an infant, Rivkah's mother says to them, "You must remember." Another woman emphasizes that "We must fight to stay alive so we can tell our story." The cultural significance of storytelling, which Hannah had ignored back in New York, is further reinforced when the young women sacrifice to perform a Seder in the camp. Having watched their fellow inmates gassed or hanged for their rebellion, Hannah and the other young women relish the familiar story of an earlier rebellion and escape from persecution. Shortly after the Seder, these women are working in the fields when

Figure 2. Kirsten Dunst (right, as Hannah Stern) opposite Brittany Murphy (Rivkah) in *The Devil's Arithmetic* (1999).

Rivkah, visibly ill, is selected along with many of the other women. Quickly changing garments with Rivkah, Hannah enters the gas chamber carrying a younger child in her arms. Even as the gas pellets are falling on them, she tells about the wonders of a beautiful future in America, where Jews will be safe.

Dying in the gas chamber, Hannah awakes in her Aunt Eva's home, where she participates fully in the Seder and its aftermath, noting solemnly, "I will always remember what happened." Seeing a framed photograph in Eva's room, she recognizes the familiar faces of herself and Rivkah in the image that had been recorded prior to the wedding. Aunt Eva reveals that the one girl is Rivkah, the name by which Eva was known before coming to America. The other is her friend Chaya who died at Auschwitz and for whom Hannah had been named. Hannah also learns that Chaya means "life."

Even though *The Devil's Arithmetic* provides a happy ending to Chaya's story, allowing her to be reborn in a new land, the film also allows its audience to confront the reality of the Holocaust, a reality that was especially grim for children, as Paul A. Shapiro notes in his "Forward [*sic*]" to *Children and the Holocaust*[9]: "Although all Jews were marked for death, only between six and eleven percent of Jewish children survived versus thirty-three percent of adults." Shapiro adds that "over a million children were murdered in the Holocaust," including "Jewish children, Romani children, institutionalized children, and handicapped children."[10] Other essays in this volume explore the treatment or significance of children during the period.

Many people in the United States want to protect children today from the horrors of the past, and one thinks of the way the exhibits in the U.S. Holocaust Museum were constructed to prevent children from seeing all aspects of them. It can be argued, however, that children, especially older children, are not served by such protection. The awareness of what is real is something storytellers have always known. Certainly Homer knew it, as did the writer(s) of Exodus and the Grimm Brothers. Bruno Bettelheim, himself a Holocaust survivor, writes in *The Uses of Enchantment* (1977)[11] that children are already prepared to understand about the evil in the world. They already know from their experiences with their parents and other children that cruelty is often random and unexpected.

Even though Yolen's novel, on which the film is based, received praise and numerous awards, it was also criticized largely for its use of fantasy elements. Among the most prominent critics was Roger Sutton, associate editor of the *Bulletin of the Center for Children's Books*, who focused his editorial in the October 1988 issue on Yolen's novel.[12] Although Sutton objects to a number of things in *The Devil's Arithmetic*, including both Hannah's safe return and Yolen's use of the American expression, "Ready or not, here we come!" as Hannah prepares to enter the gas chamber, it's clear that Sutton believes that Yolen's use of the fantasy genre of time travel somehow trivializes the horrors of the Holocaust. Taking an opposite stance, science fiction writer Orson Scott Card defended the novel in his review column for *The Magazine of Fantasy and Science Fiction*,[13] writing of his anger that critical reviews might prevent children from finding the book in their library.

The controversy over Yolen's novel raises the issue of whether the use of fantasy does trivialize her important message about remembering and about using storytelling to communicate important truths with various audiences. Perhaps the real issue here is that adults are more uncomfortable with the use of fantasy than children are.

Children are familiar with the use of fantasy and are comfortable with the interplay of fantasy with ordinary life. Even before they can talk, babies are read Margaret Wise Brown's soothing *Goodnight, Moon*, which presents a loving rabbit family in a comfortable suburban setting. Aesop's Fables and Grimm's Fairy Tales include talking animals. Roald Dahl introduces youthful readers to witches and the BFG, and the Spider-Man comics suggest that nerdy Peter Parker has acquired spider traits.

There may be more substantial reasons for the use of fantasy than simple familiarity, however. Gary K. Wolfe argues in "Fantasy as Testimony" (reproduced in this volume) that using fantasy to present the Holocaust reduces the danger of overexposure to stories of horror and observes that "the repetitions of horrific scenes and actions weaken their impact."[14] He adds, citing Kathryn Hume's essay in that issue, "we begin to need novelty to experience the shock of horror afresh."[15]

Literary representations of the Holocaust must do more, however, than allow readers and viewers to be shocked and horrified. Exactly what that something is varies with the particular respondent. For example, Michael Bernard-Donals and Richard Glejzer write in "Teaching (after) Auschwitz: Pedagogy Between Redemption and Sublimity" about the most frequent responses among educators:

> We begin by asking a simple question: what do we think we teach when we write about, or give classes on, the Shoah? In the years since 1945 we have heard a lot of answers: so that we never forget; so that something like this could never happen again; so that we can heal or redeem the damage done to the world through anti–Semitism or racial hatred or any number of other symptoms of genocide.[16]

Because both the novel and film versions of *The Devil's Arithmetic* are aimed at a youthful audience, one might assume that both are designed to teach readers and viewers about the Holocaust and about a culture that is gone, and we might ask ourselves also whether either or both versions do what Bernard-Donals and Glejzer describe. Certainly the film concludes with the previously indifferent Hannah observing solemnly, "I will always remember what happened."

Although remembering the Holocaust must precede any kind of healing response, *The Devil's Arithmetic* is a veiled recommendation for some kind of action. Indifference to what was going on around them in 1941 is what allowed people to become victims. Indeed Yolen and her film adapters demonstrate Hannah's transformation from present-day complacency as well as her general ignorance of historical conditions to a greater commitment to her family and her culture. The transformation may serve to parallel a similar complacency in her predecessors. One thinks of the ordinary Germans and Poles who sat back and watched their neighbors taken away, and of the *Judenrat* who participated in the destruction of their culture as well. Hannah's indifference to the stories that her relatives want to tell her is very similar to the indifference of people whose general comfort blinded them to the suffering of others. As Hannah's eyes are opened, members of the American film audience share in her understanding as we too are swept out of our comfortable lives into a past we can know only through history books and commercial films.

In the post–World War II period, writers and filmmakers have approached the past in multiple ways. German writers in particular have focused more on the dangers of forgetting the Nazi past. For example, Alf Lüdtke speaks specifically of West Germany in "'Coming to Terms with the Past': Illusions of Remembering, Ways of Forgetting Nazism in West Germany" and suggests that, during the post-war years, most West Germans "colluded in forgetting if not repressing those recollections of fascism that might recall its violent and murderous practices."[17] Lüdtke adds that it was especially important to forget "one's own role and activity during fascism ... their own acceptance, support, and complicity."[18] Since the post-war period, however, Germans have been more interested in coming to terms with their past ("*Vergangenheitsbewältigung*").[19] Indeed Moishe Postone observes in "The Holocaust and the Trajectory of the Twentieth Century" that since "the 1960s and early 1970s, the Holocaust in particular, and issues of historical memory in general, have become increasingly central to public discourse."[20]

By contrast, people in the United States have fewer immediate reasons to wrestle with their past. In fact, one of the best discussions of the uniquely American response to the Holocaust is found in Judith E. Doneson's study, *The Holocaust in American Film*. Doneson begins her study with a series of questions: "How and why has the Holocaust entered into the popular imagination of the American people to such a degree that it seems to have become almost a part of the American experience?"[21] She follows that question with the observation that because most Americans did not personally experience the Holocaust, it "enters America as a 'refugee' event. Following the traditional path of refugees, the event had to be shaped and molded in order to make it comprehensible to an American public."[22] Her explanation brings us back to the larger question of this essay, the use of fantasy to depict the horror of the Holocaust. While Doneson doesn't speak of fantasy specifically, she does explain that the response of most Americans has—quite literally—been mediated, something that Americans have confronted at a distance rather than experienced:

> The immediate impact of the Final Solution came largely through the media. Camera teams filmed the horrors that remained of the concentration camps after the liberation—piles of bodies, crematoria, stacks of

personal possessions—and the skeletal survivors. It was the shock of seeing these pictures and reading accounts in the press of what was discovered in the camps that brought the reality of the Holocaust to the attention of the public.[23]

Those dramatic images brought the truth of the Holocaust home to people who hadn't experienced it, and it remains important to teach young people about the Holocaust today and to use every method at our disposal. The character of Hannah is a dramatic reminder that twentieth and twenty-first century Americans are too interested in their own present lives to care about what happened a half century (or many centuries) ago.

The Devil's Arithmetic does one more important thing. By using novelty, most obviously time travel and fairy tales, it transports viewers back in time to watch what happened when people denied painful truths. It begins where the audience is, comfortable in a world where one encounters violence only in television or in film, transports them to Poland on the eve of the Holocaust, and gradually introduces the full horror of the camps. At the same time, it demonstrates that the people who experienced the Holocaust were human beings very much like themselves. While some were heroic, many others simply wanted to live their lives unencumbered. Each was a distinct individual, and that individuality is what is lost when we see only the photographs of victims whose suffering has robbed them of individuality.

Only through magic is a significantly wiser Hannah allowed to return to her family's Seder with a greater appreciation of what her relatives had gone through and of a village culture in Eastern Europe that had been lost. Reborn in her Aunt Eva's home, she participates fully in the Seder and its aftermath, concluding, "I will always remember what happened." The film's use of fantasy elements provides a contemporary American audience with a fresh way of seeing the Holocaust and a caution concerning what happens to the overly complacent. Because Americans tend to be both optimistic and forward-looking, there is danger that, as Holocaust survivors grow old and die, we will forgot them and their stories and ignore the fact that such things could happen again. *The Devil's Arithmetic* addresses that danger by the judicious use of fantasy.

NOTES

1. Ellen R. Weil, "The Door to Lilith's Cave: Memory and Imagination in Jane Yolen's Holocaust Novels," in *Journal of the Fantastic in the Arts* 5, no. 2 (1993): 90–104.

2. Alan Mintz, *Popular Culture and the Shaping of Holocaust Memory in*

America (Seattle: University of Washington Press, 2001), 131. Mintz is quoting John Gross, "Hollywood and the Holocaust," *New York Review of Books* 16, no. 3 (Feb. 3, 1994): 3–5.

3. Jane Yolen, "The Devil's Arithmetic," *JaneYolen.com*, accessed May 21, 2013, http://janeyolen.com/works/the-devils-arithmetic/.

4. Hoffman's comments are from the introduction to the DVD of the film. *The Devil's Arithmetic*, dir. Donna Deitch (Showtime, 1999).

5. Judith Doneson, *The Holocaust in American Film* (Philadelphia: The Jewish Publication Society, 1987), 6.

6. The Dunst interview was originally linked from Jane Yolen's blog (http://janeyolen.com/works/the-devils-arithmetic/); that interview is no longer available anywhere so far as I can find.

7. Another Hannah, Hana Volavkava published children's drawings and poems in *I Never Saw Another Butterfly: Children's Drawings and Poems from Terezin Concentration Camp 1942–1944* (New York: Schocken Books, 1993). Dr. Elizabeth Kubler-Ross wrote about her visit to the children's barracks at Maidanek concentration camp in Poland after World War II, where she saw hundreds of butterflies drawn on the wall. In *The Wheel of Life, a Memoir of Living and Dying* (New York: Scribner, 1998), she writes that listening to hundreds of terminally ill patients helped her understand that the butterflies were important to the prisoners in the camps because they reminded the prisoners of the process of death and dying.

8. Lawrence Baron, "Not in Kansas Anymore: Holocaust Films for Children," *The Lion and the Unicorn* 27 (2003): 402.

9. Paul A. Shapiro, "Forward [*sic*]," *Children and the Holocaust: Symposium Presentations* (Washington, D.C.: United States Holocaust Memorial Museum Center for Advanced Holocaust Studies, 2004), i.

10. Ibid.

11. Bruno Bettelheim, *The Uses of Enchantment: The Meaning and Importance of Fairy Tales* (New York: Vintage, 1977).

12. Roger Sutton, "Editorial," *Bulletin of the Center for Children's Books* (Oct. 1988): 23.

13. Orson Scott Card, "Books to Look For," *The Magazine of Fantasy and Science Fiction* 74–76 (April 1989): 36–39.

14. Gary K. Wolfe, "Fantasy as Testimony," *The Journal of the Fantastic in the Arts* 5, no. 2 (1993): 8.

15. Ibid.

16. Michael Bernard-Donals and Richard Glejzer, "Teaching (After) Auschwitz: Pedagogy Between Redemption and Sublimity," in *Witnessing the Disaster: Essays on Representation and the Holocaust*, ed. Michael Bernard-Donals and Richard Glejzer (Madison: University of Wisconsin Press, 2003), 245.

17. Alf Lüdtke, "'Coming to Terms with the Past': Illusions of Remembering, Ways of Forgetting Nazism in West Germany," *The Journal of Modern History* 65, no. 3 (Sept. 1993): 554.

18. Ibid.

19. This highly specific term comes from Martin Swales, "Sex, shame and guilt: reflections on Bernhard Schlink's *Der Vorleser* (*The Reader*) and J.M. Coettzee's *Disgrace*," *Journal of European Studies* 33 (March 2003): 7–22. The word in German combines "*Vergangenheit*" or past and "*Bewältigung*" or coming to terms with the past. Although the general term can describe the attempt to grapple with any element of the past, it is used most frequently to describe the German attempt to come to terms with the atrocities perpetrated during the Third Reich.

20. Moishe Postone, "The Holocaust and the Trajectory of the Twentieth Century," in *Catastrophe and Meaning: The Holocaust and the Twentieth Century*, ed. Moishe Postone and Eric Santner (Chicago: University of Chicago Press, 2003), 97.

21. Judith E. Doneson, *The Holocaust in American Film* (Philadelphia: The Jewish Publication Society, 1987), 6.

22. Ibid.

23. Ibid., 6–7.

A Holocaust Education in Reverse

Stephen King's "The Summer of Corruption: Apt Pupil"

LEON STEIN

Underneath this reality in which we live and have our being,
another and altogether different reality is concealed.
  If you gaze long enough into an abyss, the abyss will gaze
back into you.

—Friedrich Nietzsche

Stephen King is the most popular writer of horror and fantasy alive today. Over the last fifteen years, eighty million copies of his books have been printed worldwide.[1] Some of his novels have been made into equally popular movies. He has his avid admirers and contemptuous detractors. But he is a figure to be reckoned with, for by reaching his huge audience he is helping to shape their outlook and their feelings, even their view of reality. This is especially important with regard to the possible impact of King's portrayal of the Holocaust, one of the few real events he deals with in his shorter works.

His one work directly connected with the Holocaust is one of four novellas in a collection entitled *Different Seasons*. It is called "The Summer of Corruption: Apt Pupil." Although the collection appeared in 1982, this story was written in 1975. King spent two weeks of intensive effort writing this story, and later claimed that he had worked harder on it than anything

149

he had written up until that point. Indeed, "Apt Pupil" is the longest of the four novellas, almost two hundred pages. Perhaps King felt that only a substantially developed story could begin to do justice to his subject.

King's concern with Nazism was underscored in an interview in *Playboy* with Eric Norden in June of 1983. King's views about the Nazis and Nazism are worth quoting in some detail:

> Well, the nature of evil is a universal preoccupation for any horror writer, and Nazism is probably the most dramatic incarnation of evil. After all, what was the Holocaust but the almost literal recreation of hell on earth, an assembly-line inferno replete with fiery furnaces and human demons pitchforking the dead into lime pits? Millions have also died in the Gulag and in such places as Cambodia, of course, but the crimes of the communists have resulted from the perversion of an essentially rational and apollonian nineteenth century philosophy, while Nazism was something new and twisted, and when it exploded into the German scene in the twenties, I can see how it exercised a dangerously compelling appeal. That werewolf in us is never far from the surface, and Hitler knew how to unleash and feed it. So yes, if I had been in Germany in the early thirties, I supposed I might have been attracted to Nazism. But I've got a pretty sure feeling that by 1935 or 1936 I'd have recognized the nature of the beast and would have gotten out. Of course, unless you're in a similar situation like that you never know how you'd respond. But you can see echoes of the mad Dionysian engine that powered the Nazis all around you.[2]

King sees some of these tendencies in some of the rock groups of the past decade that let loose "just the wild frenzied mob emotions" of the Nürnberg rallies. He is concerned with the effects of such groups on young people.

From the standpoint of a historian on the Holocaust, King's observations contain some valuable insights on the unique, extreme intentionality of the Nazis, on the assembly-line methods of killing during the Holocaust, and on the charismatic appeal of Hitler and the Nazis to the German people. However, such characterizations of the Nazis as "human demons," "twisted," and "werewolves" would be dismissed today as inaccurate and convenient clichés.

Still, the history of the Holocaust has inspired a literature of fantasy and horror that has sometimes helped to communicate the immediacy of the Holocaust to the reader, and has raised some important issues that will not rest. Whether a popular work such as King's novella has done so is an important issue in its own right. "Apt Pupil" does live up to its title, theme, and significance. However, it is different from the majority of King's work, as well as other works of fantasy dealing with the Holocaust in the past decade—Lisa Goldstein's *The Red Magician* (1982), Bari Wood's best-selling *The Tribe* (1981), Dan Simmons's massive *Carrion Comfort* (1989), and Jane Yolen's fine evocation of the Holocaust for young people, *The Devil's Arithmetic* (1988). What makes "Apt Pupil" different from all these works is a pointed absence of spirituality and the supernatural. There are no golems, demons, ghosts, vampires, and hauntings to be found here, none of the traditional trappings of horror and fantasy. The subject of King's novella even contradicts his own "Afterword" to *Different Seasons*: "I hope you liked [the stories], reader, that they did for *you* what every good story should do—make you forget the real stuff weighing on your mind for a little while and take you away to a place you've never been. It's the most amiable sort of magic I know."[3]

This statement cannot apply to "Apt Pupil." For the backdrop of the story is based exactly on the horrifying "real stuff" of recent history, hardly capable of causing a feeling of "amiable magic." Still, the Holocaust can sometimes take one away "to a place you've never been." Its often unimaginable horror is unbearable because it *actually* happened. In the words of Michiko Kakutani, "The Holocaust represents the first time in history that reality exceeded the imagination."[4] The literature of the Holocaust is vital to prod the imagination, to evoke and confront an often unbearable reality. King states his goal as a writers: "I've tried as hard as I can, always, to give good weight."[5] In "Apt Pupil," the weight of the past provides a weight of its own. But it is definitely not an "amiable sort of magic."[6]

"Apt Pupil" is the story of a four-year (summer of 1974–summer of 1978) association, in King's words, between "an old man and a young boy locked up in a gruesome relationship based on mutual parasitism."[7] Joseph Reino, a perceptive students of King's work, considers the title "Summer of Corruption" to be a variation on the "Winter of our discontent" in the opening line of Shakespeare's *Richard III*.[8] The corruptible "apt pupil" in the summer of 1974 is Todd Bowden, a thirteen-year old all–American, towheaded, WASP boy fro the affluent suburbs of Los Angeles, California. Todd's name is a variant of *Tod,* the German word for death. Bowden suggests the German word *Boden,* meaning earth, nature, rootedness. Todd's corruption actually starts when he reads about the death camps in *Men's Action,* a pulp magazine that sensationalizes the horrors of the Holocaust. His fifth-grade teacher Mrs. Anderson had talked to the students about finding "YOUR GREAT INTEREST." Todd has found his. He writes a paper about the death camps, receives an unheard of "A+," and begins an almost obsessive interest in the lurid particulars of the Holocaust. This coincides with his ambition to be a detective.

Todd's interests become translated into reality when he is traveling in a local bus and spots by chance a major Nazi death-camp commandant. He recognizes that "blood-fiend of Patin" concentration camp from his photo in the magazine. The Nazi's name is Arthur Dussander. Todd goes to Dussander's little bungalow after having obtained Dussander's finger-prints from his mailbox with a detective kit. He pretends to deliver a news-paper, introduces himself, and proceeds to confront the commandant, who is now a seedy old man of seventy-six.

Dussander professes surprise, insisting that his name is "Denker" and that Todd is gravely mistaken about his identity. Again, King indulges in some interesting word symbolism here. In the German language *denker* could mean a "thinker" in the sense of a clever person, in this case applying to one who has skillfully concealed his identity and managed to elude his Israeli pursuers. The word could also apply to one who has thought things through, and this could certainly be said for Denker who traveled the stan-dard escape routes of Nazi war criminals from Germany to South America and sometimes to the United States. More significantly, the word could be associated with the nineteenth century characterization of the Germans as a country of *Dichter und Denker* (poets and thinkers). For in its terri-fying way, the Holocaust was a product of a system of German thought, of *Denker*.

In a clever stroke of irony, King is suggesting that Todd's initial Amer-ican innocence can, under certain circumstances lead down the road to self-destruction and death (*Tod*), and that the suave and "cultured" Euro-pean Dussander-Denker can conceal a murderous philosophy. "Apt Pupil" is not only an investigation into the mutual corruption of an all–American teenager and an old Nazi war criminal, but an exposure of the ruinous encounter of the worst elements of twentieth century American and Euro-pean culture.

A gaggle of empty American clichés and the superficial icons of American culture come under attack by Stephen King throughout the novella. The only ways in which Todd can interpret reality are through the familiar images of American pop culture. Thus, when Todd first encounters Dussander he thinks that "the man looked like a cross between Albert Einstein and Boris Karloff."[9] As for Dussander's accent, "It didn't sound ... well, authentic. Colonel Klink on *Hogan's Heroes* sounded more like a Nazi than Dussander did."[10] For Todd, the media is truly the image of reality. Todd's use of slang clichés is equally empty and annoying. He confronts Dussander with a detailed account of the Nazi's gruesome deeds but admits "I really groove on all that concentration camp stuff."[11] For King, the empty clichés and the shallowness of American popular culture can be a form of the "banality of evil," perhaps a counterpart of the euphemisms the Nazis used when they performed their evil deeds.

Todd decides to blackmail Dussander. He will not expose him as long as the old man recites, in the words of Todd, all the "goosby stuff." For that is Todd's only version of the Holocaust. As so, day after day, night after night, Dussander relates the stories of the gas chambers, the medical experiments, the tortures and interrogations he conducted, the ceaseless killings. All this, while Todd smiles and consumes chocolate ring-dings. We learn that Dussander "sent thirty-five hundred people a day into the ovens," having succeeded in his career in carrying out the murder of seven hundred thousand Jews, and having merited SS chief Heinrich Himmler's accolade as an "efficiency expert." Still, though awed by Dussander's account, Todd is disappointed by the former commandant's portrayal of the banal appearance of Nazi murders. True to form, Dussander justifies his crimes by arguing that he was only "given orders and directives which he followed." He also states that he did no worse than what the Americans were doing in Vietnam. King is right to have Dussander mouth these words; Nazi war criminals and their apologists have used these arguments since 1945.

As Todd listens to Dussander's account and gets to know him, Todd's interest in Nazi atrocities becomes a full-fledged obsession. The relationship between Todd and Dussander becomes a bizarre symbiosis. They do not trust each other, but are tied to their increasing immersion in evil. By failing to expose the Nazi and by developing a perverse fascination and even an identification with the perpetrators of the Holocaust, Todd becomes a party to Dussander's past.

As Dussander unearths his former existence, he (like the overwhelming majority of Nazi war criminals) expresses no remorse whatsoever. He also boasts of his disdain for the inaction and stupidity of the Americans in permitting Nazi war criminals to exist under their noses. This is certainly a reflection of King's views about American laxity toward Nazi war criminals in the sixties and seventies.

Over the next year, Todd's increasing corruption becomes manifest in a slippage of his grades and social life, frequent lurid nightmares, and an increasing dependence on Dussander. Todd Bowden and Arthur Dussander become locked in a mutual death grip. Each considers the possibility of killing the other, but decides that the possible consequences are too risky. Both would be too vulnerable to discovery. Todd explains his prolonged absences from home to his parents by claiming that he is helping lonely, old Mr. Denker by reading *Robinson Crusoe* and *Tom Jones* to him.

As Todd reopens the past, Dussander begins to experience a nostalgia for his days as an SS killer. When Todd presents the old Nazi with an SS officer's uniform, Dussander puts it on. This seems to trigger Dussander's return to his former life:

> Todd felt like the sorcerer's apprentice, who had brought the brooms to life, but who had not possessed enough wit to stop them once they got started. The old man living in genteel poverty was gone. Dussander was there. for the first time the corpses in the ditches and the crematorias seemed to take on their own reality for Todd.[12]

Todd's dreams become ambivalent. In one he is a victim chosen for the gas chambers by Dussander and in another he is wearing an SS uniform. Dussander is increasingly in control of Todd.

In early 1975 Todd's parents invite Dussander to dinner. Indulging in his own Hitlerian "big lie," Dussander claims to have been in the regular German army reserves during the Second World War and blames the disasters of the Germany and the eternal shame of the camps on "one madman in particular, of course"—a cliché repeated ten years later by President Ronald Reagan on his visit to Germany's Bitburg military cemetery.

Todd Bowden's parents, ostensibly middle-class, educated people, are portrayed by King as shallow, hopelessly optimistic, and naïve. When Todd's father remarks that the villagers who lived in the surrounding areas of Auschwitz thought that the death camps was a sausage factory, Dussander can only marvel at their ignorance and naïveté.

One of the subsidiary themes of "Apt Pupil" is the failure of American parenting. Unlike some future serial killers who were abused and abandoned as children, Todd's upbringing has been comfortable, but amazingly empty. Todd's father thinks he can "read his son like a book." His mother thinks her son has turned out wonderfully. His parents pride themselves on raising their son "without all those needless guilts." They never spanked him because "it raises more problems than it solves." Todd's father voices the pseudoprofundity that "life is a tiger that you have to grab by the tail and if you don't know the nature of the beast it will eat you up alive."[13] It is disgustingly obvious that Todd's parents are completely out of touch with their son. Says Joseph Reino,

> King is not saying that the clichés are wrong but rather that benevolent philosophies reduced to thoughtless aphorisms and innocuous clichés are utterly powerless against the boy's adamantine malevolence.[14]

Dussander has his own more sophisticated European clichés, but they are far more dangerous and sinister. Upon being offered a second glass of mediocre cognac by Scott's mother, Dussander graciously declines, saying, "One must never outdo the sublime."[15]

When Todd's grades plummet his father angrily reads Todd's report card, accidentally spelling out the word *Dad*, perhaps unwittingly revealing the kind of twisted paternalism Dussander has exercised over his son. Dussander shrewdly strengthens his control over Todd by helping the boy to study properly to improve his grades. Todd realizes what is happening:

> "I wish they *would* hang you," Todd muttered, "...I was crazy to get mixed up with you in the first place."
> "No doubt," Dussander said, and smiled thinly. "But you *are* mixed up with me."[16]

Filled with a new boldness, Dussander volunteers to pose as Todd's grandfather, and to speak with Todd's guidance counselor Ed French, about the boy's problems. Dussander reasons that if he could elude that dangerous hunter of Nazi, Simon Wiesenthal, he could easily fool an American schoolteacher. Like Todd's parents, Ed French is depicted as a superficial person who wears Keds sneakers to his job to ingratiate himself with the boys. He falls for Dussander's story about Todd's family problems as the cause of the boy's bad grades, his gullibility reinforced by the fact that the elderly "Mr. Bowden" reminds him of the venerable television character Lord Peter Wimsey. If a school guidance counselor uses the figures of popular culture for his frame of reference, what hope could there be for his students?

The now rejuvenated Dussander reverts to his former existence. He captures a stray cat and roasts it alive in his oven. He them obtains a German shepherd puppy from the dog pound. The dog pound supervisor tells Dussander what will happen to the unclaimed animals after sixty days:

> "We give them gas. It's very humane. They don't feel a thing."
> "No," Mr. Denker said, "I'm sure they don't."[17]

Todd begins to pay his price for his immersion in evil. He has his first wet dream in which his sexual climax coincides with his electrocution of a young girl. In his 1983 *Playboy* interview, King explained why he included that episode: "That was consonant with the kid's twisted character." Todd explains his dream this way: "*This is what they can't show in those magazines about the war he thought, but it's there, just the same.*"[18]

Perverted fantasy beings to displace reality for Todd. Dussander senses a change in Todd, and begins to blackmail the boy by telling him that he has hidden accounts of his meetings with Todd in a safe-deposit box. Again drawing on the images of American popular culture, Todd can only picture his predicament in the following way: "He thought of a cartoon character with an anvil suspended over its head."[19]

By now Todd and Dussander have reinforced each other sufficiently to the point where they dream and behave identically. It is no accident that to confirm their own existence they choose to kill "winos." For the teenager and the Nazi the derelicts have becomes, in the noted words of Holocaust scholar Richard Rubenstein, "superfluous people, not worthy of life."[20] This also extends to others. When the subject of the American blacks comes up in a conversation, Dussander slyly remarks to Todd: "Oh yes, the *Schwarzen*.... For twenty years this country has worried about the *Schwarzen*. But we know the solution don't we, boy?"[21]

Todd kills the derelicts near a freeway, while Dussander lures them to his home, kills them there, and disposes of them in his basement. It is now 1977, three years after that first "summer of corruption." Todd is now sixteen and has killed four more derelicts. But in that space of time, he has also become an All-Conference football players, wins the American Legion Patriotic Essay Contest, and will soon be selected as salutatorian of his class. He has integrated killing into his normal existence.

The teenager and the Nazi quickly speed to their doom once Dussander suffers a heart attack while dragging his latest victim down to the basement. Todd rushes to Dussander's home, telling his parents than Dussander has received a letter from his relatives in Germany. Todd panics because Dussander is still holding the "anvil" over him. In addition, Todd is nonplussed by the fact that Dussander has never called him by his name, having referred to him only as "boy." This indicates, of course, that Dussander past has conditioned him to have contempt for people and to view them as things.

"Apt Pupil" began with a chance meeting in sunny California when Todd spotted Dussander on a bus. It ends with another unlikely, yet conceivable encounter when Dussander is placed in a hospital bed alongside Morris Heisel, a survivor of the Patin camp who had broken his back on the same day Dussander had suffered his heart attack. Having revealed something about the mentality of the perpetrators, King devotes three vivid, detailed pages to the fate of the victim, Morris Heisel, tattoo number P499965214.

Heisel's wife and children died in the gas chambers and the crematoria of Patin, and Morris has lost his Jewish faith. When he looks at Dussander, memories of the camp begin flooding back. And when he reads a newspaper headline about the recent killings of the derelicts, his memory is jump-started and he recognizes Dussander's voice and his distinctive turns of phrase: "The voice of an urbane man: A cultured man. But there was a threat in the voice."[22]

Meanwhile, Todd's school counselor sees Lord Peter Wimsey on television, is reminded of Todd's grandfather who visited him, and calls Todd's real grandfather to inquire about Todd's progress. The old man hears Ed French's story and remarks, ominously, "The past don't rest so easy. Why else do people study history?"[23]

Now Dussander is tortured by a dream of the death camp inmates breaking down a fence and chasing him. At that point he awakens to the voice of Weiskopf, an Israeli hunter of Nazis standing over him. This is no dream. Dussander's worst fears have been realized. Like some of his Nazi associates, Dussander commits suicide by overdosing on sleeping pills, wishing he could leave a note for the "boy" whom he has come to respect. As he drifts into oblivion, he consoles himself with one of Todd's pat American phrases that he is "pegging out" and foiling Morris Heisel and his captors. But a last-minute thought of everlasting dreams terrifies him: "In sudden terror he tried to struggle awake. It seemed that hands were reaching eagerly out of the bed to grab him, hands with hungry fingers."[24]

Joseph Reino traces this image to the passage of the wrathful souls of the River Styx in the Seventh Canto of Dante's *Inferno*, and the dream reference to Hamlet's famous fear ("for in this sleep of death what dreams may come").[25] Could this be an example of what a *Time* reviewer, Paul Gray, called an example of King's technique of "plugging directly into the prefabricated images ... of post-literate prose"?[26]

By now the Israeli agent Wieskopf, and his American counterpart, Richler, are on to Todd. They have found his fingerprints in Dussander's apartment. To cinch their case a derelict walks into the police station and identifies the picture of the all-star football player and class salutatorian as the person he saw fleeing from the scene of the murder of a fellow wino.

When the story of the exposed Nazi war criminal and serial killer hits the papers, Todd's counselor Ed French realizes that Todd's fake grandfather did not look like Lord Peter Wimsey at all! Ed drives up to Todd's home to confront him about his fake grandfather and doctored report cards. "More and more it seemed to Ed that there was a vicious downside of American life ... a morality that grew cloudier every year."[27]

He asks Todd, "How did it happen?"

"'Oh, one thing just followed another,' Todd said, and picked up the .30-.30."[28]

After killing Ed French, Todd wore "the ecstatic smile of tow headed boys going off to war."[29] Equipped with four hundred rounds of ammunition, he goes to his favorite place above the freeway: "It was five hours and almost dark before they took him down."[30]

When "Apt Pupil" first appeared it was criticized on many grounds. Some reviewers called the writing clumsy and overpadded. King himself singled out his story as an example of "literary elephantiasis." Other criticisms were aimed at the simplistic crudity of the characters, the multitude of unconvincing situations, and the far-fetched plot.

King defenders such as Clive Barker, Joseph Reino, and Douglas Winter take these arguments and turn them around. To Paul Gray's criticism that Todd's sole perceptions of reality through the images of popular culture "spare readers the task of puzzling them out" and "short-circuit though," Reino and Winter counter that King intended this as an attack on the shallow perceptions, fake images, and "pseudoprofundities" of American popular culture. The further argue that "Apt Pupil" also pillories empty American educational philosophies, middle-class parenting practices, and the "superb American self-confidence" that Dussander accuses Todd of causing their mutual undoing. Joseph Reino remarks, "What distinguishes King from a mere hack writers grinding out novels for popularity of a fast back is that in 'Apt Pupil' he himself never gets self-deceived by the clichés of his own conceptions."[31] One study called the story "a scathing indictment of modern society."[32]

A more serious issue that must be raised whenever a work of popular fiction about the Holocaust appears, is this: Has the Holocaust been sensationalized and trivialized? In one important respect, the story is an object lesson in what can happen when the Holocaust is approached, certainly in Todd's case, as an endless accumulation of horrors and tortures. In a recent work about King's shorter fiction, Collins and Engbretson argue that "King's story ... avoids being exploitative by its close character analysis—both of the former death-camp commander and the putatively innocent young boy.... The story asks not, 'Who corrupted who?', but 'How did they corrupt each other, and why?'"[33]

Another example that would seem to show that this work rises above mere trivialization is the extended discussion between the Israeli and American government officials at the end of the book. It is they who take over the task of narration at the end of the story:

> Weiskopf comments, "Do you suppose, I ask myself, that the very atrocities in which Dussander took part formed the basis of some attraction between them? Maybe there is something about what the German did that exercises

a deadly fascination over us—something that that opens the catacombs of the imagination. Maybe part of our dread of horror comes from a secret knowledge that under that right or wrong set of circumstances, we ourselves would be will to build such places and staff them?.... Maybe we know that under the right set of circumstances the things that live in the catacombs would be glad to crawl out. And what do you think they would look like? Like mad Fuhrers with forelocks and shoe-polish mustaches heiling all over the place?".... "I think most of them would look like ordinary accountants," Weiskopf said. "Little mind-men with graphs and flow-charts, and electronic calculators, all ready to start maximizing the kill rations for that *next* time they could perhaps kill twenty or thirty millions instead of six. And some of them might look like Todd Bowden.[34]

In his novel *Firestarter* King developed this train of thought: "Bureaucrats running out of control.... And they love their fucking work!" And in an interview: "The thing that worries me more than monolithic authority is that there may be no such thing, and that if you could meet Hitler at the end, you would find this harried little bureaucrat saying, 'Where are my maps? Where are my armies? Gee whiz, gang, what happened?'"[35]

These statements reveal that "Apt Pupil" was written in the shadow of the American crises of the nineteen seventies—the Vietnam War, the Watergate affair, the arms race, and the sense of drift and malaise that gripped the country.

But the question remains, does the dialogue between Weiskopf and Richler contain the very "pseudoprofundities" (albeit on a higher scale) that King seems to condemn in the characters of "Apt Pupil?" From a literary standpoint, the implications of the dialogue are suspenseful and even terrifying. But again, from the standpoint of the historian of the Holocaust, King's conclusions contain only part of the truth and some half-truths as well. It is true that the Holocaust could not have been perpetrated without hordes of bureaucrats. And King is correct in speculating that if it happened once, it could happen again, and in a supposedly "civilized," industrialized country such as the United States. The story has made some frightening points that it *could* happen here. But Hitler was much more than a "harried little bureaucrat." He was a charismatic dictator who, especially in his role of ordering the Holocaust and seeing that it was carried out, retained his monolithic fanaticism and authority. Hitler took the question of the Jews personally. Nothing mattered more to him than their complete extermination. To his credit, King was embarking on an important theme when he wrote "Apt Pupil." He wrote his story at a time when the magnitude of the Holocaust was being discovered by American culture and when there was renewed interest in the event. But because a *real* event was the backdrop of his story, King, rather than Todd, should have done the real research on the Holocaust.

Another crucial issue that arise from the concluding dialogue of "Apt Pupil" is whether the study of the Holocaust as a school subject is worth the intellectual, emotional, and moral challenge it offers. Implicit in King's story are two very important points. First, that if the Holocaust is approached only from the standpoint of harping on countless morbid and frightening atrocities, it can, under certain circumstances, exert a meaningless and dangerous fascination—particular if the only means of learning about it are trashy and exploitative magazines and films. Second, it raises the question of *how* and *why* the Holocaust should be studied. At the outset of "Apt Pupil," Todd was

> trying to cope with the idea that *they had really done those things*, that somebody *had really done those things*, and that *somebody had let them do those things* ... 6,000,000: That's twice as many people as there are in L.A.[36]

One could conclude from King's story that the Holocaust was not studied in schools in the 1970s. What were the values expressed by Todd in his A+ paper on the death camps? What books did he consult? Why was Mrs. Anderson so impressed with it? From his later behavior, it is likely that Todd studied the inhumanity of the perpetrators to the exclusion of the humanity of the victims, to the exclusion of the hows, the whys, and the significance of the events. Had he perhaps read *The Diary of Anne Frank*, or even an account written by Morris Heisel, Todd's view of the Holocaust would probably have been different.

Had "Apt Pupil" been a story built around a standard horror theme, it could be interpreted as an object lesson in the dangers of reading horror fiction, just as Gustave Flaubert's *Madame Bovary* has been viewed as the destruction of a young married woman who has been raised on escapist romantic novels, the nineteenth century equivalent of today's Harlequin Romances. But the Holocaust *happened*, and therein lies both its awesome presences *and* the need to face it with intelligence and sensitivity.

"Apt Pupil" threatens to founder on two contradictions that are built into the novella. First, simply because it is entrapped in a straitjacket of popular horror fiction, it runs the risk of becomes fixated on the very atrocities that corrupt Todd and reactivate Dussander. The story of Morris Heisel and his family calls for more in-depth detail, as the Holocaust itself. But that might have defeated the storyline of the novella. Second, and most importantly, King has used the appealing forms of popular culture to expose the dangers of deriving a vision of reality (in this case the crucial reality of the Holocaust) from a popular culture unaided by serious reading, thinking, and feeling. Some literary critics are aware of King's good intentions here. *But is his audience?* Will they overlook King's message and, like Todd, be carried away by the shocking details? More dangerously, will they identify the Holocaust solely with these details and because of this either become "turned off" or morbidly fascinated? In brief, can King have his cake and eat it too?

In King's full-length novel, *The Dead Zone* (1979) written shortly after "Apt Pupil," the hero, Johnny Smith, an "everyman" who is the moral and intellectual opposite of Todd Bowden, develops psychic powers and can foresee the future. When he witnesses a political rally for a pseudo-populist, psychopathic, and neo–Nazi candidate Greg Stillson and touches Stillson's hand, he experiences a terrifying revelation of the future: Stillson will becomes the President of the United States and will launch an all-out nuclear war. Johnny Smith becomes obsessed with the question: *"If you could jump into a time machine and go back to 1932, would you kill Hitler?"*[37]

Confounding the "wheel of fortune" (fate, determinism), Smith makes his choice, directly contributes to Stillson's downfall, prevents a possible disastrous future. Presumably, Johnny Smith would have had to have known something about the incomparable consequences of Hitler's coming to power to take the desperate step of trying to stop a future disciple of Hitler. A hypothetical question: Did Johnny Smith read "Apt Pupil?" If he had, would he have acted as he did because he read it? In the end, only the readers can draw their only conclusions.

NOTES

1. George Beahm, ed. *The Stephen King Companion* (Kansas City: Andrews and McMeel, 1989), 4.
2. Ibid., 39–40.
3. Stephen King, Afterword to *Different Seasons* (New York: Viking, 1982), 527.
4. Michiko Kakutani, *New York Times*, Dec. 5, 1982, 1.
5. King, Afterword, 526.
6. Ibid., 527.
7. Ibid., 526.
8. Joseph Reino, *Stephen King: The First Decades, Carrie to Pet Sematary* (Boston: Twayne, 1988), 122.
9. Stephen King, "Summer of Corruption: Apt Pupil," in *Different Seasons* (New York: Viking, 1982), 107.
10. Ibid., 109.
11. Ibid., 114.
12. Ibid., 139–40.

13. Ibid., 115.

14. Ibid., 123.

15. Ibid., 149.

16. Ibid., 161.

17. Ibid., 179.

18. Ibid., 205.

19. Ibid., 205.

20. Richard Rubenstein, *Approaches to Auschwitz: The Holocaust and Its Legacy* (Atlanta: John Knox Press, 1987), 251–53.

21. King, "Summer of Corruption," 200.

22. Ibid., 24–28.

23. Ibid., 267.

24. Ibid., 257.

25. Ibid., 126.

26. Paul Gray, Review of *Different Seasons*, by Stephen King, *Time* 120.9 (August 30, 1982), 87.

27. King, "Summer of Corruption," 257.

28. Ibid., 295.

29. Ibid., 296.

30. Ibid.

31. Reino, *Stephen King*, 125.

32. Michael Collins and David Engbretson, *The Shorter Works of Stephen King* (Mercer Island, WA: Starmont House, 1985), 89.

33. Ibid., 84.

34. Collins and Engbretson, *The Shorter Works of Stephen King*, 286–88.

35. Ibid., 83–84.

36. King, "Summer of Corruption," 115.

37. Stephen King, *The Dead Zone* (New York: Viking, 1979), 349.

Holocaust-as-Horror, Science Fiction and the "Look" of the "Real/Reel" in *V* (1983)[1]

JOHN EDGAR BROWNING

Shadows of the Holocaust in V: *Classic and Conflicted Frames*

The theoretical groundwork for this essay is partially derived from Caroline Picart and David Frank's *Frames of Evil: The Holocaust as Horror in American Film*.[2] Picart and Frank argue that cross-fertilizations have evolved that bind Holocaust films, usually shot in a documentary or docudramatic mode, with horror films, which, in turn, are usually visually coded as drawing from the Gothic fictional tradition. Picart and Frank also argue that there is a "Gothic criminological" element that enables this cross-fertilization across the realms of fact and fiction. "Gothic criminology gestures toward an account that moves in between the realms of Gothic fiction and film, which entertains its horrified and fascinated readers with unreal horrors attended upon a realistically/cogently imagined fictional world and factual cases ... framed in Gothic terms, which are essential to plotting the social construction of where evil resides in modernity."[3] The point of Picart and Frank's argument is not to show that there is no such thing as "fact" or "fiction," but rather to show that there is a mode of narrativizing that privileges, unmistakably, the *look* of the "real," even in the use of horror-derived cinematic techniques or motifs.[4] Picart and Frank conclude that "realistic" documentary modes actually draw from "fictional" Gothic modes, which themselves have a complex relationship with the real: that is, all fictional cinematic serial killers, beginning with the iconic Norman Bates from *Psycho*, in some way draw their heritage from the historically real Ed Gein. Yet the appropriation of fictional Gothic modes into factual documentary or docu-dramatic modes is acceptable or convincing as "true" only if these cinematic footnotes masquerade as partaking of the look of the "real."

Crucial to our understanding of how the television miniseries *V* uses the cinematic mode of science fiction, as a "technology" for re-imagining the Holocaust, is a tool (again derived from Picart and Frank's *Frames of Evil*[5]), that lies in between what the authors distinguish as a "classic horror frame" and a "conflicted horror frame." The classic horror frame, being more characteristic of early Hollywood cinema, demands the monster be so completely "other" that closure may only be rendered with his or her killing or sacrifice, and with that, the restoration of normalcy to the story. The conflicted horror frame, on the other hand, views evil as residing within the "normal." Whereas classic horror monsters, like Frankenstein's Monster, "breach the norms of ontological propriety,"[6] as Noël Carroll points out, monsters of the conflicted horror frame seem "ordinary" at first glance, much like the disguisedly innocent Norman Bates. While the classic horror frame breaches the realm of "normalcy," the conflicted horror frame merges the realms of normalcy and alterity seamlessly into one another, until the two have become terrifyingly indistinguishable.

In what follows, I examine how director/screenwriter Kenneth Johnson has represented the horrors of the Holocaust on television using a fantastic mode of narration like science fiction while incorporating, to some degree, the cinematic techniques of horror and documentary filmmaking. More critically, this more fantastic mode of narrativizing diverges from historical and cinematic depictions of the Shoah like *Schindler's List* and *Apt Pupil* that rely more heavily on the cinematic techniques of horror and documentary filmmaking. What we find is that by using the grammars of both science fiction and horror, *V* challenges the dominant or classic representation of the monstrous in Holocaust narratives. Whereas the focus in Picart and Frank's *Holocaust as Horror* was in showing the differences between the two frames, the focus of this essay is in mapping how the classic and conflicted frames in the science fiction mode are more symbiotically paired than diametrically opposed. The resulting narrative in *V*, because it is not as constrained by "documentary" or "moral" demands, is much more complex, and has much to tell us, about the re-imagination of the horrors of the Holocaust and its iconic monster, the Nazi.

The Visitor-as-Nazi

First, a brief sketch of *V*'s plot is beneficial. It is the 1980s, and citizens from around the world watch helplessly as fifty disc-shaped alien space-craft, each measuring three miles across, descend upon Earth's major cities. The "Visitors," as they come to be called, emerge from the large spacecraft and appear markedly humanoid, save for strange reverberating voices and an acute sensitivity to light. Theirs is a "mission of peace," they claim, and Earth's abundance of raw materials is vital to the survival of their home world. In exchange for some of Earth's resources, the Visitors promise knowledge, advanced technologies, and medical cures. However, in reality, they harbor a terrible agenda: they have come to rape Earth of its water and harvest human beings for food. The Visitors are actually reptilian, disguised behind suits of synthesized human flesh. Soon after their arrival, the Visitors, fearing that members of the science community on Earth will unmask their true identity, begin using various media outlets to stage a "Goebbelian" propaganda campaign. The whisper campaign alleges that scientists are secretly plotting to sabotage the Visitors' "peace-ful mission," threatening to jeopardize the exchange of technological and medicinal knowledge the Visitors have promised. The public turns a blind eye while the Visitors summarily order all scientists to register themselves and their families with Visitor officials. Some citizens obey, some go into hiding, but many more disappear, carted off *en masse* by transport ship. Much of the public believes the Visitors' ruse—that is, all but a small band of resistance fighters. They are everyday citizens, and they are humanity's only hope.

As Douglas Gomery aptly points out: "Because the turnaround time from production to presentation is so short, made-for-tv movies can deal with topical issues and even, like the immensely popular *The Day After* (1983), provoke discussion of important ideas."[7] In the director's commen-tary, Kenneth Johnson acknowledges that "*V* was a retelling of the rise of the Third Reich" that attempted to grapple with critical issues like the horrors of the Holocaust.[8] The Visitors, like the Nazis, are fascist militants; their uniforms are laden with (or, as the director puts it, "reminiscent of") Nazi-period imagery—all red with black trim, and black knee-high boots—visually mirroring, and inverting, the black/red uniforms worn by the SS (see Figure 3). The Visitor laser sidearm is patterned after the German P08 Pistol, or "Luger," Johnson notes; and even the Visitor insignia, John-son adds, is "Nazi-esque" in design and features prominently in black on tall red draping banners that adorn publicized orations by Visitor officers.

Referencing another powerful allusion, the Visitors refer to their ruler back on their home world as "our *Leader*" or "the *Leader*," which is the English meaning of *Der Führer*.

Johnson points out in the director's commentary that his original script did not initially call for aliens, but instead considered the Chinese or the Russians to play the adversary.[9] Johnson recalls that in junior high school, he had viewed the film footage used as evidence at the Nuremberg trials, and it made "a startling impression upon [him.]"[10] He recalls further: "It [the footage] was so stunning to me that I think that's part of what shaped a lot of my work about intolerance and prejudice. I went to Auschwitz. I've stood there. It's an astonishing experience that you literally can't get your arms around. It's enormous."[11] Given the popularity of the Star Wars franchise at the time, Johnson elected a science fictional land-scape to "work through"[12] the Holocaust (in particular, the registration and subsequent abduction of the scientists), which for *V* is the catalyzing event or rallying point for the resistance movement.

The Visitors and the Gothic

V's narrative operates within the conventional genre framework of science fiction. Yet, there are moments in which the film employs a Gothic vocabulary and classic horror conventions to "act out"[13] the representation of not only the perpetrators, but also the victims themselves. As Johnson describes it, the film works through the Final Solution to the "scientist question"[14] (in this case, the mass abduction, and harvesting, of scientists and other undesirables). In accord with the Gothic theme, the Visitor spacecraft, for example, or "mother ships" as they are called in the film, hover ominously over Earth's major cities. At first glance, the exterior of the ships, an off-white or light grey, appears unobtrusive, as does the lim-ited view of the interior to which we are given access. After a news crew is brought on board the Los Angeles mother ship for the first time, a reporter comments, "[F]or those of us accustomed to the likes of *Close Encounters* and Darth Vader's star destroyer, our first glimpses inside of the spacecraft of the Visitors were somewhat unexpected, even disap-pointing.... The docking bay looked rather like the hanger deck of one of our big aircraft carriers." However, the exterior of the mother ships, though seemingly inconsequential, deceptively masks a Gothic infrastructure. After news cameraman Mike Donovan (Mark Singer) infiltrates the inte-rior of the Los Angeles mother ship by sneaking into an air duct—a

Figure 3. Visitors Peter Nelson (Brian, left), Andrew Pine (Steven), wearing the laser ("Luger") sidearm, and Jane Badler (Diana) in *V* (1983).

labyrinthine system of dimly lit, Gothic tunnels—we are confronted by the Visitors' macabre eating practices and true reptilian identity (Donovan captures both on camera through vents that line the air ducts), thus markedly framing these crucial plot moments within a Gothic aesthetic. The film goes on to reveal that these same Gothic elements constitute the entire central region of the mother ship(s). Johnson uses a mixture of low-lighting, dark color palette, steam, and shadow (creating a chiaroscuro effect) to construct the Gothic *mise en scène* that make up the mother ship's interior.

Johnson envisioned "a whole different feel to [the interior] ... a darker feel."[15] Perhaps the most startling scene in *V* that visibly references one of the more grisly facets of the Holocaust occurs when Martin (Frank Ashmore), a seasoned Visitor lieutenant who opposes the Leader's Earth initiatives, leads Donovan inside the mother ship's Gothic interior to an immense room containing vast stores of human bodies in suspended animation (see Figure 4). The scene visually gestures to the footage taken at liberated concentration camps (*Konzentrationslager*) in Europe. In the director's commentary, Johnson states that he intended this scene to convey "the immensity ... the enormity of the *process* that the alien Visitors were involved with [emphasis added]."[16] The use of shadowplay and "fingernails on a blackboard ... bone-chilling" music, Johnson explains, are to us recognizable conventions of horror cinema that serve to heighten the ominous feeling in this scene.[17] Another strong component of contemporary horror presented here is the connotation of vampirism and cannibalism, particularly the scene's "fixation on the use of human beings reduced to cattle, as sources of meat and leather" which is a "Holocaust-derived Gothic artifact"[18] (see, for example, *Silence of the Lambs* [1991]). This shows how the Gothic functions easily and productively as a dominant frame in American Holocaust films for "working through" some of the more macabre elements of the Shoah.

While the Gothic mode and classic horror frame can influence the way in which American Holocaust narratives represent the spectacle of the victims and their demise, these narrative elements can also restructure the ways in which Holocaust narratives configure the perpetrator as monstrous. No character in *V* is more pronouncedly monstrous than Diana (Jane Baddler), John's second in command and essentially the "real power" on Earth. Regarding the classic horror film, Picart and Frank write, "In every way, including sexual orientation, the monster is portrayed as radically different; despite some crossover into the realm of humanity, at the point at which the narrative demands that they be destroyed, they are essentially and irreducibly other."[19] Although Diana is "superficially" human, collapsing the distinction between victim and monster that is characteristic of the conflicted frame, traditional concepts of the Nazi-as-monster motif clearly inform *V*'s portrayal of Diana, ultimately "reifying stereotypic links between horror and the Holocaust."[20]

Figure 4. Marc Singer (Mike Donovan, left) and Frank Ashmore (Martin) stand before a vast store room of human bodies in the interior of the Los Angeles mother ship in *V* (1983).

Diana's classic configuration as "other" becomes clearer as we examine specific features of her character in detail. An amalgam of several monstrous traits, Diana is both attractive and alluring, so much so that her femininity is dangerously threatening towards men. Nevertheless, structurally, her configuration is also masculinized: she is often the bearer of "the gaze," usually conceived as "the male gaze," and she is sadistically homoerotic towards women. The emphasis placed on Diana's monstrous or othered sexuality supplants an ethic of response with a more traditional Hollywood horror schematic. To borrow from Picart and Frank, Johnson, like Steven Spielberg in *Schindler's List*, "ultimately acts out, rather than works through, a representation of the Holocaust by reducing it to yet another backdrop for the unfolding of a set of perversions ... that render Nazism monstrous."[21] One scene from *V* in particular shows Donovan and Kristine Walsh (Jenny Sullivan) in the foreground engaging in sexual foreplay, while in the background, a television (the dominant position in the room from which to overlook the couple) begins airing a press interview with Diana, before moving to a close-up on Diana's face. At this point, Diana peers eerily, and smilingly, into the camera, and by extension, into the living room, where she assumes the role of voyeur to the sexual display before her (a motif that is repeated elsewhere in the film and in subsequent installments). "Uncomfortable" moments like this one regularly occur between Kristine and Diana. Two instances show Diana ambiguously placing her hand on Kristine, once on her arm, then another time on her shoulder, in a manner that, at one point, verges on the homoerotic, and at other times, on the violated. Johnson notes in the director's commentary that he intended these scenes to relate Diana's "many appetites,"[22] and that one such appetite might include a sexual attraction for Kristine.

Picart and Frank point out that the relation between the resilient nature of the "Nazi-as-sexualized-monster," the fetishization of Nazi symbology, and erotized violence continues to circulate internationally as a "visual narrative currency,"[23] a grammar now familiar to multiple viewing publics. Diana's character is a conflation of these three formidable themes. The tendency to concentrate several deviant "markers" within a single character (like Diana), as is common in classic horror, has the effect of elevating narratologically "the stakes of evil"[24] in the monstrous. Thus, the image of the Nazi as the site of Judith Halberstam's notion of a "Gothic economy" (the "ability to condense many monstrous traits into one body"[25]) has proven to be a common enterprise among Hollywood filmmakers. Unfortunately, the trend in Holocaust historiography to silence or play down the atrocities committed against thousands of homosexual men, lesbians, and bisexuals under the edict of the Final Solution is clearly evidenced by the conflation of these sexual (monstrous) identities with the conception of evil. Formations of monstrous sexuality such as those we find in Holocaust narratives prove fundamentally problematic because "they rely on the same heterocentric assumptions," note Picart and Frank, "that give rise to fascist values, that is, the criminalization and extermination of individuals on the basis of sexuality."[26] Robin Wood contends that "The reason why patriarchal capitalist society is so reluctant to confront this aspect of Nazism is clearly that it has its own stake in the same assumptions."[27]

Yet, Diana's role as Nazi-as-sexualized-monster comprises only one element of her pathology. "Diana," Johnson remarks, "is sort of my combination of Mengele, and Göring, and Himmler."[28] Later in the film, Diana figures prominently in key scenes that visually reference narrative horror methods typically used in portrayals of Josef Mengele, which, given Mengele's relation to the Holocaust, is more revelatory than Diana's sexuality. In one such scene, Diana's terror chamber—outfitted with scalpels, a flame inducer, and a harnessing apparatus reminiscent of dentist's chair (a visual footnote to *Marathon Man* [1976] perhaps)—echoes stories Johnson had read about Nazi interrogation.[29] In another scene that is both visually striking and sexually ambiguous, Diana employs the "male gaze" during a medical experiment she authorized and choreographs herself. Through a two-way mirror, Diana observes as Brian (Peter Nelson), a youthful Visitor lieutenant, and Robin Maxwell (Blair Tefkin), a human detainee aboard the Los Angeles mother ship, engage in coitus, the fruition of which becomes a major subplot in the next installment, *V: The Final Battle* (1984). The re-gendering of the male gaze here invokes another crossover of Diana's with other common visualizations of the monstrous feminine.

The imbrications of power and gender in Diana place her in the realm of the "third shadow," that is, the female monster or the *feminine-as-monstrous*: a natural offshoot of Janice Rushing and Thomas Frentz's framework[30] (which, in general, does not occur in the decidedly less progressive strain of straight "Holocaust-as-horror" films, Picart and Frank point out[31]). Perhaps Diana's inclusion in *V*, a "Holocaust-as-[science fiction]" film that does not have a strict horror classification (but instead merely incorporates cinematic horror conventions), is made possible precisely because she inhabits a Mengele-type (i.e., masculinized) role, one that is firmly, and "safely," bound within the landscape of science "fiction" rather than "real/reel" horror.

Conclusion: Classic and Conflicted Frames— Redux

To close my analysis of *V*, it is necessary to review some of the complex interrelationships that bind the classic and conflicted frame in the film. By the end of the next installment, *V: The Final Battle*, and in the opening episodes of *V: The Series* (1984–1985), in which Diana is tried for crimes against humanity (a media spectacle the humans liken to Nuremberg), we begin to see her vulnerable side. Diana, like the exterior of the mother ship(s), or like the Visitors themselves, has many faces that blend seamlessly into the natural order.

In addition to classic elements of horror, *V* simultaneously invokes the conflicted frame, where: 1.) the Visitors' "natural" façade, 2.) the humans who, during the course of the film, "look the other way" in exchange for power, and 3.) Visitor factionists (like Martin and others) who oppose the Leader's initiatives on Earth, all actively "interrogat[e] the binaries (e.g., normality-abnormality, active monster-passive victim) at the base of traditional conceptualizations of evil and mass murder."[32] Johnson intended the Visitor faction "to show good Nazis and bad Nazis."[33] He goes on to say, "The aliens, just as, indeed, all the members of the *Wehrmacht* in World War II, were not out to kill everybody. They were people just like us."[34] In short, while other Holocaust narratives that appropriate the conflicted frame in isolation often resort to merely questioning dominant portrayals of the monstrous as "abnormal," *V* challenges, to some extent, the culturally dominant mode often used to simplistically narrativize the monstrous in the Holocaust. In so doing, *V* forms complex cross-fertilizations between the classic and conflicted frames, resisting easy binaries.

V offers a different way in which to re-visualize the face of evil, using the grammars and narrative techniques of science fiction and horror to move across the classic as well as the conflicted frames—to visualize stories of monsters and heroes. The film's strategic use of handheld shots frequently invokes the "docudramatic" or "authentic look" of the Holocaust, albeit within the more fluid structure of a science fictionalized narrative. The resulting collision of "real/reel" worlds allows for a much more complex narrative capable of breaching the realm of fiction to address "real" concerns by working through the numerous horrors of the Holocaust and imaginatively reworking them into a vision of brave new worlds.

NOTES

1. This essay was presented at the 31st International Conference on the Fantastic in the Arts in March 2010, as part of a panel, with Judith Kerman and Carol A. Senf, entitled "Elements of the Fantastic in Film and Media Explorations of the Holocaust." Later, in slightly different form, this chapter comprised part of a longer essay, collaboratively written with Caroline Joan (Kay) S. Picart and Carla Maria Thomas, entitled, "Where Reality and Fantasy Meet and Bifurcate: Holocaust Themes in *Pan's Labyrinth*, the *X-Men*, and *V: The Original Miniseries (1983)*," in *Speaking of Monsters: A Teratological Anthology*, ed. Caroline Joan S. Picart and John Edgar Browning (Palgrave Macmillan: 2012), 271–90, reproduced with permission of Palgrave Macmillan (the full published version of this publication is available from: http://us.macmillan.com/speakingofmonsters/CarolineJoanS Picart). Considerable thanks are due to Picart for laying the initial groundwork for this essay.

2. Caroline Joan (Kay) S. Picart and David A. Frank, *Frames of Evil: The Holocaust as Horror in American Film* (Carbondale: Southern Illinois University Press, 2006).

3. Caroline Joan (Kay) Picart and Cecil Greek, *Monsters In and Among Us: Toward a Gothic Criminology* (Madison, NJ: Fairleigh Dickinson University Press, 2007), 12.

4. For a concise exposition of this argument, see Caroline J.S. Picart and David Frank, "Horror and the Holocaust: Genre Elements in *Schindler's List* and *Psycho*," *The Horror Film*, ed. Stephen Prince (New Brunswick, NJ: Rutgers University Press, 2003), 206–23.

5. Picart and Frank, *Frames of Evil*, 5–8. See also Isabel Cristina Pinedo, "Postmodern Elements of the Contemporary Horror Film," in Steven Prince, ed. *The Horror Film* (New Brunswick, NJ: Rutgers University Press, 2004), 85–117.

6. Noël Carroll, *Philosophy of Horror, or Paradoxes of the Heart* (New York: Routledge, 1990), 16.

7. Douglas Gomery, "The Economics of the Horror Film," in *Horror Films: Current Research on Audience Preferences and Reactions*, ed. James B. Weaver, III and Ron Tamborini (Mahwah, NY: Lawrence Erlbaum Associates, 1996), 46–62.

8. Kenneth Johnson, "Feature-Length Commentary by Writer/Director," *V: The Original Miniseries*, Side A, DVD, Warner Home Video (1983/2001).

9. Ibid.

10. Ibid.

11. Ibid.

12. For a complete discussion of "working through," see Dominick LaCapra, *Writing History, Writing Trauma* (Baltimore MD: Johns Hopkins University Press, 2001); LaCapra, *Representing the Holocaust: History, Theory, Trauma* (Ithaca, NY: Cornell University Press, 1994); and LaCapra, *History and Memory After Auschwitz* (Ithaca, NY: Cornell University Press, 1998).

13. For a complete discussion of "acting out," see Dominick LaCapra, *Writing History, Writing Trauma* (Baltimore, MD: Johns Hopkins University Press, 2001); LaCapra, *Representing the Holocaust: History, Theory, Trauma* (Ithaca, NY: Cornell University Press, 1994); and LaCapra, *History and Memory After Auschwitz* (Ithaca, NY: Cornell University Press, 1998).

14. Johnson, "Feature-Length Commentary by Writer/Director," Side A.

15. Ibid.

16. Ibid.

17. Ibid.

18. Picart and Frank, *Frames of Evil*, 28.

19. Ibid., 7.

20. Ibid., 125.

21. Ibid., 102.

22. Johnson, "Feature-Length Commentary by Writer/Director," Side A.

23. Picart and Frank, *Frames of Evil*, 133.

24. Ibid., 124.

25. Judith Halberstam, *Skin Shows: Gothic Horror and the Technology of Monsters* (Durham, NC: Duke University Press, 1995/2006), 88, 102–05.

26. Picart and Frank, *Frames of Evil*, 124.

27. Robin Wood, "Nuit et Brouillard," in *International Dictionary of Films and Filmmakers* 1, ed. Christopher Lyon (Chicago: St. James Press, 1984), 332.

28. Johnson, "Feature-Length Commentary by Writer/Director," Side A.

29. Ibid.

30. See Rushing and Frentz, *Projecting the Shadow: The Cyborg Hero in American Film* (Chicago: University of Chicago Press, 1995). For further discussion on the "third shadow," see Caroline Joan Picart, *The Cinematic Rebirths of Frankenstein: Universal, hammer, and Beyond* (Westport, CT: Praeger, 2002).

31. Picart and Frank, *Frames of Evil*, 131.

32. Ibid., 127.

33. Johnson, "Feature-Length Commentary by Writer/Director," Side A.

34. Ibid.

A Dishonest Reckoning

Play-"Acting Through" Personal Trauma and the Shoah in Martin Scorsese's Shutter Island (2010)

Kristopher Mecholsky

> *Our dried voices, when*
> *We whisper together*
> *Are quiet and meaningless*
> *As wind in dry grass...*
> *Shape without form, shade without colour,*
> *Paralysed force, gesture without motion.*
> > —T.S. Eliot, "The Hollow Men"
>
> *Remember us, for we too have lived, loved and laughed.*
> > —Martin Scorsese, *Shutter Island* (2010)

In the case of traumatic events, forgetting is not the *absence* of memory but work *against* it. Forgetting actively masks memory. Thus, remembering trauma is a re-direction of that work. It uncovers memory by directly working *on* the covering up, giving shape and vitality to that "gesture without motion" that is repetitive acting out—the acting out which Freud described as "transference of the forgotten past."[1] How then can the "paralysed force" of the traumatized, illustrated by Teddy Daniels's (Andrew Laeddis's) delusion in *Shutter Island* (2010), transform into remembrance?[2] The work of forgetting *and* the work of remembering trauma *both* imply a break with the ordinary, in the same way a traumatic event is itself broken out of the ordinary. Historical traumas of the magnitude of the Shoah consequently demand *extra*ordinary representations, and we should not be surprised that the fantastic has come to be not only defended but embraced in depictions of the Shoah.

The Holocaust and the fantastic, the relationship that draws this anthology together, were thus always entwined, for few other events in human history have come so close to being utterly unbelievable, to the degree that even some who were imprisoned and sent to their deaths could not accept its basic veracity as it happened. But what exactly is "the fantastic?" This answer unfortunately is difficult to articulate since it has been defined in so many ways and it yet remains debated. Tzvetan Todorov defined it first, and calls it a genre, clarifying that he means it is the duration of "that hesitation experienced" in choosing between natural and supernatural explanations for narrative events. For Todorov, a genre is defined by "a principle operative in a number of texts."[3] Kathryn Hume calls the fantastic an impulse born of a twin desire for both mimesis and fantasy, while Judith Kerman thinks of it more as a process.[4] Much of the problem with its definition, I believe, lies in a poorly communicated understanding of words like "genre" and "mode" among critics and theorists of different disciplines and sub-disciplines. As Daniel Chandler points out, "One theorist's genre may be another's sub-genre or even super-genre (and indeed what is technique, style, mode, formula or thematic grouping to one may be treated as a genre by another)."[5]

At any rate, these theorists all maintain similar views on the effects of the fantastic in fiction: it produces a hesitation in the reader and/or characters about the realistic nature of the content of the text. Thus, while I think of the fantastic as a mode, it is in such a way that I would also incorporate those who think of it as an impulse and process and even Todorov and his particular idea of genre. Mode means at least two things to literary critics: in rhetoric, it is considered a way of using language, as when writing persuasion, exposition, argument, or narration; and in critical theory, it has been traditionally the manner and attitude the writer takes toward the audience and subject. In both cases, mode arises based on a certain kind of intent by the author toward the subject at hand; in this case, that intent is to make the reader and/or characters fundamentally hesitate about the reality of what is presented. As a mode, then, it is obviously an impulse, process, *and* principle operative in at least parts of a number of disparate works.

In any case, reckoning with the use of the fantastic in Holocaust fiction is really no longer much of a concern for the small portion of the public that studies the fantastic or Holocaust fiction—but it remains a major concern for nearly everyone else. In representations of the Shoah—

and in film more than literature, too—audiences have demanded a certain level of "legitimacy" and "decorum," however vague those terms and concepts are. While the widely acknowledged canon of Holocaust literature has gradually incorporated apparently indecorous, experimental novels into its fold (such as *See Under: Love* [2002] and *Everything Is Illuminated* [2002]), what some have deemed indecent Holocaust films (such as Uwe Boll's *Auschwitz*, Paul Schrader's *Adam Resurrected*, or Quentin Tarantino's *Inglourious Basterds*) have been less able to escape criticism.

Consequently, use of death-camp imagery in a psychological thriller like Scorsese's *Shutter Island* appears emphatically indecent to most, a despicable and exploitative capitalization on one of the greatest horrors of humankind for the purposes of evoking an audience thrill. In a podcast discussion of the movie, critics Dana Stevens and Troy Patterson of *Slate* contend that the film is filled with "deliberately horrible clichés throughout" leading to scenes of "untoward luridness," noting that part of the luridness is the inclusion of apparently unnecessary shots of scenes from Dachau, which they consider unsuccessful, tacky, and tawdry in their evident presence as necessary psychological back-story.[6] For the most part, even more charitable critics seemed to agree that the film was a waste of time and talent or at best a celebration of excess. As Anthony Lane wrote in *The New Yorker*, Scorsese's goal in the film is to "pillage all the B movies he has ever seen (including some that were forgotten by their own directors), and to enshrine the fixations and flourishes of style on which they relied." Following Umberto Eco's observation that "two clichés make us laugh but a hundred clichés move us, because we sense dimly that the clichés are talking among themselves, celebrating a reunion," Lane suggests that *Shutter Island* "is that reunion, and that shrine."[7]

Thus on the one hand, audiences and critics might simply praise the film's celebration of, and genius with, style; and on the other hand, they might decry what apparently amounts to exploitation of Holocaust imagery purely for style. But beyond the question of the film's own use of the Shoah, the critical response to it speaks for other questions regarding fictional responses to the Holocaust that still resound: What are the limits of fiction in representations of the Shoah? Can genre fiction ever appropriately or legitimately represent it? What is appropriate and legitimate when it comes to Holocaust representation? In the course of exploring *Shutter Island*'s use of Holocaust imagery, I focus on these crucial questions, but first I turn to some theoretical foundations of narrative representation of historical trauma.

Historical and Fictional Representation and the Shoah

Any fictional response to the Holocaust "invariably provoke[s] controversy by inspiring revulsion and acclaim in equal measure," as Sue Vice argues in *Holocaust Fiction*: "To judge by what many critics have to say, to write Holocaust fictions is tantamount to making a fiction of the Holocaust."[8] At the same time, if Western culture should be remembering the Shoah, fictionalizations at least of personal testimonies need to have room to disseminate. But questions remain, with each publication or distribution of such fictionalizations, about the limits of artistic depictions of the Holocaust. Should there ever be anything aesthetic about it? When those who lived through the experience have died, are we doomed to forget that they lived? How can cultures continue to remember without personal witnesses? Gilead Morahg argues in "Creating Wasserman: The Quest for a New Holocaust Story in David Grossman's *See Under: Love*," that frequently "the lives of Holocaust victims are sanctified and their experiences in the ghettos and the camps are deemed inaccessible and incomprehensible to those who did not actually live through them."[9] As respectful as this approach to trauma is, it also constricts collective memory, cutting it short and emptying it of its initial impulse. So who will remember the rememberers? And how?

Continuing representations of the Holocaust are absolutely vital, not only for survivors but for future generations. Despite Adorno's often misquoted statement about poetry after Auschwitz (that there is none), he affirmed in *Negative Dialectics* that "perennial suffering has as much right to expression as a tortured man has to scream," and Paul Ricoeur argues in *Time and Narrative* that "there are perhaps some crimes that must not be forgotten, victims whose suffering cries less for vengeance than for narration."[10] Still, Ricoeur argues a little earlier in that work that the kind of horror and victimization associated with historical traumas *like* the Shoah is (ironically) incomparable. What kind of narration does that leave for memorialization?

Making narratives out of discrete events has been historically a natural human response to make sense out of the passage of time. But experience and testimonial are the backbone of historiography, and since we use narratives (fictional or otherwise) to make sense of events, history tends to reflect the narratives we already have, particularly those we identify with most, until "we learn to see a given series of events *as* tragic, *as* comic, and so on."[11] We collect documents and other written traces, select and summarize them according to some organizing principle, and narrate them for some specific purpose. Yet the Shoah and other events of traumatic import are

> the other side of history that no cunning of reason can ever justify and that, instead, [reveal] the scandal of every theodicy of history ... [because] horror isolates events by making them incomparable, incomparably unique, uniquely unique.... The more we explain in historical terms, the more indignant we become; the more we are struck by the horror of events, the more we seek to understand them.[12]

Thus, not only are depictions of the Holocaust vital, they are also inevitable. History and narrative make sense of the already-forced unity of time, and will keep trying to do so even when no sense can be made out of the events. So this need brings us back again and again to the historical trauma of the Shoah, even when no common narrative makes it understandable.

What narrative representations can do justice to the *narratological* trauma that historical traumas impose? Can any mass-market, generic representations achieve such justice? Shouldn't those depictions (if they should exist at all) be just as "authentic" and "true-to-life" as possible? Not necessarily; *representing* such authenticity is impossible. Representation selects and loses information and shifts agency to the narrator from the subject. Only unadulterated documents (visual, aural, or textual) can communicate even a semblance of authenticity, of the past *wie es eigentlich gewesen* ("as it actually happened"), as Leopold von Ranke called it. Melanie Wright argues that in the case of mass-market films, for instance,

> events like the *Shoah* are [inevitably] presented in simplified, distorted ways. Some degree of cliché is unavoidable in the attempt to seduce the mass market.
> Moreover, the evidence of many Holocaust films themselves suggests that the underlying artificiality of film does not fit easily with the facticity of the suffering of six million. Many directors have attempted to take a realistic approach to the events. But where efforts are made to create an "authentic" picture of the death camp, questions are raised not just about bad taste but also about immorality.[13]

It would seem that in the case of Holocaust narratives meant to reach a wide audience, "authenticity"—history *wie es eigentlich gewesen*—may be impossible. Not only might such attempts be in "bad taste," they may be unethical and immoral. And in terms of historiography, no generic narrative will be able to accurately depict or represent the Holocaust by the very nature of the unique narratological trauma it imposes.

Thinking Through Trauma, Thinking Through Genre

So far I have argued that genre-bending, "unrealistic" fictional depictions of the Holocaust are not only "legitimate," they may be one of the most honest ways of approaching the Holocaust fictionally. At the same time, mass-market narratives *are* important in terms of cultural remembrance, and mass markets rely on generic simplification. Can these conditions be reconciled in one work? I believe Martin Scorsese's *Shutter Island* is that reconciliation. Tied up in the "dishonest" packaging of a cheap-thrill money-maker is an honest confrontation with a number of very serious and pressing national concerns. Scorsese thrusts *Shutter Island* into the mode of the fantastic to illustrate the echoing effects of cultural trauma, cultural memory, and cultural forgetting. Traumatic events break up the ordinary and understandable, but those who confront them still feel compelled to fit them into generic narratives for easy comprehension, which inevitably do not work. Thus, the memory and forgetting of trauma echoes and repeats. The film, like the novel, tries to make the audience experience that echoing, that persistence of traumatic memory. Teddy Daniels's acting out of his personal trauma is encrypted into a patchwork of numerous genres of the 1950s, appropriately destabilizing the audience's sense of reality in the face of great trauma, while also visually linking Teddy's personal family trauma with his war trauma. Thus, when Scorsese delves into those postwar genres in the latter half of the film, Teddy's delusional paranoia actually demonstrates how his personal denial is similar to America's cultural denial. Teddy has buried his trauma so deep it returns to the surface of his life everywhere, in a similar way to America's relish of postwar paranoia genres. Thus, Scorsese ultimately offers a response to repressed cultural trauma through a narrative of repressed personal trauma.

But the persistence of the problem of "bad taste" would still seem to discount a "genre" work like *Shutter Island* as an appropriate response to the Holocaust. "Bad taste" is a very relative term, though, associated with the ending of a work: something is in "bad taste" if its *purpose* is excessively pejorative or crassly opportunistic, neither of which describe *Shutter Island*, as I will demonstrate. Rather, the film's clever use of genre is precisely what makes it an honest reckoning with past historical trauma. Again, it is Martin Scorsese's particular adaptation of Dennis Lehane's novel that makes this honest reckoning possible because its play on genre generates the fantastic, producing hesitation in the audience (and in the protagonist) about the veracity of the events unfolding—which is the very essence of the response to psychological trauma. As Bilge Ebiri says at the end of his review of the film, "There's a way more interesting and powerful movie lurking beneath *Shutter Island*'s pulp trappings."[14]

An overview of the whole narrative is necessary at this point to continue this argument. The book and film versions differ in the presentation and depiction of events in some definite ways, but the basic events themselves in both are the same. In 1954, two U.S. marshals—Edward "Teddy" Daniels and his new partner, Chuck Aule—take a boat to Shutter Island in Boston Harbor to investigate the disappearance of a woman who drowned her three children and was imprisoned in the otherwise uninhabited island's psychiatric prison (Asheliffe Hospital). The marshals are increasingly rebuffed by the hospital staff in their attempts to investigate the matter. Rachel's psychiatrist, Dr. Sheehan, has evidently been allowed to leave the island; the liaison to the board of directors, Dr. Jeremiah Naehring, will not release the records of the staff for investigation; and the director, Dr. John Cawley, will not allow them to search one of the wards (Ward C) and discourages them from going to the lighthouse, which he claims has already been searched. With little assistance from the hospital, Teddy calls off the investigation, but is prevented from leaving by an approaching hurricane. By this time, Teddy has begun to have migraine headaches, as well as vivid memories of his experience liberating Dachau and dreams of his wife, Dolores Chanal, who was killed in a fire set by an arsonists named Andrew Laeddis.

Stuck on the island, the two marshals continue their search, and Teddy reveals to Chuck that he is actually also searching for Laeddis, who is supposed to be imprisoned there. Ashecliffe denies that he is a patient, and Teddy has come to find him. But Teddy also tells Chuck that he discovered an ex-patient of Ward C named George Noyce who claims that the psychiatrists at Ashecliffe are experimenting on the patients. Teddy wants to find Laeddis and reveal what is happening on Shutter Island to the public, disgusted as he is by the notion that the United States might be employing such similar tactics to the Nazis's. As the storm rages more, Dr. Cawley tells Teddy and Chuck that Rachel has been suddenly found. Both men become even more suspicious, and when the storm wrecks power on the island, they sneak into Ward C, where the most violent patients are held. The marshals are separated, and Teddy finds George Noyce, who claims everyone on the island—including Chuck Aule—are staging an elaborate game for Teddy. When Teddy finds Chuck again, he tells him he is going to the lighthouse by way of the cliffs. The men separate, and as Teddy climbs along the rock face, he finds a woman hiding out in the cliff caves. Paranoid and alone, she claims to be the real Rachel Solando, a former psychiatrist at Ashecliffe who was discredited and committed after discovering other staff were performing mind control experiments with psychotropic drugs and brain surgery. She suggests that Teddy has been given the drugs, too, and must trust no one, even his partner.

Teddy makes his way back to the hospital where Dr. Cawley and the other staff claim that Teddy came to the island alone. Convinced he will be captured and experimented on, Teddy escapes to the lighthouse to find out if all Noyce and the woman in the cliffs said was true. At the lighthouse, Teddy only finds Dr. Cawley, who tells Teddy that Teddy is actually Andrew Laeddis, a prisoner at Ashecliffe for shooting his wife (Dolores Chanal) after she drowned their three children. Cawley tells Teddy that he concocted an entire fantasy world—using anagrams and mixing up his own history—because he blames himself for his family's tragedy since he never got Dolores the psychiatric help she needed. Cawley also reveals that the entire hospital has played along with Teddy's fantasies in order to get him to face his own traumas, in one last attempt to help him before the other doctors lobotomize him to pacify his violent tendencies. His apparent partner, Chuck Aule, is actually his psychiatrist, Dr. Lester Sheehan, whom Teddy believed was Rachel's psychiatrist. The narrative concludes with Teddy/Andrew as a patient at the hospital, possibly having regressed into his fantasy world again and headed for a lobotomy.

Scorsese's version of the foregoing events actually amplifies the impact of the traumas Teddy experiences, which is his major stylistic innovation over Lehane's novel. Scorsese employs the fantastic mode that Lehane also uses, but does so on a broader and more in-depth scale in order to effectively impart a sense of the echoing effects of cultural trauma, cultural memory, and cultural forgetting. His use of genre to confront response to psychological trauma can be traced effectively in the opening scenes of the film, culminating with Doctors Naehring and Cawley rejecting the marshals' request for the staff's records. I will proceed chronologically through these scenes to note and evaluate Scorsese's shifting use of genre that elicit a sense of the fantastic, ultimately demonstrating that the very genres Teddy tries to understand his trauma through reveal his own culture's failing attempts to understand its own psychological traumas.

As indicated earlier, trauma is everywhere in the film. Although the film and book are both noted for their twists and turns, upon reflection, everything is entirely on the surface. In the first shot of the film, the island itself juts out of the water (and later, events take place during the most traumatic of weather events: a hurricane). Normal has been torn asunder. Teddy Daniels goes to the island to investigate the disappearance of a patient, but his encounters and discoveries there tear apart his very worldview to such a degree that he cannot accept it. In fact, the entire narrative experience, which the reader supposed was reality, has been an elaborate pageant by the psychiatrists on the island to try and *make* Teddy accept what he actually did live through. It has been an experimental "working through" of Andrew's trauma; an attempt, as the asylum's director Cawley says, to understand the mind "not by way of ice picks through the brain or large doses of dangerous medicine but through an honest reckoning of the self."[15] Cawley and Sheehan have reenacted the very fantasy Andrew concocted for himself in the hopes they might transform the repetition into a confrontation: effectively, an Aristotelian acting out *toward* a working through, wherein the acting out is repeated, indulged, and shifted so it can play itself out into a recovery. The result is a narrative that is a complete and sustained use of the fantastic, wherein the main character as well as the audience are kept steadily in a state of uncertainty about the reality of the events. It is a mode that allows Lehane and Scorsese to reflect part of the traumatic experience in the reader. But in ways a contemporary novel has much more trouble producing reliably, a contemporary film can easily invoke a number of identifiable genres through a series of visual and aural cues.

So what genres, exactly, does Scorsese begin using to generate a sense of the fantastic? And why do his depictions more effectively depict trauma than Lehane's? Whereas Lehane opens his novel with a description by Dr. Lester Sheehan of Ashecliffe Hospital as sitting "benignly" on its island, looking "nothing like a hospital for the criminally insane and even less like the military barracks it had been before that,"[16] Scorsese's film opens with ominous music over a shot of a thick fog sitting on water. When we first get a glimpse of the eponymous island, it is to the dark accompaniment of three low, sustained chords played on cellos and basses. The island looks very foreboding and very *much* like it holds a hospital for the criminally insane.[17] Thus, while Lehane draws on a modernist literary device (depicting nature as aloof, unsympathetic, and utterly unreflective of Teddy's inner turmoil), Scorsese indulges in simplified narrative conventions as he begins to accumulate a series of various stock genre elements that force the audience to switch between different genres.

In this opening scene alone, Scorsese draws on at least three distinct film styles, triggering different genre responses (sometimes simultaneously) for the audience. The opening shot most directly alludes to Hitchcockian suspense films since the non-diegetic music used is Ingram Marshall's "Fog Tropes," which employs a mildly howling wind as a baseline for a soundscape of eerie horns and strings. The wind is punctuated by low horn blasts that sound like foghorns, after which a slowly undulating horn arpeggio plays against sustained string chords that fluctuate slightly in pitch. The next shot is of Teddy throwing up in the bathroom in the interior of the boat, and as he leaves the head to return to the main deck, he is framed in the back of a long shot filled with hanging, nineteenth-century shackles that are in focus before Teddy himself comes into focus, as the camera tracks in on him. The shackles briefly invoke horror, particularly given their unexpected appearance with someone in mid-twentieth-century clothing. When Teddy meets up with Chuck, the film's dialogue and costuming invoke the "G-men" films of the 1940s and 1950s that glorified federal agencies like the FBI and the Treasury Department. While they are talking, however, Scorsese interjects a flashback as Teddy discusses his dead wife. The flashback is steeped in bright color with no diegetic sound, accompanied instead by the dissonant, non-diegetic "Fog Tropes," whose volume increases when the flashback begins. The sharp juxtaposition in color and soundtrack invokes shades of the Italian horror films of Mario Bava and Hitchcock's *Vertigo*, but it also jars even the uninformed viewer from the genres so far conjured up. Scorsese further disrupts the audience's sense of continuity by cutting back from the memory to a shot of the water at the side of the boat and then back again to a still shot from the flashback—Teddy's wife smiling—just before Teddy reveals to Chuck that she died.[18]

This first scene takes place over four minutes, and not only has Scorsese kept the viewer unstable regarding genre, the viewer has already seen the first visual association of the twin traumas of Teddy's life: his wife's tragedy and his witness at Dachau. During the flashback, which shows Teddy's wife giving him a tacky tie, only one image sticks out inexplicably. While the rest of the flashback sequence reveals different points-of-view of her giving him the tie, Scorsese also curiously incorporates one shot of a spinning record, although it appears to have no bearing on the memory.[19] A little later, though, a spinning record is revealed to have more significance for Teddy.

The next several scenes of *Shutter Island* repeat the overall pattern of this first one: Scorsese introduces genre elements and disrupts them with peculiarities that tie Teddy's traumas together. For instance, a number of varying kinds of suspense and horror tropes are incorporated into the story as the men enter the facility—a looming, dark, anachronistic fortress;

a thin-haired, balding woman with a red scar across her neck making a "shushing" sign and smiling; a suspicious psychiatrist with ties to government intelligence agencies. The most stable genre slowly establishes itself as a blend of detective films noir: a patient has escaped from a locked room, and the marshals begin questioning the staff and prisoners to find her, while the main detective battles the intrusion of his own personal difficulties.[20] As becomes clear to Chuck, Teddy has ulterior motives in his investigation: he seems to be chasing down his wife's killer.

As the investigation becomes the main action of the story, and a stable genre seems to establish itself, Scorsese again interrupts his own genre play with more associations between personal and cultural trauma. As Dr. Cawley gives background information on Rachel Solando, giving Teddy her picture, which triggers a sudden flashback for him. It is Teddy's second flashback, in fact, but instead of his wife, he now recalls a series of images from what the relatively knowledgeable viewer will recognize as a Nazi death camp (see Figure 5). Like the previous flashback, this sequence is marked by a drastic shift in color tone (predominantly blue, contrasting with Cawley's warm, greenish office) and soundtrack (a recording of children playing backward). In terms of editing, the flashbacks are linked as similar ruptures in the filmic narrative, both compositionally and in terms of their effect on the protagonist. Moreover, the explicit close-up of barbed wire recalls an earlier comment by Teddy about the barbed wire at Ashecliffe: "I've seen this before."[21]

As the frequency of flashbacks increases, the storm intensifies, and the number of suspense genre allusions increases. All of this further disrupts the audience's sense of narrative and reality. After Teddy and Chuck question the staff, they learn that communication to the mainland has been lost, and Dr. Cawley invites them to his quarters (a Civil War mansion, of course) for drinks and conversation.[22] Although their investigation ostensibly continues, suspense now emerges as the new dominant genre. The answers to the marshals' questions are inconsistent, and it is clear that the entire hospital staff is hiding something. The color palate of the film shifts to vibrant colors (again, in the vein of late Mario Bava and Hitchcock). Once Chuck and Teddy meet the German psychiatrist Dr. Naehring—in a mansion in a storm, of course—the film begins to lose its grip on the detective genre entirely. The establishing shot of the mansion sequence is accompanied by the sound of a Mahler quartet, and Teddy has an extended montage flashback, longer than the previous two flashbacks—and ultimately far more significant.[23]

At this point, in terms of the overall narrative, the dreams, flashbacks,

Figure 5. Nazi death camp imagery in *Shutter Island* (2010).

and delusions become vitally important for understanding how the film works through trauma. Structurally, after the night at the mansion, the film steadily transforms into a suspense/horror thriller, as Teddy and Chuck seem to become the pursued in a complex conspiracy. But the audience and Teddy are pretty well shaken in their hold on reality by now and remain in constant suspense as they try to decide its underlying truth—which is how Scorsese realizes the fantastic for the audience. Consequently, the narrative impulse for cohesion that arises while following the events compels the audience (and Teddy) to try to decide the correct genre for the action. The apparently free-floating signifiers of dream, memory, and delusion take on increasing importance as they become the only anchors for deciding what course the "true" narrative will take. In this regard, the mansion scene is crucial.

In this scene, the destabilized genre of the film shifts most decidedly, and Teddy's flashbacks and dreams coincide, connecting his personal trauma with the historical trauma of the Holocaust and ultimately demonstrating how the psychiatrists are deliberately associating those traumas for Teddy since the film associates them for us. As Teddy walks into the mansion and Dr. Cawley talks about its history, the Mahler quartet gets louder. As the camera frames Teddy's face in medium close-up, the film cuts to a shot tracking in on the record player. This is the second shot of a spinning record, and its blue Odeon label immediately recalls the only other record shown in the film so far: the blue Odeon record in Teddy's very first flashback of his wife. When Teddy corrects Chuck about the composer ("Nice music. Who is that? Brahms?" "No. It's Mahler"), the film cuts to a flashback of prisoners at Dachau, just after Teddy says "No."[24] In this third flashback, the viewer gets the first definitive evidence that Teddy is remembering a death camp. What is more striking about this third flashback, however, is its soundtrack, which is *continuous* with the diegetic music in the mansion. The Mahler quartet continues during the marshals' discussion with Cawley and Naehring, and it continues during Teddy's next flashback to the death camp and to a Nazi commander's slow suicide, which Teddy witnessed and passively permitted.[25]

This change in the flashback structure is notable. Given the entirety of the narrative, Cawley and Naehring's choice to play Mahler's Quartet for Piano and Strings in A minor is not accidental.[26] In Lehane's book, the music *is* relatively incidental to Teddy's meeting with Cawley and Naehring. In fact, they are already in discussion with him and Chuck, and Teddy has looked around, before Cawley puts music on. When he does, its "Prussian" sound triggers Teddy's memory of the suicidal commandant, but only because the music reminds him "of cafés overseas and a record collection he'd seen in the office of a subcommandant at Dachau, the man listening to it when he'd shot himself in the mouth."[27] In Scorsese's adaptation, the music is apparently the very piece that played while Teddy watched the subcommandant die, and it drifts along between Teddy's present and past, linking the two. The spinning record reminds the audience of Teddy's other trauma: his wife. Furthermore, it is clear in Scorsese's version (at least in a second viewing) that the doctors are deliberately triggering a traumatic memory of his from the war. After Naehring names the piece, which Teddy clearly remembers, Cawley claps his hands together conspicuously and asks the men what they want to drink, broaching the problem of Teddy's drinking—which is revealed in more depth in the dream sequence that occurs when Teddy goes to sleep after visiting the mansion. The psychiatrists are playing directly into Teddy's acting-out fantasy, but they are also trying to direct it. By triggering successive traumatic memories while Teddy masks his most personal trauma, the doctors hope to make him confront *all* of his repressed memories.

For the viewer, the flashbacks are occurring more frequently and are blended more imperceptibly with what is ostensibly happening in reality. Not only is the distinction between the diegetic and non-diegetic music now blurred, but the falling rain in the back of the shots of the marshals talking is matched with falling snow at Dachau, falling paper in the commandant's office, and the falling ash in his dream that night about his wife. In conjunction with the image of the spinning record in Teddy's flashback to his wife as well as his memory of his experience at Dachau, the sequential matchcut and the confusion caused by indistinct diegetic/non-diegetic music visually link the first several flashbacks together.

Since dream sequences are less burdened with generic constraints, the pile-up of visual allusions draws together many of the events Scorsese has been alluding to, further strengthening their relationship and conflating cultural and personal trauma for the audience. As Teddy goes to sleep after his talk with Cawley and Naehring, he begins to dream. Most noticeably, an echoing version of Johnnie Ray's "Cry" blasts forth on the soundtrack. But before the audience enters into very much of the dream—the first shot of the sequence is the camera tracking in down the hallway of the Laeddis's apartment—Scorsese immediately cuts to a tracking-in shot of a record player spinning a blue-label record.[28] The shot is almost identical to the two previous shots of a record in Teddy's first flashback on the boat and in his flashback at the mansion. Soon Teddy sees his wife (played by Michelle Williams) in their apartment, where she accuses him of continuing his alcoholism. He admits it, citing his killing in the war as its cause. In retrospect, the discussion of alcohol in the mansion becomes clear. Ash begins to fall around them as Rachel talks to him, and she moves off into another room that unrealistically looks out onto a lake where she says they summered one year. The amount of ash increases as the dream continues, and Scorsese weaves in many more allusions to Teddy's many traumas and realities. Williams turns around to reveal her back smoldering, recalling her supposed death in a fire. But she is later soaking wet, recalling her murder of her children. When Teddy holds his wife, blood pours from her stomach, indicating his shooting her. All the while, ash falls increasingly, signaling the Nazi death camp as much as his wife's supposed death in a fire. In retrospect, the dream emerges as one of the most significant *visual* junctions in the film for the personal and collective trauma that Andrew reflects.[29] Along with this scene, Teddy's conversation with Chuck in a mausoleum in the prison cemetery links Teddy's difficulty concerning his military involvement with his inaction regarding his mentally imbalanced wife.

After the dream, Scorsese teases out the mystery behind Teddy's hallucinations, dreams, and obsessions, but he does so through the genres he has so far invoked. Now that Teddy's traumas have been imperceptibly blended—another example: Ruby Jerins portrays Rachel Laeddis, Teddy's actual drowned daughter, as well as the "missing patient" Rachel Solando's drowned daughter and a dead girl in his visions of Dachau—when the plot advances, fully inhabiting the tropes of 1950s horror and Frankenheimer-like conspiracy thrillers, it parallels Teddy's personal traumas. In this way—by focusing on Teddy's manic use of genre as a mask, as a desperate attempt to understand—the film directly address a number of problems of the postwar era and immediately yokes them to Teddy's problems.

Scorsese makes his equation of personal and cultural trauma evident most explicitly through a few key lines of dialogue throughout a number of isolated scenes. For instance, when Teddy and Chuck are exploring Ward C, looking for the pyromaniac that Teddy believes killed his wife, the marshals find out patients are running loose in the ward after the storm. In full horror mode, Scorsese depicts the men searching dark corridors filled with disembodied screaming, while creepy people (a laughing guard and a shirtless, bloody prisoner) appear out of nowhere. One patient, Billings, jumps Teddy, strangling him with his elbow while whispering harshly in his ear:

> Listen to me! Listen! I don't want to leave here, all right? I mean, why would anyone want to? We hear things here about the outside world. About atolls, about H-bomb tests. You know how a hydrogen bomb works?.... Other bombs explode, right? Not the H-bomb. It implodes, creating an explosion to the thousandth, the millionth degree! Do you get it?[30]

This is one of many references by patients to the atrocities committed by outside society. This apparently psychotic and murderous patient doesn't want to leave the ghastly hell Scorsese so ably depicts because the United States has developed the H-bomb, and such horror is more fearful to him. And in the context of the struggle over Teddy's self-identity, Billings' "ramblings" have even further importance. Teddy himself is imploding to such a degree he is causing a far worse outward explosion. This is an admirable level of thematic reinforcement added to the film, but it would be a mistake to forget the importance of the surface meaning here: the United States has developed mass-killing bombs that even a murderous psycho finds frightening.

The tie between Teddy's ghosts and the U.S.'s own dark past is reinforced further when Teddy meets the Rachel Solando hiding in the cliffs. Claiming to be a former psychiatrist of Ashecliffe, she explains to Teddy that they labeled her crazy to discount everything she said: "That's the Kafkaesque genius of it. People tell the world you're crazy, but your protests to the contrary just confirm what they're saying!" She likens the practices she claims are happening on Shutter Island to the North Koreans in the 1950s:

Marshal, the North Koreans used American POWs during their brainwashing experiments. They turned soldiers into traitors. That's what they're doing here! They're creating ghosts to go out in the world and do things sane men never would [....] Fifty years from now, people will look back and say, "Here, this place is where it all began. The Nazis used Jews, the Soviets used prisoners in their own gulags, and we tested patients on Shutter Island."[31]

The Communist conspiracies of various postwar thrillers are equated with Teddy's memories of the concentration camp, as well as the experiments he thinks his own government is performing.

But the bond between Teddy's personal history and America's postwar problems is made most explicit when Teddy and Chuck are stuck in the mausoleum during the hurricane while they are out looking for Andrew Laeddis's grave.[32] First, Chuck asks if Teddy is there to kill Laeddis. Scorsese frames them in a two-shot, with Teddy foregrounded and slightly out of focus. The film remains in this shot for Teddy's response, which comes after he thinks for a moment: "I'm not here to kill Laeddis." The film cuts suddenly to a winter scene in a forest, as soldiers come walking out of a fog. The motif from Penderecki's "Passacaglia," from the opening shot when the island emerged in the fog, reappears on the non-diegetic soundtrack and continues into the cross-cut back to the two-shot of Teddy and Chuck. This juxtaposition of shots emphasizes the importance of the flashback to Chuck's question by keeping Chuck in focus and by decentering Teddy visually and narratively. When Chuck responds, "If it were my wife, I'd kill him ... twice," Teddy gives a short laugh and Scorsese cuts back to the winter scene, now specifically a shot of a Nazi concentration camp where German soldiers are surrendering. The cross-cutting continues as Teddy tells his story about the German guards surrendering at Dachau,

> When we got through the gates at Dachau, the SS guards surrendered. The commandant tried to kill himself before we got there, but he botched it ... took him an hour to die. When I went outside, I saw all the bodies on the ground. Too many to count. Too many to imagine. So yeah, the guards surrendered, we took their guns, and we lined them up.

Most of this dialogue is spoken over a Dachau montage, images which the audience has already glimpsed. As Teddy speaks the last sentence, the music builds in volume and tension, and then one of the Allied soldiers shoots an escaping German soldier. In the flashback, Teddy begins firing, as do all of the American soldiers. Scorsese tracks quickly to the right as the German soldiers are shot brutally. The shot is entirely unrealistic since such a shooting would occur all at once. Instead, the viewer witnesses the shooting begin on the left and continue along the line synchronized with the camera's tracking. The lengthened shot intensifies the moment, stretching the massacre to fifteen seconds what would have happened much faster. Teddy concludes his story saying, "It wasn't warfare. It was murder. I've had enough of killing. That's not why I'm here."[33] But this story is not just about killing; it's about killing as a response to atrocity. He participated in the mass murder of the surrendered SS guards at Dachau after witnessing the infamous "death train," and he killed his wife for drowning their children. The acts committed by those Teddy murdered are two of the most horrific acts of humankind, but Teddy's response to them haunts him *because he was complicit in allowing them to go on.*

Conclusion

Scorsese's greatest trick in *Shutter Island* is that everything is entirely on the surface—even as it's not. Traumatic memories are usually suppressed in such a way that they remain at the surface, only masked. Similarly, the film tries to do precisely what Teddy is trying to do: examine Americans' confrontation with human atrocity to keep it from happening again. He is trying to uncover the truth at the hospital, but his "work" is misdirected. He should be uncovering his own truth first. While Cawley and his staff have indeed deceived Teddy by allowing him to play out his own fantasy, they are trying to operate just below that play of masking signifiers to use the acting out against itself. And Scorsese is actually imitating Cawley's plan. His film draws on the acting out by American culture, done through simplified, schematic genre narratives, in order to equate Teddy's obsessive repetition with America's postwar generic repetition. The American audience is positioned as an historical witness to the collective trauma of the Shoah by being drawn in "dishonestly" to a genre film, in order to encourage an honest reckoning with collective guilt over the past. The layering use of multiple genres creates an atmosphere of the fantastic, which in turn produces a structural trauma—a more honest way for *contemporary* Americans to confront the collective trauma of the Shoah, which most did not experience. Teddy is a metonym for the mythic American hero, masked by delusions and haunted by repressed traumatic memories. Ultimately, this association suggests that the problems and solutions for one might be the problems and solutions for the other: the way out for Teddy is the way out for America.

The ending remains a puzzler then, but for different reasons. As Teddy sits on the steps of one of the buildings, Dr. Sheehan comes up to him and they chat, after which Teddy tells him, "We've gotta get off this rock, Chuck." Apparently, he has regressed, so Dr. Sheehan signals to Dr. Cawley, Dr. Naehring, and the Warden to come for him, presumably to give him a lobotomy since the working-through pageant did not work. But maybe Teddy sees all of this—it's hard to tell—and he looks somewhat knowingly at Dr. Sheehan when he then says, "You know, this place makes me wonder... Which would be worse: to live as a monster or to die as a good man?"[34] He gets up to meet the men coming to take him. If Martin Scorsese has equated Teddy's traumas with America's, what does this say about our chances?

NOTES

1. Sigmund Freud, "Remembering, Repeating and Working-Through," in *The Standard Edition of the Complete Psychological Works of Sigmund Freud*, vol. 12, trans. and ed. James Strachey (London: Hogarth Press, 1958), 151.

2. Throughout this essay, I will refer to the character of Teddy Daniels/ Andrew Laeddis as simply "Teddy Daniels."

3. Tzvetan Todorov, *The Fantastic: A Structural Approach to a Literary Genre* (Ithaca, NY: Cornell University Press, 1975), 25, 3.

4. Kathryn Hume, *Fantasy and Mimesis: Responses to Reality in Western Literature* (London: Methuen, 1984), 21; Judith Kerman, "Drawing Lines in the Sand: The Fantastic Considered as an Instance of Liminality," in *Flashes of the Fantastic: Selected Essays from* The War of the Worlds *Centennial, Nineteenth International Conference on the Fantastic in the Arts*, ed. David Ketterer (Westport, CT: Greenwood Press, 2004), 178.

5. Daniel Chandler, "An Introduction to Genre Theory," last modified 2000, http://www.aber.ac.uk/media/Documents/intgenre/chandler_genre_theory.pdf.

6. Dana Stevens and Troy Patterson, "Shutter Island," episode 94, *Slate*'s Spoiler Specials, *Slate*, podcast audio, February 18, 2010, http://feeds.feedburner.com/SlateSpoilerSpecials.

7. Anthony Lane, "Behind Bars," review of *Shutter Island* and *A Prophet*, *The New Yorker*, March 1, 2010, http://www.newyorker.com/arts/critics/cinema/2010/03/01/100301crci_cinema_lane.

8. Sue Vice, *Holocaust Fiction* (London: Routledge, 2000), 1

9. Gilead Morahg, "Creating Wasserman: The Quest for a New Holocaust Story in David Grossman's *See Under: Love*," *Judaism* 51, no. 1 (Winter 2002): 52, Academic Search Complete (6502821).

10. Theodor Adorno, *Negative Dialectics*, trans. E.B. Asthon (London: Routledge, 1973), 362; Paul Ricoeur, *Time and Narrative*, vol. 3, trans. Kathleen Blamey and David Pellauer (1988; Chicago: University of Chicago Press, 1990 [1988]), 189.

11. Ricoeur, *Time and Narrative*, 185.

12. Ibid., 187–88.

13. Melanie J. Wright, "'Don't Touch My Holocaust': Responding to *Life Is Beautiful*." *The Journal of Holocaust Education* 9, no. 1 (Summer 2000): 21.

14. Bilge Ebiri, "*Shutter Island*, Scorsese's longed-for leap into low-down

genre filmmaking, isn't the potboiler you expect—to its credit," review of *Shutter Island*, *Nashville Scene*, February 18, 2010, http://www.nashvillescene.com/ nashville/shutter-island-scorseses-longed-for-leap-into-low-down-genre-filmmak ing-isnt-the-potboiler-you-expect-andmdash-to-its-credit/Content?oid=1227237.

15. Dennis Lehane, *Shutter Island* (2003; New York: HarperTorch, 2004 [2003]), 346.

16. Lehane, *Shutter Island*, 2.

17. Chapter 1, *Shutter Island*, dir. Martin Scorsese (Hollywood, CA: Paramount Pictures, 2010), DVD.

18. Ibid.

19. Ibid.

20. Ibid., Chapter 2.

21. Ibid.

22. Ibid., Chapter 3.

23. Ibid., Chapter 4.

24. Ibid.

25. Ibid.

26. Lehane's use of the Mahler quartet is anachronistic. There would have been no recording of this work extant during World War II because the manuscript had been lost and was not rediscovered until the 1960s.

27. Lehane, *Shutter Island*, 76.

28. Chapter 5, *Shutter Island*, DVD.

29. Ibid.

30. Ibid., Chapter 10.

31. Ibid., Chapter 13.

32. Ibid., Chapter 7.

33. Ibid.

34. Ibid., Chapter 19.

Going Beyond Horror
Fantasy, Humor and the Holocaust[1]
Caroline Joan (Kay) S. Picart

Introduction: Classic and Conflicted Frames

The theoretical framework of this essay begins with one of my co-authored books, *Frames of Evil: The Holocaust as Horror in American Film*.[2] In this book, I and David Frank, a historian and rhetorician, discuss the cross-fertilizations that have evolved, binding Holocaust films, usually shot in a documentary or docu-dramatic mode, and horror films, usually visually coded as drawing from the Gothic fictional tradition. Yet the point of *Holocaust as Horror* is not to show that there is no such thing as "fact" or "fiction" but that there is a mode of narrativizing that clearly privileges the look of the "real," even in the use of horror-derived cinematic techniques (such as in *Schindler's List* [1993], where the Nazi Goeth's [Ralph Fiennes] roving and penetrating gaze upon Helena [Embeth Davidtz], his maid, in the basement scene, are reminiscent of shots seen from the point of view of Hannibal Lechter [Anthony Hopkins] in *Silence of the Lambs* [1991]) or motifs (*Schindler's List*'s visualization of the Schindler women's descent into the "showers" is reminiscent of *Psycho*'s [1960] shower scene, with a reverse ending: the Schindler women are saved, rather than killed).[3] Part of the book's conclusion is that "realistic" documentary modes actually draw from "fictional" Gothic modes, which themselves have a complex relationship with the real: all fictional cinematic serial killers, beginning with the iconic Norman Bates from *Psycho*, in some way draw their heritage from the historically real Ed Gein. Yet the appropriation of fictional

Gothic modes into factual documentary or docu-dramatic modes is acceptable or convincing as "true" only if these cinematic references masquerade as partaking of the look of the "real." As such, this essay converges with Dominick LaCapra's aspiration for an "ethic of response"[4] to those who have suffered from and continue to suffer from the trauma of the Holocaust. The methods employed by this essay shift the focus to critical practices of viewership and interpretation,[5] and ultimately inquire whether there is any kind of responsibility that accompanies our enjoyment of films that draw from, and yet imaginatively diverge from, the traumatic heritage of the Holocaust. In thus deploying these tools, I ask, drawing from Daniel Schwarz, whether "the intelligibility of history, even the place of evil in history, depends on reconfiguring its imaginative and aesthetic terms."[6]

But how does one analyze cinematic genres that reference the Holocaust, but defy the privileging of the documentary mode, for more fantastic (or at least, non-realistic) modes of narrativizing? What do the cinematic modes of fantasy, magic realism, and comedy, for example, tell us about how the legacy of the Holocaust has seeped into the way that we collectively imagine and tell stories about heroes and monsters, and "good" and "evil?" From whose perspective do we tell these stories? Is there an ethics of spectatorship that can be glimpsed through science fiction, fantasy, and comedic referents to the trauma of the Holocaust? What do, for example, *Pan's Labyrinth* and *Life Is Beautiful* tell us about how we collectively work through the trauma of the Holocaust through less realistic formats, as opposed to the documentary mode of narrativizing?

An important conceptual tool in tackling this set of questions is partially derived from Isabel Cristina Pinedo.[7] This tool lies in the distinctions drawn between a "classic horror frame" and a "conflicted horror frame."[8] The classic horror frame, more characteristic of Hollywood horror films of the thirties and forties, demands the creation of a monster so utterly Other that only his/her killing/sacrifice can render closure, and with that, the restoration of normalcy, to the story. As Pinedo writes: "the boundary between good and evil, normal and abnormal, human and alien is as firmly drawn as the imperative that good must conquer evil, thus producing a secure Manichean worldview in which the threats to the social order are largely external and (hu)man agency prevails, largely in the figure of the masterful male subject."[9] In contrast to the classic horror frame, the conflicted horror frame views evil as residing within the "normal." Whereas classic horror monsters "breach the norms of ontological propriety,"[10] such as the classic Hollywood Frankenstein Monster(s), monsters of the conflicted horror frame seem "ordinary" at a first glance, much like

Norman Bates. While the classic horror frame breaches the ontology of "the normal,"[11] the conflicted horror frame, as Steffen Hantke observes "violates the integrity and separateness of the two spheres"[12]—the normal and the fantastic.

Whereas the focus in *Holocaust as Horror* was in showing the differences between the two frames, the focus of this essay is in mapping how the classic and conflicted frames, in fantasy, magic realist and comedic modes, are less diametrically opposed than paired in mirror-imaging ways, like Siamese twins. The resulting narratives, because they are not as overtly constrained by "documentary" or "moral" binaries, are much more complex, and have much to tell us, about the teratological re-imagination of the Holocaust and its iconic monster, the Nazi.

Pan's Labyrinth: *Myth, History and Fantasy*

Marketed as a fairy tale for adults, *Pan's Labyrinth* (*El Laberinto del Fauno*) juxtaposes the horrors of two worlds: the horrors of fantasy in an archetypal world of fairies and fauns, and the horrors cemented by a fascist regime, of psychopathic military men and their minions. Its story can be simply sketched, as a starting point. Nearing the end of the bloody Spanish Civil War, 10-year-old Ofelia (Ivana Baquero) is ordered to go to an isolated mansion along with her extremely pregnant mother, Carmen (Ariadna Gil). Lonely and alienated from her new stepfather, Captain Vidal (Sergi López), Ofelia, summoned by a grasshopper-fairy, discovers an ancient labyrinth where she meets the Faun, who recognizes her as the long-missing "Princess Moanna" and regales her with stories of the fairy world. The plot takes an unexpected twist when Ofelia's mother, Carmen, suddenly becomes ill because of what seems like a pregnancy worthy of Mary Shelley's Frankensteinian nightmares. Devoted to her mother, Ofelia makes an agreement with the Faun to save her mother. Yet to prove that Ofelia/Princess Moanna's spirit has remained "whole" and uncontaminated by her mortal flesh, Ofelia/Princess Moanna also has to perform three tasks. Much like all mythical quests, these challenges launch her on an Odyssean journey, where she must use her guile and wit, and trust her own instincts to overcome all monsters who stand in the way of her reclaiming her royal status in the fairy world.

The plot of the film meanders across these two worlds: one rooted in fairy tales and the other in Franco-ite Spain. The two worlds initially seem completely separate, but then slowly begin to infiltrate and influence each other, as evidenced, for example, by the filters used to shoot the two worlds. Despite the hypersaturated color of the daytime world of Franco-ite Spain, its night scenes have a cold, bluish-gray tint. In addition, the camera work in the world of the diegetic real has a linear, less active perspective. In contrast, the nocturnal underworld or labyrinth scenes predominantly have a light green sheen that lights up the moss that seems to populate not only the background, but also the trees and the figure of the Faun himself. In general, the color palette of the Faun's world is more vibrant: its reds and golds are particularly luminous, and the camera work in this fantasy world initially seems more active and meanders about imaginatively.

Later, as the film develops toward its climactic conclusion, the two worlds begin to bleed into each other, with the turning point being Carmen's near-miscarriage and descent into a fever that induces delirium. Interestingly, it is the fantasy world that influences the real world first, as Ofelia, following the Faun's instruction, immerses a mandrake root, shaped like a boy, in a bowl of milk, feeds it two drops of blood, and slips it underneath her ailing mother's bed. Increasingly, the reds and golds of the fantasy world seep into the real world as her mother begins to recover.

Yet when Ofelia's stepfather, Vidal, finds what appears, to his eyes, to be a decaying root soaked in putrefying milk, another turning point ensues. Choosing her second husband over her daughter, Carmen rejects her daughter's impassioned pleas and disciplines her by throwing the mandrake into the fire. As the mandrake transitions, through Ofelia's gaze, from being simply a root to becoming a human-like creature that writhes in pain and lets off a shrill cry, Carmen's fate, which she has chosen by rejecting the fantasy world in favor of the real, becomes clear. Carmen dies as she gives birth to Vidal's son, and the color palette of the film again begins to shift. The golden color undertone is replaced by an ash grey that predominantly marks Captain Vidal's harsh universe and seems reminiscent of the color tones of Picasso's *Guernica*.[13] The colors of the diegetically real become more dominant as Ofelia is forced to report to the Faun that she failed to heed his advice in the accomplishment of her second task, and she experiences utter despair.

On the one hand, *Pan's Labyrinth* seems to have a clear, practically literal reference to the nightmare of the Holocaust through the figure of Captain Vidal, who is clearly a sadist in military uniform. He has set up camp in an isolated farmhouse in northern Spain to stamp out the pestilence of leftover anti–Fascist rebels from the Civil War. Vidal's only other obsession, all too reminiscent of the Nazis, is to produce a pure blooded son.

One of the most violent scenes, shown very early, and one of the very few sequences visibly referencing horror methods of narration in relation to the Holocaust, illustrates how the captain indifferently tortures one of two captured "rebels" who turn out to be innocent peasants hunting rabbits. Shot in Gothic low key lighting, and seen from a high angle shot, from the point of view of Vidal, we see an extreme close-up of the prisoner's face, systematically mashed into a pulp by a bottle, which, unlike the prisoner's face, does not break.[14] Then, with the same degree of aloofness, the captain simply shoots the protesting father of the man he just killed. When an examination of the now-deceased prisoners' belongings reveals two dead rabbits (and thus proves the alleged rebels' story to be true), Vidal simply shrugs and walks away, expressing irritation that his staff has even bothered him with such an inconsequential matter.

Yet it is less the captain, a clear appropriation of the Nazi-as-monster type, who is of interest to us. Rather, it is the second of the monsters, the "Pale Man," who bears closer scrutiny, precisely because his connection to the monstrosities of the Holocaust is more oblique, and therefore, given the vividness of director Guillermo del Toro's imaginative universe, more revelatory. The original design of the "Pale Man," according to the director's notes, was an obese man who suddenly lost a lot of weight, leaving the excess flesh hanging over an extremely tall, skeletal frame.[15] Del Toro changed the face, such that only the nostrils and bloody mouth remained; the creature's eyes became bloodshot eyeballs that could be inserted into slits in the palms of his hands. To see, the monster would then hold his hands, fan-like, against his head.

The result was a character both mythic and historical. The Pale Man was a creature, akin to the many wondrous beasts encountered by Odysseus during his journey back home, who is forever hungry. He is surrounded by luxuriant supplies of food, yet he consumes only the flesh of innocents (as evidenced by the pile of children's shoes—a historical reference to the Holocaust), and ironically is never full (See Figure 6). Del Toro, in the director's commentary,[16] was clear that he wanted the *mise en scène* of the Pale Man to resemble both a "church" (meaning something that commands dread and reverence, much like Otto's notion of the *Mysterium Tremendum*[17]) and "the Holocaust" (principally through the pile of shoes—now an iconic synechdoche for the millions killed during the Holocaust). Del Toro's interpretation of Ofelia's catabasis into the Pale Man's lair therefore parallels some Holocaust historians' description of the descent into the gas chambers as a "negative sublime."[18]

Del Toro was also at pains to make the diegetic real world (Franco-

Figure 6. Ivana Baquero (Ofelia) opposite Doug Jones (Pale Man) in *Pan's Labyrinth* (2006).

ite Spain) and the fantasy world within *Pan's Labyrinth*, increasingly mime each other. In one pivotal scene, Captain Vidal sits at a long, rectangular table, where, as a show of wealth and power, he superciliously feeds the town officials with luxuriant supplies of food during wartime conditions when food is scarce and heavily rationed. In a mirror-imaging way, the Pale Man also sits at a long, rectangular table decked with appetizing displays of food, essentially as alone as the captain is, despite the small crowd gathered around Vidal, engaging in self-serving political small talk. Del Toro takes pains to explain that the predominant visual lines of the camera, in both table scenes, were long and linear, in contrast to the usually circular lines that animate the fantasy world.[19] The lighting in both had a yellow, harsh glare, quite unlike the soothing, golden color of Ofelia's story of the rose, which she narrates to her brother, sleeping in her mother's womb.

Del Toro was meticulous in emphasizing that all of his artistic designs had an allusion to fine art rather than "comic book" references. For instance, he embedded a visual allusion to one of Francisco Goya's horrifying Black paintings: that of Saturn devouring one of his sons.[20] In *Pan's Labyrinth*, the Pale Man devours two fairies: a grotesque form of justice, as Ofelia had willfully devoured two juicy grapes from the Pale Man's table despite the fairies' and the Pale Man's warnings. But this is a form of excessive "justice" the Nazis would have well understood, in their attempt to stamp out all rebellion or resistance, much as, interestingly, the Faun later attempts to extract blind obedience from Ofelia for her third task.

Del Toro emphasizes that it is not so much whether Ofelia "succeeds" at her tasks, but her coming to trust her judgment enough to rebel, that is important.[21] It is as much a "coming of age" as it is a paean of praise for those who dared to be disobedient to the Nazis. Del Toro, at the end of his commentary on the film, reveals that he deliberately chose the same actor for both the Pale Man and the Faun because in his mind, the Pale Man, the Faun, and the Giant Toad were all the same character.[22] In other words, even the sacrifice of the blue and red fairies to the Pale Man's ravenous revenge was simply a ruse to test Ofelia's/Princess Moanna's spirit. As proof, del Toro states that in the final scene, when Princess Moanna has entered into her kingdom, not only is her mother restored as Queen, beautiful in full regalia beside her king, but also, all three fairies are present, vibrantly alive.[23]

What emerges, upon a deeper analysis, are the complex interrelationships binding a classic and conflicted frame, particularly in the figures of the Faun and Ofelia, the two characters who cross most easily across the two diegetic realms of the real and the fantastic. Del Toro was careful to emphasize that "Pan" was referenced in the title only of the U.S. English release. To him, the Faun was a creature more ambiguous—a "neutral" character, neither "good" nor "bad."[24] In the diegetic "real world," the Faun seems a monster both "classic" and "conflicted." With his imposing appearance and agelessness (the reference to Cronos pops up again, when the Faun states that he has many names, some so old that only the trees can pronounce them), the Faun appears completely "other." Yet because the Faun initially seems so bent in helping Princess Moanna regain her rightful place, he seems wise and good, and therefore, sympathetic enough to understand Ofelia's mortal plight (therefore, in spirit, passing as humane). It is important to see that the Faun ages backwards, such that he seems oldest (practically blind with cataracts and bent over, perhaps in mimicry of an archetype like the Greek figure of Tiresias, the blind seer) when he is most benevolent. Later, as he gets more tyrannical (and demands that Ofelia sacrifice her younger brother—the brother whose birth has caused her mother's painful pregnancy and eventual death), he becomes younger and more attractive, much like Lucifer. When Ofelia resists the Faun's final command/offer, he surrenders the girl-woman to his diegetic real life counterpart in this scene. Captain Vidal, who seems an extension of the

Faun in this darkest of moments, shoots Ofelia, and claims his son—only to be assassinated by the triumphant rebels. Much like the Nazis, who prized a severe Aryan form of beauty, the Faun, during the final temptation/challenge in the diegetic real world, appears most attractive and tyrannical. It is in this scene that the Faun appears to be the monster of the conflicted frame: someone more akin to the Nazi psychopathic human beasts, who delight in the suffering of innocents.

Yet the story does not end there. In a temporal loop that begins in the thick of the action and returns to the beginning, where the blood dripping from Ofelia's nose and hand had flowed backwards, the blood now drips in a slow but steady stream, forming rivulets that fill the lacunae of the labyrinth, resembling a Mayan sacrifice. As the diegetically "real" Ofelia dies, a hero mourned, the Princess Moanna returns to her kingdom, hailed by her magical royal parents and all the strange and wondrous creatures of the fantastic realm, including, of course, the Faun, who bows to her, much as a devoted courtier does. The Faun, in the fantastic realm, ultimately ends up not a monster, but his counterpart, a citizen-emissary: a catalyst whose function was to help reawaken Ofelia/Moanna's true self.

As Del Toro acknowledges in his commentary on the film,[25] it is important that Ofelia is a girl-woman: someone who has not yet crossed completely over into sexual maturity and motherhood. As such, there is no contradiction for her between being a true princess (as opposed to the apparent "princess" in the green dress and shiny black shoes her mother wanted her to be, in order to display her as an obedient spectacle of femininity at the captain's long table) and going on these masculine adventures of battling monsters. While Ofelia/Moanna, within the diegetic fantastic world, initially appears as the unambiguous heroine of a classic frame (human/Good versus Other/Evil), especially in her battle against the giant Toad, in her battle against the Pale Man, her "goodness" becomes questionable. She appears to have a perverse streak for disobedience, as she does not heed the Faun's earlier warning not to become distracted, and she refuses to follow the directives of the fairies in choosing which door to open to claim an ancient dagger, and eventually in stealing two luscious grapes from the forbidden table of the apparently sleeping Pale Man. Her punishment: the bloody devouring of the two fairies and her apparent banishment by the Faun. Thus, Ofelia, during her second test or challenge appears, more akin to characters who populate narratives of the conflicted frame: she knows evil can lurk within, and she knows the despair of the Fall, with its curse of mortality.

Nevertheless, during the third and final test, Ofelia, though she swears total and absolute obedience to the Faun, defies him, refusing to spill the blood of an innocent (her brother, who inadvertently caused her mother Carmen much pain during pregnancy and eventually kills Carmen when he is born). Ofelia's "perverse streak" of disobedience thus becomes revaluated, within this context, as a rebellion against Evil and as a finding of her true self: a "coming home." Indeed, Del Toro, in his commentary, praises the value of learning to become disobedient and to trust one's own sense of inner decency, in contrast with, in his view, the codified "fairy tales" of politics and organized religion.[26]

To close this analysis of *Pan's Labyrinth*, it is important to notice that Mercedes, the maid/militia spy (Maribel Verdú), survives Ofelia in the diegetic real world. As Del Toro notes in his commentary, Mercedes and Ofelia, in some crucial ways, "are the same" (in contrast to the compliant Carmen, Ofelia's mother).[27] Both Ofelia and Mercedes have secret lives and engage in dangerous adventures; both have a propensity to disobey outer directives and honor their inner selves. Mercedes, in some ways, is the grown up version of Ofelia.

But there are two crucial differences between Mercedes and Ofelia: 1.) Mercedes no longer believes in fauns and magic, as Ofelia does; 2.) Mercedes is capable of a great deal of violence, as revealed in the scene in which she stabs Captain Vidal and guts his cheek, calling him a "pig," thus momentarily turning the tables on her would-be torturer and escaping.

In contrast, Ofelia not only believes in Fauns and magic: to her, they are the more compelling reality. Unlike Mercedes, Ofelia is incapable of any violence, even against the brother who has caused her beloved mother's suffering and death, or against Captain Vidal, who seems the very embodiment of Evil. A Christ-like figure, she absorbs violence into herself rather than choosing to direct it outwards, to save herself or to gain entry into the fantastic world through the sacrifice of another, however justifiable it may seem. Ofelia/Moanna is a character who can only survive within a classic frame as she is, in the final choice, incapable of making compromises with evil and violence. Mercedes, because she has been willing to make such compromises, can survive in the diegetic real world and thus become a "hero" of the conflicted frame. And it is ultimately through her eyes that we survive Del Toro's fantastic and mythic deformation of the nightmare of Spanish Nazism, to look forward with something resembling hope.

From the fantastic world of *Pan's Labyrinth*, we next move into the magic realist and comedic world of *Life Is Beautiful* to see how we have collectively attempted to go beyond the horror of the Holocaust to brave new worlds that acknowledge this trauma but do not remain trapped in it.

Life Is Beautiful: *Magic Realism, History and Humor*

To make the transition into the magical realist and comedic reinterpretation of the Holocaust in *Life Is Beautiful*, I borrow from Arthur Koestler's theoretical schema visualizing the continuum binding the "Haha" experience (comedy) and the "Aha" instance (artistic creation and scientific discovery).[28] Briefly sketched, Koestler held that the psychological "mechanics" of comedy are essentially the same as other "creative" acts: these mechanics involve the sudden clash between two mutually exclusive codes of rules, or associative contexts, which are suddenly juxtaposed. What results is "bisociation"—a condition, Koestler explains,[29] that compels us to interpret the situation in "two self-consistent but incompatible frames of reference at the same time; it makes us function simultaneously on two different wave-lengths."[30] The tension caused by bisociation is purged either through laughter, scientific fusion, or artistic confrontation. As Koestler writes:

> The conscious or unconscious processes underlying creativity are essentially combinatorial activities—the bringing together of previously separate ideas of knowledge and experience. The scientist's purpose is to achieve *synthesis*; the artist aims at a *juxtaposition* of the familiar and the eternal; the humorist's game is to contrive a *collision*.[31]

Koestler draws up a continuum binding humor (the "Ha-Ha" experience, where the tension of juxtaposing two planes of meaning normally kept apart is exploded), scientific discovery (the "Aha" experience where this tension is resolved in a cause-effect relation) and artistic creation (the "Ah" experience, where the tension is held).

What I do in this later section of the chapter is explore how bisociation, as well as an uneasy and complex tension between the "monstrous" and the "all too human," constitutes the fulcrum upon which the comedic, the fantastic and the horrifying converge in fluid interrelationship. In *Life Is Beautiful* (1997) (Italian, *La Vita è bella*), that tension is created through the juxtaposition of a magic realist and comedic point of view (the story of the persecution of the Jews and the Holocaust from the point of view of a child, who is told this is simply a game), with a tragic storyline (the loss of a beloved father, and the inhumane treatment and near-extermination of a race). That creative tension, to mangle a phrase from Thomas Kuhn's *The Essential Tension*, is compounded by the bisociation of a deliberately inauthentic form (hyper-enhanced color, characteristic of fantasy films) with a historical event (the Holocaust).

As an essay[32] published in *The Holocaust Film Sourcebook* shows, David Bathrick argues that the charges brought against Holocaust films generally fall across three categories: trivialization, visualization, and fictionalization.[33] The charge of trivialization involves, for Bathrick, the ways in which Holocaust films aimed at mass audiences have the capacity to turn the Holocaust into a commodified consumer event. Bathrick notes that Miramax, for example, launched a seven million dollar advertising campaign to promote the American release of *Life Is Beautiful*,[34] and many critics responded to the film's popular success with sentiments echoing an Art Spiegelman cartoon in *The New Yorker* that depicted a concentration camp prisoner holding an Oscar.

While trivialization is certainly a problematic for many of the film's critics, visualization seems above all else to have incited revulsion against *Life Is Beautiful*. For Bathrick, the concern with visualization is really one of "authenticity," a term that repeatedly surfaces in critical responses to *Life Is Beautiful*.[35] Interestingly, the film's introductory voiceover mirrors James Whale's defensive prologue in *Bride of Frankenstein* (1935), in that it acknowledges its limitations as an "authentic" representation of the Holocaust by dubbing the ensuing story as "like a fable."[36] Nevertheless, the film is presumptively viewed against an assumed scale of verisimilitude or "authenticity."

One aspect of such expectation involves the film's depiction of an almost benign concentration camp, one in which Nazis are caricaturized as "the mean guys who yell" and violence is rendered invisible, hinted at as taking place behind the scenes. Though we are left to intuit the camp's violence, the film's representation of the gas chambers is limited to a scene in the antechamber in which prisoners are asked to undress. In addition, when the film's central character, Guido, is shot, the action occurs off-screen, and we infer his death only through the soundtrack's gunfire. Critics who note the lack of realism in the absence of on-screen violence typically focus on a brief point-of-view shot of a mound of bones, which is only visible momentarily, and even then, glimpsed briefly through a thinning fog. The criticisms leveled against this single and vivid moment of "real" on-screen horror are often that the corpses appear surreal, or that

Guido, based on factual occurrences, surely would have detected the stench of the dead bodies long before this revelatory scene could take place, thus effectively canceling its surprise/shock element, as well as its verisimilitude.[37] In the end, perhaps the most common charge against the film concerning authenticity lies with the survival of Guido's son, Giosue, which would have been impossible in the concentration camps.

Roberto Benigni, the film's director, co-screenwriter, and lead actor, taking an opposing view to the rhetorical strategies Steven Spielberg employs in marketing *Schindler's List* (1993), has addressed critical insistence on verisimilitude in interviews:

> This is not a historical document by any means.... According to what I read, saw, and felt in the victims' accounts, I realized nothing in a film could even come close to the reality of what happened. You can't show unimaginable horror—you can only ever show less than what it was. So I didn't want audiences to look for realism in my movie.[38]

Though Benigni consulted survivors, researched histories and personal accounts, and was under advisement by historian Marcello Pezzetti through Milan's Center for Contemporary Jewish Documentation, Benigni realized the inevitable insufficiency of any attempt to represent the Holocaust in a realist manner. Benigni conducted the preliminary research necessary to reconstruct a realist film, but subsequently made a judiciously measured authorial choice in favor of creating an "unrealistic" film instead. Historical advisor Pezzetti notes, "The historian has to be a historian, but at the end the artist must choose what to do and how. He did not follow all of the analysis and recommendations I provided. He was very careful to keep his own counsel and decide according to his own sensibility."[39] Benigni's artistic choices included the "reconstruction of the camp as a stone building rather than a more realistic wooden frame complex ... [to add] to the fairy tale setting,"[40] as well as intentionally portraying the dead bodies as surreal or unreal.[41]

Life Is Beautiful, then, deliberately defies the use of documentary and horror-derived cinematic modes of story-telling, but for what purpose? One could argue that the film's lack of verisimilitude helps the audience to establish a distance from the historical reality of the Holocaust in order to allow for what Dominick LaCapra has termed the "working through" of Holocaust trauma. Unlike more sober film treatments of the Holocaust that compulsively repeat or "act out" the trauma of the Holocaust on-screen (and by extension, urge us to continue "acting out" the trauma as well), *Life Is Beautiful* and other comedic (and fantastic) film representations of the Holocaust offer, one could argue, the potential for "working through" the trauma of the Holocaust by juxtaposing audience understandings of the historical reality of the Holocaust—which are informed by popular representations and images so widespread that they have become part of the collective (un)conscious—against the humorous fictions perpetuated in the films. Such humorous (and fantastic) representations, through their juxtaposition of conventionally non-associated modes of representation, potentially allow new understandings or relationships, even if fragile and fleeting, to emerge. One is never entirely finished with "acting out," and "working through"[42] is never absolutely closed, if the trauma runs so severely, particularly collectively, as in the case of the Holocaust; but there are moments of catharsis, insight, and potential healing, if subjects, as a matter of degree rather than completion, work through rather than act out.[43]

Along a parallel track with the themes of working through and bisociation, the act of interpreting humor in Holocaust films relies, to some extent, on the Incongruity Theory of Humor, which "holds that we laugh when we experience a certain discrepancy between what a situation is and what we expect it to be."[44] This theory, in turn, relies on the presupposition, along the lines of Koestler's notion of bisociation, that there exist at least two frames of reference, and the understanding that a comic situation "belongs simultaneously to two altogether independent series of events and is capable of being interpreted in two entirely different meanings at the same time," termed "dissociation."[45] Correspondingly, Sidra Dekoven Ezrahi refers to the distance between these two meanings as a

> cognitive dissonance in the foreground *vis-à-vis* the events enacted in the background ... informed by a *self-conscious* editing out of unacceptable historical reality.... The editing-out takes place *at the time* of danger as expression of displacement or dissociation ... and *at a distance* from danger as the second stage in the collective recovery from catastrophe.[46]

Thus, while in *Life Is Beautiful* Guido Orefice (Roberto Benigni) intentionally, diegetically, edits Holocaust historical reality to create a fantastic game for his son during their internment in a concentration camp, the audience, looking in, also re-edits historical reality, simultaneously displacing it from the on-screen action and yet imaginatively sustaining it as present.

This paradoxical interplay between presence and absence of historical reality is, in the film, nowhere more evident perhaps than in Guido's "translation" of the brutal camp rules and regulations as a Nazi corporal delivers them after Guido and Giosue (Giorgio Cantarini) first arrive in the camp. In this scene, Guido pretends to understand German so he can "translate" the corporal's instructions into a game in which his son must accumulate points in order to win a tank. Thus the corporal's statement, "Any sabotage is punishable by death, sentenced carried out right here in the yard, by machine gun in the back!" is comically rendered, in Guido's translation, "Scores will be announced every morning on the loudspeakers outside! Whoever is last has to wear a sign that says 'jackass'—here on his back!"[47] While Guido mimics the corporal's gestures and tone of voice, the audience, unlike Giosue, is aware of the disparity between the horror of the corporal's statements—which, though delivered in German, are still able to be inferred even by non–German-speaking audiences—and Guido's lighthearted game. The game's humorous aspect relies "on this blend of formal mimicry and willed ignorance of the horror, this ability to acknowledge the external forms of camp life while denying (and obstructing) their murderous intent."[48] The multiple reaction shots of Giosue's amazement that interrupt the shots of Guido "translating" allow the audience to identify with Giosue's wonder while remaining aware of the disparity between his understanding of the camp and the historical reality of the camps.

Similarly, Millicent Marcus analyzes the comic function of this disparity, citing Luigi Pirandello's *L'umorismo* as central to understanding how the comedy of *Life Is Beautiful* revolts against the urge to "act out" the trauma of the Holocaust. Marcus explains, "While the comic, for Pirandello, resides in the "avvertimento del contrario"—the awareness of disparate perspectives—the humorous resides in the "sentimento del contrario"—the concomitant philosophical reflection on the meaning of that disparity.[49] Thus, in Pirandellian terms, the inner audience (Giosue) laughs at the *avvertimento del contrario* while simultaneously we laugh at its *sentimento*. It is this doubling that grants Pirandellian humor its "philosophical and ethical *gravitas*."[50] Marcus applies Pirandello's theory to Guido's game, citing those moments in *Life Is Beautiful* in which the audience is most aware of the *sentimento del contrario*:

> [E]very time that Guido must invent a new gimmick to accommodate another instance of horror into his game plan, we must re-travel the distance between the Nazi original and the "Italian" translation, between atrocity and life-sustaining misinterpretation. We re-traverse that distance when Guido.... displays the tattooed number on his arm as evidence that he is enrolled in the game, when he explains that the back-breaking work of carrying anvils to the blast furnace is for the soldering of the plates for the tank, and when he concludes that all the children have disappeared because they are simply hiding. Every time we laugh, every time we make the cognitive leap that enables us to "get it" we re-trace the distance separating Guido's signifier from the Nazi signified.[51]

Conclusion: Working Through
Beyond Horror

In relation to the popularization of Holocaust representations, Alan Mintz observes:

> We are desperately in need of a way to understand this daunting complexity [of interpretations]. Yet the model we now have at our disposal is a rigid rhetoric of purity and impurity that compounds the difficulty.... We construct an ideal of authenticity and are quick to identify betrayals and exploitations.... The result is a contentious politics of blame and self-righteousness rather than a broadening cultural dialectic. The perpetuation of Holocaust memory is hardly served thereby....[52]

Pan's Labyrinth and *Life Is Beautiful*, in their own ways, offer different ways in which to re-memorialize the trauma of the Holocaust, but in a manner contrary to the usual documentary and horror-derived cinematic techniques. Both films deploy principally the grammars and narrative techniques of fantasy, magic realism and comedy to move across the classic as well as the conflicted frames, in order to re-imagine stories of monsters and heroes. In *Pan's Labyrinth*, the use of contrasting color palettes infused with mythic as well as Holocaust references creates a delicate balance between fantasy and history. In *Life Is Beautiful*, the imaginative rendering of historical accounts into a personal story humorously incorporating the point of view of a child forges an aesthetic that mixes the vivid brightness of magic realism, the rebellious energy of humor, and the darkness of traumatic memory. The result, in both, is the collision of "real/reel" worlds, which allows for a much more complex narrative capable of breaching the realm of "reel" fiction to address "real" concerns. Both films work through the unspeakable horrors of the Holocaust and imaginatively recreate them into visions of brave new worlds, thus inviting us, as imaginative spectator-participants, to critically examine our enjoyment of and identification with these worlds of conflicted frames. Much like the heroes of the conflicted frame, we know there are no easy binaries, both aesthetically and morally. Although we know that the notion of what is "heroic" can no longer be recaptured as "classic" or "pure," such heroism, however conflicted, can be glimpsed and lived, as it is in these films.

NOTES

1. Parts of this essay have appeared in: Caroline Joan (Kay) S. Picart, John Edgar Browning, and Carla Maria Thomas, "Where Reality and Fantasy Meet and Bifurcate: Holocaust Themes in *Pan's Labyrinth* (2006), *X-Men* (2000), and *V*

(1983)," in *Speaking of Monsters: A Teratological Anthology*, ed. Caroline Joan S. Picart and John Edgar Browning (New York: Palgrave Macmillan, 2012), 271–90, reproduced with permission of Palgrave Macmillan (the full published version of this publication is available from: http://us.macmillan.com/speakingofmonsters/CarolineJoanSPicart); and Caroline Joan (Kay) Picart and Jennifer Perrine, "Laughter, Terror and Revolt in Three Recent Holocaust Films," *The Holocaust Film Sourcebook* 1 (Westport, CT: Praeger, 2004), 402–13. I wish to thank ABC-Clio, Inc. for providing a complimentary license to reprint an adapted, excerpted version of the *Holocaust Film Sourcebook* essay, incorporated into this chapter. In addition, I dedicate this chapter to my two families, the Philippine Picart family and Tallahassean Terrell family, and especially my loving and supportive husband, Jerry Rivera, without whose patience and devotion I would not be able to accomplish as much. I also wish to thank Professors Raymond Fleming and John Stuhr for their continued mentorship and friendship, and John Edgar Browning and Professor Judith Kerman for inviting me on board this worthy project as well as being very patient with the time constraints and competing priorities under which I've had to work. Especially to John, I owe much, for his friendship, faith, patience, and collegiality.

2. Caroline Joan (Kay) S. Picart and David A. Frank, *Frames of Evil: The Holocaust as Horror in American Film* (Carbondale: Southern Illinois University Press, 2006).

3. For a concise exposition of this argument, see Caroline J.S. Picart and David Frank, "Horror and the Holocaust: Genre Elements in Schindler's List and Psycho," in *The Horror Film*, ed. Stephen Prince (New Brunswick, NJ: Rutgers University Press, 2003), 206–23.

4. Dominick LaCapra, *History and Memory After Auschwitz* (Ithaca, NY: Cornell University Press, 1998), 199–210.

5. Alan Mintz similarly advocates a constructivist, rather than a "realist," model of interpreting what the Holocaust has come to mean, springing from the active engagement of the "overlapping communities of interpretation in American society." See Alan Mintz, *Popular Culture and the Shaping of Holocaust Memory in America* (Seattle: University of Washington Press, 2001), 171.

6. Daniel R. Schwarz, *Imaging the Holocaust* (New York: St. Martin's, 1999), 37.

7. Isabel Cristina Pinedo, "Postmodern Elements of the Contemporary Horror Film," in T*he Horror Film*, ed. Steven Prince (New Brunswick, NJ: Rutgers University Press, 2004), 85–117.

8. Pinedo contrasts "postmodern" to "classic," but given the many rhetorical valences that freight the word "postmodern," Frank and I prefer to use "conflicted."

9. Pinedo, "Postmodern Elements of the Contemporary Horror Film," 89.

10. Noël Carroll, *Philosophy of Horror, or Paradoxes of the Heart* (New York: Routledge, 1990), 16.

11. Within the context of the filmic reinterpretation of a historical event, like the Holocaust, time is front and center to the project. But within the context of the "fantastic," time is irrelevant as it is a timeless sphere or one that does not adhere strictly to linear time. In the original context (Holocaust as horror, and film as historical [realistic-looking] revisualization), the theme of time is central.

12. Steffen Hantke, "The Kingdom of the Unimaginable: The Construction of Social Space and the Fantasy of Privacy in Serial Killer Narratives," *Literature/Film Quarterly* 26 (1998): 179–95.

13. Ruthe Stein writes: "Whether intentional or not, 'Labyrinth' bears a

resemblance to Picasso's 'Guernica.' Del Toro uses a similar palette—the color is so faded that some scenes appear to be in black and white with shades of gray—and his eerie mythical characters sport multiple eyes in unusual locations as on the famous mural." See Ruthe Stein, "The horror of the underworld (and this world)," *San Francisco Chronicle*, December 29, 2006, http://www.sfgate.com/cgi-bin/article.cgi?f=/c/a/2006/12/29/DDGH7N4LSM22.DTL.

14. In the director's commentary, Guillermo del Toro mentions that this scene is inspired by both a real incident from the civil war, and his own personal experiences that unlike Hollywood movies, where bottles constantly break, in real life, the bases of bottles prove extremely sturdy as instruments of violence. Guillermo del Toro, "Feature Audio Commentary by Writer/Director," *Pan's Labyrinth* (*El laberinto del fauno*), Disc One, New Line 2-Disc Platinum Series (MMVII New Line Entertainment, Inc., 2007).

15. Guillermo del Toro, "Pan and the Fairies (El Fauno y Las Hadas), *Pan's Labyrinth* [*El laberinto del fauno*], Disc Two, DVD, New Line Entertainment, 2007.

16. Del Toro, "Feature Audio Commentary by Writer/Director," Disc One.

17. Rudolf Otto, *The Idea of the Holy* (Oxford: Oxford University Press, 1923).

18. For a review of this perspective, see A.D. Moses, "Structure and Agency in the Holocaust: Daniel J. Goldhagen and His Critics," *History and Theory* 37 (1998): 194–220, especially 204. See also Daniel Goldhagen, *Hitler's Willing Executioners: Ordinary Germans and the Holocaust* (New York: Knopf, 1996) and Bruno Chaouat, "In the Image of Auschwitz," *diacritics* 36, no. 1 (Spring 2006): 86–96.

19. Del Toro, "Feature Audio Commentary by Writer/Director," Disc One.

20. Ibid.

21. Ibid.

22. Ibid.

23. Ibid.

24. Ibid.

25. Ibid.

26. Ibid.

27. Ibid.

28. Arthur Koestler, *Janus: A Summing Up* (London: Hutchinson, 1978), 112–13.

29. Other works that elaborate on similar themes are Arthur Koestler, *Insight and Outlook: An Inquiry into the Common Foundations of Science, Art and Social Ethics* (New York: Macmillan, 1949), and Arthur Koestler, *The Ghost in the Machine* (New York: Macmillan, 1967).

30. Koestler, *Janus*, 112–13.

31. Ibid., 129.

32. I acknowledge Jennifer Perrine's insightful contributions to this analysis of *Life Is Beautiful*. Nevertheless, there are both parallel and alternative modes of explanation explored by other critics that are reminiscent of this approach. For example, Michael Bernard-Donals and Richard Glejzer see less the comedic in *Life Is Beautiful* than the failure of the fabular form to convey historical experience. They write: "The initial voice-over's insistence that this is a difficult story to tell comes out in the comparison to a fable: 'Like a fable, there is sorrow ... / and, like a fable, it is full of wonder and happiness.' This 'like' quality to the film ... suggests that what follows is inadequate to the experience, that the fabular form itself won't get at its story." See Michael Bernard-Donals and Richard Glejzer, *Between Witness and Testimony, The Holocaust and the Limits of Representation* (Albany: State

University of New York Press, 2001), 126. It is this "formal inadequacy" that for them, explains contradictory critical responses of both irritation and comic redemption (Ibid.)

33. David Bathrick, "Rescreening 'The Holocaust': The Children's Stories," in *New German Critique: An Interdisciplinary Journal of German Studies* 80 (Spring-Summer 2000): 44.

34. Ibid., 45.

35. Ibid., 48.

36. Much ink has been spilled regarding the insistence of Miramax's Harvey Weinstein on the inclusion in the American release of the film of the voiceovers that serve as the film's narrative frame. While most sources credit Weinstein as the reason for the voiceover, in contrast, Radu Mihaileanu, the director of *Train of Life* (1998) (a.k.a. *Train de vie*), claims that the voiceover was the brainchild of Cannes festival director Gilles Jacob, who, according to Mihaileanu, recommended the use of the auditory framing device to Benigni after viewing *Train of Life*, which has a similar non-realistic narrative frame. See Anne Thompson, "The Evolution of 'Life,'" *Premiere Magazine* (April 1999): 1–2.

37. Stuart Liebman, "If Only Life Were So Beautiful." *Cineaste* 24, no. 2–3 (Spring-Summer 1999): 22.

38. Benigni, Roberto. *Press Kit 19*. Quoted in Maurizio Viano, "Life Is Beautiful: Reception, Allegory, and Holocaust Laughter," *Film Quarterly* 53, no. 1 (Fall 1999): 30.

39. Carlo Celli, "Interview with Marcello Pezzetti," *Critical Inquiry* 27 (Autumn 2000): 151.

40. Carlo Celli, "The Representation of Evil in Roberto Benigni's Life Is Beautiful," *Journal of Popular Film and Television* 28, no. 2 (Summer 2000): 77.

41. Celli, "Interview with Marcello Pezzetti," 151.

42. For a discussion of "working through," as opposed to "acting out" the trauma of the Holocaust, see Dominick LaCapra, *Representing the Holocaust: History, Theory, Trauma* (Ithaca, NY: Cornell University Press, 1994), 210. See also, generally, Dominick LaCapra, *History and Memory After Auschwitz* (Ithaca, NY: Cornell University Press, 1998) and Dominick LaCapra, *Writing History, Writing Trauma* (Baltimore, MD: Johns Hopkins University Press, 2001).

43. For a discussion of the complex (and potentially liberatory) intersection between humor and horror, refer to: Caroline Joan S. Picart, *Remaking the Frankenstein Myth on Film: Between Horror and Laughter* (Albany: State University of New York, 2003); see also the creative and tense interplay between the documentary impulse, horror, and humor in Caroline J.S. Picart, "The Documentary Impulse and Reel/Real Horror," *A Companion to the Horror Film*, ed. Harry Benshoff (Malden, MA: Wiley-Blackwell, forthcoming 2014). For a discussion of the relationship between "acting out" and "working through" as applied to *Schindler's List*, refer to Caroline J.S. Picart and David Frank, "The Holocaust as Horror-Psychological Thriller Film: Working-Through Spielberg's *Schindler's List*," *Film and History, 2003 Annual CD-ROM*.

44. Casey Haskins, "Art, Morality, and the Holocaust: The Aesthetic Riddle of Benigni's Life Is Beautiful," *The Journal of Aesthetics and Art Criticism* 59, no. 4 (Fall 2001): 380.

45. Henri Bergson, *Laughter: An Essay on the Meaning of the Comic*, trans. Bloudesley Brereton and Fred Rothwell (Los Angeles: Green Integer, 1999), 90.

46. Sidra Dekoven Ezrahi, "After Such Knowledge, What Is Laughter?" *Yale Journal of Criticism* 14, no. 1 (Spring 2001): 301.

47. Roberto Benigni and Vincenzo Cerami, *Life Is Beautiful (La Vita é Bella)*: *A Screenplay*, trans. Lisa Taruschio (New York: Hyperion-Miramax, 1998), 109.

48. Millicent Marcus, "'Me lo dici babbo che gioco é' The Serious Humor of *La Vita é Bella*," *Italica* 77, no. 2 (2000): 160.

49. Luigi Pirandello, *L'umorismo* (Milan: Mondadori, 1986), 153. Cited by Marcus, "'Me lo dici babbo che gioco é,'" 162.

50. Pirandello, *L'umorismo*, 138. Cited by Marcus, "'Me lo dici babbo che gioco é,'" 162.

51. Marcus, "'Me lo dici babbo che gioco é,'" 163.

52. Mintz, *Popular Culture and the Shaping of Holocaust Memory in America*, 171.

Bibliography

Abe, Kobo. *Secret Rendezvous*. Trans. Juliet Carpenter. New York: Knopf, 1979 [1977].

Adelman, Gary. *Naming Beckett's Unnamable*. Lewisburg, PA: Bucknell University Press, 2004.

Adorno, Theodor. "Cultural Criticism and Society." In *Prisms*. Trans. Samuel and Shierry Weber. Cambridge: MIT Press, 1981.

_____. *Negative Dialectics*. Trans. E. B. Asthon. London: Routledge, 1973.

_____. *Notes to Literature*. Trans. Samuel and Shierry Weber. New York: Columbia University Press, 1991.

_____. "Trying to Understand Endgame." In *Samuel Beckett: Modern Critical Views*. Ed. Harold Bloom. New York: Chelsea House, 1985.

Agamben, Georgio. *Open: Man and Animal*. Stanford, CA: Stanford University Press, 2004.

Allen, Brooke. "Solipsism." Review of *Everything Is Illuminated*. By Jonathan Safran Foer. *Atlantic Monthly* (April 2002).

Alter, Robert. Review of *King of the Jews*. By Leslie Epstein. *New York Times Review of Books* 84 (1979).

Arendt, Hannah. *Eichmann in Jerusalem: A Report on the Banality of Evil*. New York: Viking Press, 1964.

Baron, Lawrence. "Not in Kansas Anymore: Holocaust Films for Children." *The Lion and the Unicorn* 27 (2003).

Bathrick, David. "Rescreening 'The Holocaust': The Children's Stories." In *New German Critique: An Interdisciplinary Journal of German Studies* 80 (Spring–Summer 2000): 41–58.

Beahm, George, ed. *The Stephen King Companion*. Kansas City, MO: Andrews and McMeel, 1989.

Beckett, Samuel. *Malone Dies*, in *Three Novels: Molloy, Malone Dies, and The Unnamable*. New York: Grove Press, 1995.

_____. *The Unnamable*, in *Three Novels: Molloy, Malone Dies, and The Unnamable*. New York: Grove Press, 1995.

Belau, Linda. "Trauma and the Material Signifier." Para. 1. *George Washington University*. http://pmc.iath.virginia.edu/text-only/issue.101/11.2belau.txt.

Benigni, Roberto, and Vincenzo Cerami. *Life Is Beautiful (La Vita é Bella): A Screenplay*. Trans. Lisa Taruschio. New York: Hyperion-Miramax, 1998.

Benjamin, Walter. "Theses on the Philosophy of History." In *Illuminations*. Trans. Harry Zohn. New York: Schocken, 1985.

Bergson, Henri. *Laughter: An Essay on the Meaning of the Comic*. Trans. Bloudesley Brereton and Fred Rothwell. Los Angeles: Green Integer, 1999.

Berlin, Adele, and Marc Zvi Brettler. *The Jewish Study Bible*. Oxford: Oxford University Press, 2004.

Bernard-Donals, Michael, and Richard Glejzer. *Between Witness and Testimony, The Holocaust and the Limits of Representation*. Albany: State University of New York Press, 2001.

_____, and _____. "Teaching (After) Auschwitz: Pedagogy Between Redemption and Sublimity." In *Witnessing the Disaster: Essays on Representation and the Holocaust*. Ed. Michael Bernard-Donals and Richard Glejzer. Madison: University of Wisconsin Press, 2003.

Bernstein, Michael-André. *Foregone Conclusions: Against Apocalyptic History*. Berkeley: University of California Press, 1994.

Bernstein, Stephen. "'The Question Is the Story Itself': Postmodernism and Intertextuality in Auster's New York Trilogy." In *Detecting Texts: The Metaphysical Detective Story from Poe to Postmodernism*. Ed. Patricia Merivale and Susan Elizabeth Sweeney. Philadelphia: University of Pennsylvania Press, 1999.

Bettelhim, Bruno. *Surviving*. New York: Vintage, 1980.

_____. *The Uses of Enchantment: The Meaning and Importance of Fairy Tales*. New York: Vintage, 1977.

Blackman, Jackie. "Beckett's Theatre 'After Auschwitz.'" In *Samuel Beckett: History, Memory, Archive*. Ed. Seàn Kennedy and Katherine Weiss. New York: Palgrave Macmillan, 2009.

Bohman-Kajala, Kimberley. *Reading Games: An Aesthetics of Play in Flann O'Brien, Samuel Beckett, & Georges Perec*. Chicago: Dalkey Archive Press, 2007.

Borges, Jorge Luis. *Borges: A Reader*. Ed. Emir Rodriguez Monegal and Alastair Reid. New York: Dutton, 1981.

_____. *Labyrinths: Selected Stories and Other Writings*. Ed. Donald A. Yates and James E. Irby. New York: New Directions, 1964.

_____. *A Personal Anthology*. Ed. Anthony Kerrigan. New York: Grove Press, 1967.

_____. "The Witness." In *A Personal Anthology*. Ed. Anthony Kerrigan. New York: Grove Press, 1967.

Bosmajian, Hamida. *Sparing the Child: Grief and the Unspeakable in Youth Literature About Nazism and the Holocaust*. New York: Routledge, 2002.

Boulter, Jonathan. *Beckett: A Guide for the Perplexed*. New York: Continuum, 2008.

Boxall, Peter. *Since Beckett: Contemporary Writing in the Wake of Modernism*. New York: Continuum, 2009.

Brown, Robert McAfee. *Elie Wiesel: Messenger to All Humanity*. Notre Dame, IN: University of Notre Dame Press, 1983.

Buber, Martin. *Tales of the Hasidim: The Early Masters*. New York: Schocken Books, 1947.

Bukiet, Melvin Jules, ed. *Nothing Makes You Free: Writings by Descendants of Jewish Holocaust Survivors*. New York: W.W. Norton, 2002.

Campbell, Julie. "Moran as Secret Agent." *Samuel Beckett Today* 12 (2002): 81–92.

Card, Orson Scott. "Books to Look For." *The Magazine of Fantasy and Science Fiction* 76 No. 4 (April 1989): 36–39.

Cargas, Harry James. *Harry James Cargas in Conversation with Elie Wiesel*. New York: Paulist Press, 1976.

Carroll, Noël. *Philosophy of Horror, or Paradoxes of the Heart*. New York: Routledge, 1990.

Caruth, Cathy. *Trauma: Explorations in Memory*. Baltimore, MD: Johns Hopkins University Press, 1995.

_____. *Unclaimed Experience: Trauma, Narrative, and History*. Baltimore, MD: Johns Hopkins University Press, 1996.

Celli, Carlo. "Interview with Marcello Pezzetti." *Critical Inquiry* 27 (Autumn 2000): 149–57.

_____. "The Representation of Evil in Roberto Benigni's *Life Is Beautiful*." *Journal of Popular Film and Television* 28 No. 2 (Summer 2000): 74–79.

Chandler, Daniel. "An Introduction to Genre Theory." Last modified 2000. http://www.aber.ac.uk/media/Documents/intgenre/chandler_genre_theory.pdf

Chaouat, Bruno. "In the Image of Auschwitz." *diacritics* 36 No. 1 (Spring 2006): 86–96.

Cole, Emmet. Review of *Apikoros Sleuth*. By Robert Majzels. *Movable Type* 2 (2006): ucl.uk/graduate/issue/2/Apikoros.

Coleridge, Samuel. Chapter XIV of *Biographia Literaria*. In *The Collected Works of Samuel Taylor Coleridge: Sketches of My Literary Life & Opinions*. Vol. 7. Bollingen Series LXXV. Ed. James Engell and W. Jackson Bate. Princeton, NJ: Princeton University Press, 1983.

Collins, Michael, and David Engbretson. *The Shorter Works of Stephen King*. Mercer Island, WA: Starmont House, 1985.

Dean, Martin. *Collaboration in the Holocaust: Crimes of the Local Police in Belorussia and Ukraine, 1941–44*. New York: St. Martin's Press, 2000.

Delbo, Charlotte. *Auschwitz and After*. Trans. Rosette C. Lamont. Newport, CT: Yale University Press, 1995.

del Toro, Guillermo. "Feature Audio Commentary by Writer/Director." *Pan's Labyrinth* (*El laberinto del fauno*). Disc One. New Line 2-Disc Platinum Series (MMVII New Line Entertainment, Inc., 2007). DVD.

_____. "Pan and the Fairies (El Fauno y Las Hadas)." *Pan's Labyrinth* (*El laberinto del fauno*). Disc Two (MMVII New Line Entertainment, 2007). DVD.

Denby, David. "Darkness Out of Light." *The New Yorker*. November 16, 1998. 114–16.

Des Pres, Terrence. "Holocaust Laughter?" In *Writing and the Holocaust*. Ed. Berel Lang. New York: Holmes and Meier, 1988.

The Devil's Arithmetic. Dir. Donna Deitch (Showtime, 1999).

Doneson, Judith E. *The Holocaust in American Film*. Philadelphia: Jewish Publication Society, 1987.

Dreifus, Claudia. "The Progressive Interview: Art Spiegelman." *The Progressive* 53 No. 11 (Nov. 1989).

Ebiri, Bilge. "*Shutter Island*, Scorsese's Longed-For Leap into Low-Down Genre Filmmaking, Isn't the Potboiler You Expect—To Its Credit." Review of *Shutter Island*. *Nashville Scene*. February 18, 2010. http://www.nashvillescene.com/nashville/shutter-island-scorseses-longed-for-leap-into-low-down-genre-film making-isnt-the-potboiler-you-expect-andmdash-to-its-credit/Content?oid=1227237.

Eilach, Yaffa. *Hasidic Tales of the Holocaust*. New York: Vintage, 1982.

Englander, Nathan. *For the Relief of Unbearable Urges*. New York: Random House, 1999.

Epstein, Leslie. *King of the Jews*. New York: Coward, McCann & Geoghegan, 1979.

Ewert, Jeanne C. "'A Thousand Other Mysteries': Metaphysical Detection, Ontological Quests." In *Detecting Texts: The Metaphysical Detective Story from Poe to Postmodernism*. Ed. Patricia Merivale and Susan Elizabeth Sweeney. Philadelphia: University of Pennsylvania Press, 1999.

Ezrahi, Sidra DeKoven. "After Such Knowledge, What Laughter?" *Yale Journal of Criticism* 14 No. 1 (Spring 2001): 278–313.

_____. *By Words Alone: The Holocaust in Literature*. Chicago: University of Chicago Press, 1980.

Feinberg, Anat, trans. *Embodied Memory: The Theatre of George Tabori*. Iowa City: University of Iowa Press, 1999.

Feuer, Menachem. "Almost Friends: Post-Holocaust Comedy, Tragedy, and Friendship in Jonathan Safran Foer's *Everything Is Illuminated*." *Shofar: An Interdisciplinary Journal of Jewish Studies* 25 No. 2 (Winter 2007): 24–48.

Foer, Jonathan Safran. *Everything Is Illuminated*. Boston: Houghton Mifflin, 2002.

Fogelman, Eva. *Conscience and Courage: Rescuers of Jews During the Holocaust*. New York: Anchor, 1995.

Frankel, Glenn. "The Rabbi and the Dictator." *The Seattle Times*. February 10, 1990. A10–11

Frankl, Viktor E. *Man's Search for Meaning: An Introduction to Logotherapy*. New York: Washington Square, 1963.

Franklin, Ruth. *A Thousand Darknesses: Lies and Truth in Holocaust Fiction*. New York: Oxford University Press, 2011.

Fredericks, S.C. "Problems of Fantasy." *Science-Fiction Studies* 5 (March 1978): 33–44.

Friedländer, Saul. Introduction to *Probing the Limits of Representation: Nazism and the "Final Solution."* Ed. Saul Friedländer. Cambridge: Harvard University Press, 1984.

_____. *Reflections on Nazism: An Essay on Kitsch and Death*. Bloomington: Indiana University Press, 1984.

Freud, Sigmund. "Remembering, Repeating and Working-Through." In *The Standard Edition of the Complete Psychological Works of Sigmund Freud*. Vol. 12. Trans. and ed. James Strachey. London: Hogarth Press, 1958.

Garrison, Alysia. "'Faintly Struggling Things': Trauma, Testimony, and Inscrutable Life in Beckett's *The Unnamable*." In *Samuel Beckett: History, Memory, Archive*. Ed. Seàn Kennedy and Katherine Weiss. New York: Palgrave Macmillan, 2009.

Gary, Romain. *The Dance of Genghis Cohn*. New York: World Publishing, 1968.

Gillman, Sander. "Is Life Beautiful? Can the Shoah Be Funny?: Some Thoughts on Recent and Older Films." *Critical Inquiry* 26 (Winter 2000): 279–308.

Gitelman, Zvi. "The Soviet Union." In *The World Reacts to the Holocaust*. Ed. David Wyman. Baltimore: Johns Hopkins University Press, 1996.

Glatstein, Jacob, Israel Knox, and Samuel Margoshes, eds. *An Anthology of Holocaust Literature*. New York: Atheneum, 1975.

Golbert, Rebecca. "'Neighbors' and the Ukrainian Jewish Experience of the Holocaust." In *Lessons and Legacies, Volume VII: The Holocaust in International Perspective*. Ed. Dagmar Herzog. Evanston, IL: Northwestern University Press, 2006.

Goldhagen, Daniel. *Hitler's Willing Executioners: Ordinary Germans and the Holocaust*. New York: Knopf, 1996.

Goldstein, Lisa. *The Red Magician*. New York: Pocket Books, 1982.

Gomery, Douglas. "The Economics of the Horror Film." In *Horror Films: Current Research on Audience Preferences and Reactions*. Ed. James B. Weaver, III, and Ron Tamborini. Mahwah, NY: Lawrence Erlbaum Associates, 1996.

Gopnik, Adam. "Comics and Catastrophe: Art Spiegelman's *Maus* and the History of the Cartoon." *The New Republic* 22 (June 1987): 29–34.

Gray, Paul. Review of *Different Seasons*. By Stephen King. *Time* 120 No. 9 (August 30, 1982).

Gronbaek, Lisbeth. "Writing and Reading Beyond the Wordable: Beckett's *L'Innommable* and Perec's *La Disparition*." Ph.D. diss., Victoria University of Wellington, 2006.

Gross, John. "Hollywood and the Holocaust." *New York Review of Books* 16 No. 3 (Feb. 3, 1994): 3–5.

Halberstam, Judith. *Skin Shows: Gothic Horror and the Technology of Monsters.* Durham, NC: Duke University Press, 2006 [1995].

Hampton, Christopher. *The Portage to San Cristóbal of A.H.,* in *The Theatre of the Holocaust: Six Plays.* Vol. 2. Ed. Robert Skloot. Madison: University of Wisconsin Press, 1999.

Hantke, Steffen. "The Kingdom of the Unimaginable: The Construction of Social Space and the Fantasy of Privacy in Serial Killer Narratives." *Literature/Film Quarterly* 26 (1998): 178–95.

Harpham, Geoffrey. "The Grotesque: First Principles." *Journal of Aesthetics and Art Criticism* 34 No. 4 (Summer 1976): 461–78.

Hartman, Geoffrey. *The Longest Shadow: In the Aftermath of the Holocaust.* New York: Palgrave, 2002.

Hartman, Geoffrey H. "On Traumatic Knowledge and Literary Studies." *New Literary History* 26 No. 3 (Summer 1995): 537–63.

Haskins, Casey. "Art, Morality, and the Holocaust: The Aesthetic Riddle of Benigni's Life Is Beautiful." *The Journal of Aesthetics and Art Criticism* 59 No. 4 (Fall 2001): 373–84.

Hirsch, Marianne. "The Generation of Postmemory." *Poetics Today* 29 No. 1 (Spring 2008): 103–28.

Hume, Kathryn. *Fantasy and Mimesis: Responses to Reality in Western Literature.* New York: Methuen, 1984.

Irwin, W.R. *The Game of the Impossible: A Rhetoric of Fantasy.* Urbana: University of Illinois Press, 1976.

Iser, Wolfgang. "The Pattern of Negativity in Beckett's Prose." In *Samuel Beckett: Modern Critical Views.* Ed. Harold Bloom. New York: Chelsea House, 1985.

Jaggi, Maya. "George and His Dragons." *The Guardian.* March 16, 2001. Accessed September 15, 2012. http://www.guardian.co.uk/books/2001/mar/17/arts.high ereducation.

Johnson, Kenneth. "Feature-Length Commentary by Writer/Director." *V: The Original Miniseries.* Side A. DVD. Warner Home Video (2001 [1983]).

Kant, Immanuel. *Religion Within the Limits of Reason Alone.* Trans. Theodore M. Greene and Hoyt Hudson. New York: Harper and Row, 1960.

Kakutani, Michiko. *New York Times.* December 5, 1982.

Kenner, Hugh. *Samuel Beckett: A Critical Study.* London: Calder, 1962.

Kerman, Judith. "Drawing Lines in the Sand: The Fantastic Considered as an Instance of Liminality." In *Flashes of the Fantastic: Selected Essays from* The War of the Worlds *Centennial, Nineteenth International Conference on the Fantastic in the Arts.* Ed. David Ketterer. Westport, CT: Greenwood Press, 2004.

Kertzer, Adrienne. *My Mother's Voice: Children, Literature, and the Holocaust.* New York: Broadview Press, 2002.

King, Stephen. Afterword to *Different Seasons.* New York: Viking, 1982.

_____. "Summer of Corruption: Apt Pupil." In *Different Seasons.* New York: Viking, 1982.

Koestler, Arthur. *The Ghost in the Machine.* New York: Macmillan, 1967.

_____. *Insight and Outlook: An Inquiry into the Common Foundations of Science, Art and Social Ethics.* New York: Macmillan, 1949.

_____. *Janus: A Summing Up.* London: Hutchinson, 1978)

Kubler-Ross, Elizabeth. *The Wheel of Life, a Memoir of Living and Dying.* New York: Scribner, 1998.

LaCapra, Dominick. *History and Memory After Auschwitz.* Ithaca, NY: Cornell University Press, 1998.

_____. *Representing the Holocaust: History, Theory, Trauma*. Ithaca, NY: Cornell University Press, 1994.

_____. *Writing History, Writing Trauma*. Baltimore, MD: Johns Hopkins University Press, 2001.

Lamont, Rosette C. "Beckett's Wandering Jew." In *Reflections of the Holocaust in Art and Literature*. Ed. Randolph L. Braham. New York: Columbia University Press, 1990.

Land-Weber, Ellen. *To Save a Life: Stories of Holocaust Rescue*. Urbana: University of Illinois Press, 2000.

Lane, Anthony. "Behind Bars." Review of *Shutter Island* and *A Prophet*. *The New Yorker*. March 1, 2010. http://www.newyorker.com/arts/critics/cinema/2010/03/01/100301crci_cinema_lane.

Lang, Berel. *Holocaust Representation: Art Within the Limits of History and Ethics*. Baltimore, MD: Johns Hopkins University Press, 2000.

Langer, Lawrence. *The Holocaust and Literary Imagination*. New Haven: Yale University Press, 1975.

Langer, Lawrence L. *Versions of Survival: The Holocaust and the Human* Spirit. Albany: State University of New York Press, 1982.

Laub, Dori. "Bearing Witness or the Vicissitudes of Listening." In *Testimony: Crises of Witnessing in Literature, Psychoanalysis and History*. Ed. Shoshana Felman and Dori Laub. New York: Routledge, 1992.

Lehane, Dennis. *Shutter Island*. New York: HarperTorch, 2004 [2003].

Levi, Primo. *The Drowned and the Saved*. New York: Vintage, 1988.

Levine, Hillel. *In Search of Sugihara: The Elusive Japanese Diplomat Who Risked His Life to Rescue 10,000 Jews from the Holocaust*. New York: Free Press, 1996.

Liebman, Stuart. "If Only Life Were So Beautiful." *Cineaste* 24 No. 2–3 (Spring–Summer 1999): 20–22.

Lowry, Lois. *Number the Stars*. New York: Houghton Mifflin, 1989.

Lüdtke, Alf. "'Coming to Terms with the Past': Illusions of Remembering, Ways of Forgetting Nazism in West Germany." *The Journal of Modern History* 65 No. 3 (Sept. 1993): 542–72.

Marcus, Millicent. "'Me lo dici babbo che gioco é' The Serious Humor of *La Vita é Bella*." *Italica* 77 No. 2 (2000): 153–70.

Majzels, Robert. *Apikoros Sleuth*. Toronto: Mercury Press, 2004.

Mawhinney, Heather. "'Vol du Bourbon': The Purloined Letter in Perec's *La Disparition*." *Modern Language Review* 97 (January 2002): 47–58.

McGlothlin, Erin Heather. *Second-Generation Holocaust Literature: Legacies of Survival and Perpetration*. New York: Camden House, 2006.

McLoughlin, Kate. "'Dispute Incarnate': Philip Roth's *Operation Shylock*, the Demanjuk Trial, and Eyewitness Testimony." *Philip Roth Studies* 3 No. 2 (Fall 2007): 115–30.

Merivale, Patricia, and Susan Elizabeth Sweeney. "The Game's Afoot!: On the Trail of the Metaphysical Detective Story." In *Detecting Texts: The Metaphysical Detective Story from Poe to Postmodernism*. Ed. Patricia Merivale and Susan Elizabeth Sweeney. Philadelphia: University of Pennsylvania Press, 1999.

Meyer, Adam. "Putting the 'Jewish' Back in 'Jewish American Fiction': A Look at Jewish American Fiction from 1977 to 2002 and an Allegorical Reading of Nathan Englander's 'The Gilgul of Park Avenue.'" *Shofar: An Interdisciplinary Journal of Jewish Studies* 22 No. 3 (Spring 2004): 104–20.

Millet, Kitty. "Halakhah and the Jewish Detective's Obligations." In *Questions of Identity in Detective Fiction*. Ed. Linda Martz and Anita Higgie. Newcastle: Cambridge Scholars Press, 2007.

Milton, Edith. "Looking Backward: Six Novels." *The Yale Review* 69 No. 1 (October 1979).

Mintz, Alan. *Popular Culture and the Shaping of Holocaust Memory in America.* Seattle: University of Washington Press, 2001.

Monegal, Emir Rodriguez, and Alastair Reid. Introduction to *Borges: A Reader.* Ed. Emir Rodriguez Monegal and Alastair Reid. New York: Dutton, 1981.

Morahg, Gilead. "Creating Wasserman: The Quest for a New Holocaust Story in David Grossman's *See Under: Love." Judaism* 51 No. 1 (Winter 2002): 51–60.

Moses, A.D. "Structure and Agency in the Holocaust: Daniel J. Goldhagen and His Critics." *History and Theory* 37 (1998): 194–220.

Oliner. Samuel P., and Pearl M. Oliner. *The Altruistic Personality: Rescuers of Jews in Nazi Europe.* New York: Free Press, 1988.

Oster, Shai. "Holocaust Humor." *The Utne Reader* 95 (Sept.–Oct. 1999): 82–6.

Otto, Rudolf. *The Idea of the Holy.* Oxford: Oxford University Press, 1923.

Ozick, Cynthia. "The Rights of History and the Rights of the Imagination." In *Quarrel and Quandary.* New York: Knopf, 2000.

Patraka, Vivian M. *Spectacular Suffering: Theatre, Fascism, and the Holocaust.* Bloomington: Indiana University Press, 1999.

Perec, Georges. "Le Nouveau Roman et le refus du réel" (1962). In *L.G.: Une aventure des années soixantes.* Paris: Éditions du Seuil, 1992.

_____. *A Void.* Trans. Gilbert Adair. London: Harvill, 1994.

Perloff, Marjorie. "'In Love with Hiding': Samuel Beckett's War." *Iowa Review* 35 No. 2 (2005): 76–103.

Pfefferkorn, Eli. "The Art of Survival: Romain Gary's *The Dance of Genghis Cohn." Modern Language Studies* 10 No. 3 (Fall 1980): 76–87.

Picart, Caroline Joan. *The Cinematic Rebirths of Frankenstein: Universal, Hammer, and Beyond.* Westport, CT: Praeger, 2002.

Picart, Caroline Joan (Kay) S., Carla Maria Thomas, and John Edgar Browning. "Where Reality and Fantasy Meet and Bifurcate: Holocaust Themes in *Pan's Labyrinth*, the *X-Men*, and *V: The Original Miniseries (1983)."* In *Speaking of Monsters: A Teratological Anthology.* Ed. Caroline Joan S. Picart and John Edgar Browning. Palgrave Macmillan: 2012.

Picart, Caroline Joan (Kay) S., and Cecil Greek. *Monsters In and Among Us: Toward a Gothic Criminology.* Madison, NJ: Fairleigh Dickinson University Press, 2007.

Picart, Caroline Joan (Kay) S., and David A. Frank. *Frames of Evil: The Holocaust as Horror in American Film.* Carbondale: Southern Illinois University Press, 2006.

Picart, Caroline Joan (Kay) S., and Jennifer Perrine. "Laughter, Terror and Revolt in Three Recent Holocaust Films." *The Holocaust Film Sourcebook.* Vol. 1. Westport, CT: Praeger, 2004.

Picart, Caroline J.S. "The Documentary Impulse and Reel/Real Horror." *A Companion to the Horror Film.* Ed. Harry M. Benshoff. Malden, MA: Wiley-Blackwell, forthcoming 2014.

Picart, Caroline J.S., and David Frank. "The Holocaust as Horror-Psychological Thriller Film: Working-Through Spielberg's *Schindler's List." Film and History: 2003 Annual CD-ROM.*

_____, and _____. "Horror and the Holocaust: Genre Elements in *Schindler's List* and *Psycho." The Horror Film.* Ed. Stephen Prince. New Brunswick, NJ: Rutgers University Press, 2003.

Picart, Caroline Joan S. *Remaking the Frankenstein Myth on Film: Between Horror and Laughter.* Albany: State University of New York, 2003.

Pinedo, Isabel Cristina. "Postmodern Elements of the Contemporary Horror Film."

In *The Horror Film*. Ed. Steven Prince. New Brunswick, NJ: Rutgers University Press, 2004.

Pirandello, Luigi. *L'umorismo*. Milan: Mondadori, 1986.

Postone, Moishe. "The Holocaust and the Trajectory of the Twentieth Century." In *Catastrophe and Meaning: The Holocaust and the Twentieth Century*. Ed. Moishe Postone and Eric Santner. Chicago: University of Chicago Press, 2003.

Rabkin, Eric S. *The Fantastic in Literature*. Princeton, NJ: Princeton University Press, 1976.

Rauschning, Hermann. *Hitler Speaks*. London: Putnam, 1939.

Reino, Joseph. *Stephen King: The First Decades, Carrie to Pet Sematary*. Boston: Twayne, 1988.

Ribbat, Christoph. "'Nomadic with the Truth': Holocaust Representation in Michael Chabon, James McBride, and Jonathan Safran Foer." *Anglistik und Englischunterricht* 66 (2005): 199–218.

Ribiére, Mireille. "La Disparition/ A Void: deux temps, deux histoires?" In *Georges Perec et l'Histoire* (*Études Romanes 46*). Ed. Carsten Sestoft and Steen Bille Jørgensen. Copenhagen: Museum Tusculanum Press, 2000.

Ricoeur, Paul. *Time and Narrative*. Vol. 3. Trans. Kathleen Blamey and David Pellauer. Chicago: University of Chicago Press, 1990 [1988].

Rokem, Freddie. *Performing History: Theatrical Representations of the Past in Contemporary Theatre*. Iowa City: University of Iowa Press, 2000.

Rosenbaum, Thane. "With the Shoah, Can Tragedy Become Farce?: Considering an Italian Funnyman's Concentration Camp Comedy." *Forward*. October 23, 1998. http://www.forward.com/issues/1998/98.12.23/arts.html.

Roth, John K. *Ethics During and After the Holocaust: In the Shadow of Birkenau*. Basingstoke, England: Palgrave Macmillan, 2005.

Rubenstein, Richard. *Approaches to Auschwitz: The Holocaust and Its Legacy*. Atlanta: John Knox Press, 1987.

Ruiz, Pablo Martin. "Four Cold Chapters: On the Possibility of Literature Leading Mostly to Borges and Oulipo." Ph.D. dissertation, Princeton, 2009.

Rushforth, Peter. *Kindergarten*. San Francisco: McAdam/Cage, 2006.

Rushing, Janice Hocker, and Thomas S. Frentz. *Projecting the Shadow: The Cyborg Hero in American Film*. Chicago: University of Chicago Press, 1995.

Saltzman, Arthur M. *Designs of Darkness in Contemporary American Fiction*. Philadelphia: University of Pennsylvania Press, 1990.

Santner, Eric. "History Beyond the Pleasure Principle: Some Thoughts on the Representation of Trauma." In *Probing the Limits of Representation: Nazism and the "Final Solution."* Ed. Saul Friedländer. Cambridge: Harvard University Press, 1992.

Sartre, Jean-Paul. *Between Existentialism and Marxism*. London: New Left Books, 1974.

Schwarz, Daniel R. *Imaging the Holocaust*. New York: St. Martin's, 1999.

Schwarz-Bart, André. *The Last of the Just*. New York: Bantam, 1960.

Shapiro, Paul A. "Forward." In *Children and the Holocaust: Symposium Presentations*. Washington, D.C.: United States Holocaust Memorial Museum Center for Advanced Holocaust Studies, 2004.

Shenker, Israel. Interview with Samuel Beckett NYT. May 5, 1956. In *Samuel Beckett: Critical Heritage*. Ed. Lawrence Graver, Raymond Federman. New York: Routledge, 1999 [1979].

Shutter Island. Dir. Martin Scorsese (Hollywood, CA: Paramount Pictures, 2010). DVD.

Skibell, Joseph. *A Blessing on the Moon*. New York: Berkeley, 1997.

Skloot, Robert. "Holocaust Theatre and the Problem of Justice." In *Staging the Holocaust: The Shoah in Drama and Performance (Cambridge Studies in Modern Theatre)*. Ed. Claude Schumacher. Cambridge: Cambridge University Press, 1998.

_____. Introduction to *The Theatre of the Holocaust: Six Plays*. Vol. 2, Madison: University of Wisconsin Press, 1999.

_____, ed. *The Theatre of the Holocaust: Four Plays*. Vol. 1. Madison: University of Wisconsin Press, 1982.

Sokoloff, Naomi B. Review of *Representing the Holocaust in Children's Literature*. By Lydia Kokkola. *The Lion and the Unicorn* 30 No. 1 (Jan. 2006).

Spiegelman, Art. *Maus: A Survivor's Tale*. New York: Pantheon, 1986.

_____. *Maus II: A Survivor's Tale—And Here My Troubles Begin*. New York: Pantheon, 1991.

_____. *Metamaus*. New York: Pantheon, 2011.

Stein, Ruthe. "The Horror of the Underworld (and This World)." *San Francisco Chronicle*. December 29, 2006. http://www.sfgate.com/cgi-bin/article.cgi?f=/c/a/2006/12/29/DDGH7N4LSM22.DTL.

Steiner, George. *Bluebird's Castle: Some Notes Toward a Redefinition of Culture*. New Haven: Yale University Press, 1971.

_____. *Language and Silence: Essays on Language, Literature, and the Inhuman*. New York: Atheneum, 1967.

_____. "Through That Glass Darkly." *Salmagundi* 93 (Winter 1992): 37–50.

Stevens, Dana, and Troy Patterson. "Shutter Island." Episode 94. *Slate*'s Spoiler Specials. *Slate*. Podcast audio. February 18, 2010. http://feeds.feedburner.com/SlateSpoilerSpecials.

Suleiman, Susan Rubin. *Crises of Witnessing and the Second World War*. Cambridge: Harvard University Press, 2006.

Sutton, Roger. "Editorial." *Bulletin of the Center for Children's Books* (October 1988).

Swales, Martin. "Sex, Shame and Guilt: Reflections on Bernhard Schlink's *Der Vorleser* (*The Reader*) and J.M. Coetzee's *Disgrace*." *Journal of European Studies* 33 (March 2003): 7–22.

Tabori, George. "*Die Kannibalen*: Zur europäischen Erstaufführung." In *Unterammergau oder Die guten Deutschen*. Frankfurt am Main: Suhrkamp, 1981.

Tec, Nechama. *When Light Pierced the Darkness: Christian Rescue of Jews in Nazi-Occupied Poland*. New York: Oxford University Press, 1986.

Thompson, Anne. "The Evolution of 'Life.'" *Premiere Magazine* (April 1999): 1–2.

Thomson, Philip. *The Grotesque: The Critical Idiom*. Ed. John D. Jump. London: Methuem, 1972.

Todorov, Tzvetan. *The Fantastic: A Structural Approach to a Literary Genre*. Cleveland: Press of Case Western Reserve University, 1973.

_____. *The Fantastic: A Structural Approach to a Literary Genre*. Ithaca, NY: Cornell University Press, 1975.

Tushnet, Leonard. *The Pavement of Hell*. New York: St. Martin's Press, 1972.

Viano, Maurizio. "Life Is Beautiful: Reception, Allegory, and Holocaust Laughter." *Film Quarterly* 53 No. 1 (Fall 1999): 26–34.

Vice, Sue. *Holocaust Fiction*. London: Routledge, 2000.

Volavkava, Hana. *I Never Saw Another Butterfly: Children's Drawings and Poems from Terezin Concentration Camp 1942–1944*. New York: Schocken Books, 1993.

Warner, Marina. *From the Beast to the Blonde: On Fairy Tales and Their Tellers*. New York: Farrar, Strauss and Giroux, 1994.

Weil, Ellen R. "The Door to Lilith's Cave: Memory and Imagination in Jane Yolen's

Holocaust Novels." In *Journal of the Fantastic in the Arts* 5 No. 2 (1993): 90–104.

_____. *The Holocaust in Literature*. Chicago: Roosevelt University External Studies Program, 1990.

Weissman, Gary. *Fantasies of Witnessing: The Postwar Effort to Experience the Holocaust*. Ithaca, NY: Cornell University Press, 2004.

Wiesel, Elie. "The Holocaust as Literary Inspiration." In *Dimensions of the Holocaust: Lectures at the Northwestern University*. By Elie Wiesel, Lucy S. Dawidowic, Dorothy Rabinowitz, and Robert McAfee Brown. Anno. Elliot Lefkovitz. Evanston, IL: Northwestern University Press, 1977.

_____. *A Jew Today*. Trans. Marion Wiesel. New York: Random House, 1978.

Wolfe, Gary K. *Evaporating Genres: Essays on Fantastic Literature*. Middletown, CT: Wesleyan University Press, 2011.

_____. "Symbolic Fantasy." *Genre* 8 No. 3 (September 1975): 194–209.

Wolosky, Shira. "Samuel Beckett's Figural Evasions." In *Languages of the Unsayable*. Ed. Sanford Budick and Wolfgang Iser. New York: Columbia University Press, 1986.

Wood, Robin. "Nuit et Brouillard." In *International Dictionary of Films and Filmmakers*. Vol. 1. Ed. Christopher Lyon. Chicago: St. James Press, 1984.

Wright, Melanie J. "'Don't Touch My Holocaust': Responding to *Life Is Beautiful*." *The Journal of Holocaust Education* 9, no. 1 (Summer 2000): 19–32.

Yolen, Jane. *Briar Rose*. New York: Tom Doherty, 1992.

_____. *The Devil's Arithmetic*. New York: Viking Kestrel, 1988.

_____. "The Devil's Arithmetic." *JaneYolen.com*. Accessed May 21, 2013. http://jane yolen.com/works/the-devils-arithmetic/.

_____. "An Experiential Act." *Language Arts* 66 No. 3 (March 1989): 246–51.

Zabarko, Boris, ed. *Holocaust in the Ukraine*. Trans. Marina Guba. Portland, OR: Vallentine Mitchell, 2005.

About the Contributors

John Edgar **Browning** has a Ph.D. in American studies from the University at Buffalo (SUNY) and is currently a Marion L. Brittain Postdoctoral Fellow at Georgia Tech. His books include *Speaking of Monsters: A Teratological Anthology*, with Caroline Joan (Kay) S. Picart (Palgrave Macmillan, 2012), *The Forgotten Writings of Bram Stoker* (Palgrave Macmillan, 2012), and two forthcoming volumes.

Paul **Eisenstein** is the dean of the School of Arts & Sciences and a professor in the Department of English at Otterbein University, where he teaches courses on contemporary literature, literary theory (especially psychoanalysis), and film. His essays on the Holocaust have appeared in *History and Memory* and *German Quarterly*, and in the volume *Approaches to Teaching Elie Wiesel's* Night (Modern Language Association, 2007).

Joan **Gordon** is a professor of English at Nassau Community College in New York and the reviews editor for *Science Fiction Studies*. With Veronica Hollinger, she co-edited *The Wesleyan Anthology of Science Fiction* (Wesleyan University Press, 2010) and *Queer Universes: Sexualities in Science Fiction* (Liverpool University Press, 2010). She is a past president of the Science Fiction Research Association and winner of the SFRA's Clareson Award for outstanding service.

Judith B. **Kerman** is a professor emerita of English at Saginaw Valley State University. She was the editor of *Retrofitting Blade Runner: Issues in Ridley Scott's* Blade Runner *and Philip K. Dick's* Do Androids Dream of Electric Sheep? (Bowling Green State University Popular Press, 1991). She was a Fulbright Senior Scholar to the Dominican Republic in 2002 and is the publisher and editor of Mayapple Press, as well as founding editor of *Earth's Daughters*.

Michael P. **McCleary** holds degrees from the University of Washington. He was a lecturer at the University of Haifa from 1992 to 2006, where he taught Shakespeare, Blake, and other subjects. His publications include an essay in *Strands Afar Remote: Israeli Perspectives on Shakespeare* (University of Delaware Press, 1998) and an article in *Shakespeare Quarterly*.

Kristopher **Mecholsky** earned a Ph.D. in 2012 from Louisiana State University, where his dissertation earned both the James Olney Distinguished Dissertation Award and the Lewis P. Simpson Distinguished Dissertation Award. He is a postdoctoral teaching associate at Louisiana State University. He, with David Madden, is the author of *James M. Cain: Hard-Boiled Mythmaker* (Scarecrow, 2011).

Patricia **Merivale** is a professor emerita of English and comparative literature at the University of British Columbia and is the author of *Pan the Goat-God: His Myth in Modern Times* (Harvard University Press, 1969), and co-editor, with Susan Elizabeth Sweeney, of *Detecting Texts: The Metaphysical Detective Story from Poe to Postmodernism* (University of Philadelphia Press, 1999). She has given numerous conference papers, most recently a keynote address at "The Metaphysical Thriller/ Le Thriller Metaphysique" at the University of Liege, Belgium.

Caroline Joan (Kay) S. **Picart**, Esq., completed a Ph.D. in political philosophy from Pennsylvania State University, a postdoctoral fellowship on jurisprudence with the Cornell School of Criticism and Theory, and a joint J.D./M.A. in Women's Studies from the University of Florida. She has authored 16 books with scholarly presses and has also published 30 peer-reviewed articles in scholarly journals as well as 26 book chapters, many of which are on film, philosophy, and law.

Vandana **Saxena** received a Ph.D. from the Indian Institute of Technology Delhi. She teaches at the School of Modern Languages and Cultures at the University of Nottingham Malaysia Campus. She is the author of *The Subversive Harry Potter: Adolescent Rebellion and Containment in the J.K. Rowling Novels* (McFarland, 2012). Her research interests include adolescent fiction, fantasy literature and fairy tales and culture studies.

Carol A. **Senf** is a professor and associate chair of the School of Literature, Media, and Communication at Georgia Tech. A Victorianist by training, she has written on the Brontë sisters, George Eliot, Dickens, Hardy, and Sarah Grand. She has spent most of her academic career exploring Bram Stoker's fiction and has written two critical studies of Stoker and one critical study of *Dracula*, edited several collections of Stoker criticism, and produced two annotated editions of Stoker novels.

Leon **Stein** received a Ph.D. in 1966 from New York University. Now a professor emeritus, he was the first Mansfield Professor of History at Roosevelt University, and he continues to teach courses at the Schaumburg Campus. His teaching and research fields include history of the Holocaust, history of ideas, social movements, and nationalism. His many publications include numerous papers and articles on the Holocaust and the history of nationalism, and a curriculum on the Holocaust for the public schools of the State of Illinois.

Eric J. **Sterling** is a Distinguished Research Professor of English and Alumni Professor at Auburn University Montgomery in Alabama, where he has taught since 1994. He earned a doctorate in English from Indiana University. He is the author of *Life in the Ghettos During the Holocaust* (Syracuse University Press, 2006) and has published articles on Arthur Miller, Peter Barnes, Elie Wiesel, *Schindler's List*, Shimon Wincelberg, Holocaust bystanders, and other aspects of the Holocaust.

Ellen R. **Weil** (1944–2000), a longtime university instructor, wrote *Harlan Ellison: The Edge of Forever* (Ohio State University Press, 2002), as well as many essays, with her husband Gary K. Wolfe.

Gary K. **Wolfe** is a professor of humanities in Roosevelt University's Evelyn T. Stone College of Professional Studies. His work has focused on science fiction and other forms of fantastic literature, and he has received the Pilgrim Award from the Science Fiction Research Association, the Distinguished Scholarship Award from the International Association for the Fantastic in the Arts, the Eaton Award from the Eaton Conference on Science Fiction and the British Science Fiction Association Award for nonfiction. He has twice been nominated for the Hugo Award from the World Science Fiction Convention.

Jane **Yolen** is a distinguished American writer of fantasy, science fiction, and children's books. She is the author or editor of close to 300 books, including the Holocaust novella *The Devil's Arithmetic*. Other works include the Nebula Award–winning short story "Sister Emily's Lightship," the novelette *Lost Girls*, *Owl Moon*, *The Emperor and the Kite*, the *Commander Toad* series, and *How Do Dinosaurs Say Goodnight*. In 2010, she was awarded the World Fantasy Award for Life Achievement at the World Fantasy Convention.

Jules **Zanger** (1927–2014) was a professor emeritus of American literature and American studies at Southern Illinois University at Edwardsville. He was a former president of the Midcontinent American Studies Association and published widely in American literature. His articles and essays have appeared in *American Literature*, *American Studies*, *Modern Philology*, *Literature in Translation*, *NEQ*, and elsewhere.

Index

227